With all my

Christmas 19

Charles

It may help with the EBP. Walks!

THE MAKING OF
THE ENGLISH LANDSCAPE

THE NORFOLK LANDSCAPE

The Wash

Thornham

WELLS NEXT THE SEA
Stiffkey
Burnham Mkt
Warham all Saints
Binham

HUNSTANTON

Heacham
Docking
Lt Walsingham

Sedgeford
Fring
E Barsham
Gt Snoring
Barney

Shernborne
Gt Bircham
FAKENHAM

Dersingham
Anmer
W Rudham
E Rudham
Stibbard
Toftrees
Gt Ryburgh

Wolferton
Helhoughton

Castle Rising
Gt Massingham
Horningtoft

S Wootton
Roydon
N Elmham

Terrington St Clement
Clenchwarton
KING'S LYNN
Gayton
Litcham

E Winch
E Walton
Castle Acre
Bittering

Tilney St Lawrence
Setchey
Pentney
Narborough

Smeeth
Watlington
Sporle
Necton

Marham
SWAFFHAM
Holme Hale
Shipdham

Shouldham

Stowbridge
Beachamwell
Cranworth

Outwell
Wimbotsham
Stradsett
Ashill

DOWNHAM MKT
Denver
Wereham
Boughton
Gooderstone
Scoulton

Wretton
Stoke Ferry
Hilborough
WATTON
Griston

Hilgay
Foulden
Bodney
Merton
Caston

Northwold
Thompson

Southery
Methwold
Ickburgh
Shropham

Brandon Creek
Mundford
Gt Hockham

Feltwell

Hockwold cum Wilton
E Harling

Croxton

Shadwell

THETFORD

R Ouse

0   10
Miles

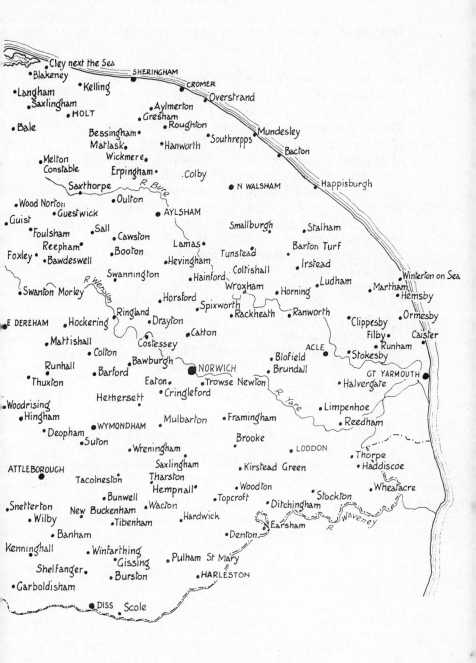

THE MAKING OF THE ENGLISH LANDSCAPE
Edited by W. G. Hoskins and Roy Millward

THE MAKING OF THE WELSH LANDSCAPE

The Norfolk Landscape

by

DAVID DYMOND

HODDER AND STOUGHTON

LONDON   SYDNEY   AUCKLAND   TORONTO

British Library Cataloguing in Publication Data

Dymond, David
    The Norfolk landscape.—(The making of the
    English landscape)
    1. Norfolk—Historical geography
    I. Title   II. Series
    911'.4261   DA670.N6

ISBN 0 340 04332 6

To my wife Mary
Who comes from Norfolk

Preface

This book on Norfolk is offered with some trepidation by one who was born in Northamptonshire, brought up in Devon, took his first job in Yorkshire and now lives, of all places, in Suffolk. I can however claim, in mitigation, to have married a Norfolk girl on a cold March day in a Norfolk church, and to have been a great admirer of the county since I first visited it twenty-two years ago. Therefore this volume, which has slowly taken shape over ten years, is written from the point of view of an enthusiastic visitor who wants to see the wood for the trees. My intention has been to highlight the main features of this highly distinctive county, and the principal historical reasons which lie behind them. My own original contribution is chiefly in the sections on medieval markets and Victorian villages, and for the rest I am heavily indebted to many other people whose work and writings I have attempted to summarise and synthesise. A growing army of students and researchers, professional and amateur, young and old, are now creating new knowledge at a hectic pace and making East Anglia a particularly exciting region to live in.

In gathering material for this book, I have received valuable help from the Norfolk and Norwich Record Office, the Colman and Rye Library and Castle Museum, Norwich, the Norfolk Archaeological Unit, the Committee for Aerial Photography, Cambridge, the university libraries of Cambridge and East Anglia, and from my own department, the Board of Extra-Mural Studies of Cambridge University. I would also like to thank the following individuals for their support: William Hoskins who originally persuaded me to undertake the task; Roy Millward who, as General Editor, has given stimulating criticism in the final shaping of the book; Margaret Body of Hodder & Stoughton for patient encouragement over many years; Christopher Barringer, a true colleague and friend who always helped when I was floundering; Paul Rutledge for wise advice in the Record Office; Peter Wade-Martins and his colleagues in that remarkable 'power house' at Gressenhall; Derek Edwards for guiding me through the intricacies of aerial photography; Graham Pooley for providing fine photographs from the equally vital man's-eye view; Barbara Green, Alan Carter and Peter Northeast for helpful comments; Elsie McCutcheon who, with her writer's eye, saved me from many a solecism; Nancy Tripp for typing endless drafts; and finally my wife and three children for allowing me, for so long, to neglect my domestic and horticultural duties.

The study of landscapes is certainly not the most important form of history, either thematically or evidentially, as it does not allow us to penetrate much beyond the technological and economic 'husk' of human life. Nevertheless, it does demonstrate how places influence people, and how in turn people shape the places in which they live and work. Furthermore, it gives us a firm physical stage on which we can reconstruct the higher themes of human life – personal, social, governmental, intellectual, religious and cultural. I hope that this book about a specially rich and immensely characterful English county will be accepted as a fair summary of knowledge as it exists in the early 1980s, and that it will itself stimulate some of the new work which must soon supplement and outdate it.

April 1984   DAVID DYMOND
                                  Grundle House
                                  Stanton
                                  Suffolk
                                  (5 miles from the border)

Contents

11

List of plates

List of maps

Editor's Introduction

DAVID DYMOND's *Norfolk* is the nineteenth volume in the *Making of the English Landscape* series, an ambitious survey of the history of our countryside and towns planned by W. G. Hoskins more than thirty years ago. The pieces of England's jigsaw of counties are beginning to fall into place. The reader can now place David Dymond's *Norfolk* beside the already published essays of Norman Scarfe and Christopher Taylor on the neighbouring counties of *Suffolk* and *Cambridgeshire*. Together the authors reveal the forces at work over the last five thousand years in the shaping of a regional landscape, that of East Anglia.

The series arose out of a dissatisfaction with much of the topographical writing of the 1930s, a discontent that is still with us in the 1980s when one scans the ceaseless torrent of guide-book journalism in the travel columns of the Sunday papers. The approach of all the authors who have contributed the eighteen published volumes of the series to date has been determined by the belief that the visible landscape is itself an expression of centuries of history, a history whose clues may be revealed through patient exploration in the field but whose full explanation can only be reached through evidence locked up in national and county records.

W. G. Hoskins laid the foundation of *The Making of the English Landscape* books when he returned to the University College at Leicester after the Second World War to establish the Department of English Local History. As a post-graduate research department it was able to turn all its energy towards local studies; after more than thirty years the harvest has indeed been rich. From the beginning it was Professor Hoskins' intention that these riches should be made accessible to those outside the walls of Academe, and the first channel through which his work became known to the general public was a series of twenty-minute talks on the BBC's Third Programme. Those talks were the inspiration for the present series of books.

Much has changed since the introductory volume and the three county essays – Cornwall, Lancashire and Gloucestershire – appeared in the mid-fifties. The series itself underwent a change of format in 1970 with the publication of Christopher Taylor's *Dorset* and Arthur Raistrick's *West Riding of Yorkshire*. The text was doubled in length, but the aim of our authors remained the same, to reveal some of the riches of our county landscapes to the ordinary reader and to encourage him to explore further through the activities and publications of local historical and archaeological groups and societies. Another, less radical change, overtook the series in 1981 with a decision to publish only in paperback.

An underlying theme of all the books has been the influence of a changing economy and society on the English landscape. The many acres of ridge-and-furrow in the Midland counties are the visible relic of a long lost medieval ordering of life. But as the series progressed into the 1970s one was made aware of the problems presented by contemporary changes in achieving a complete survey of the landscape history of England's counties. The greatest challenge came with the upheaval in Britain's local government that erased whole counties from the map. Wales and Scotland suffered most. Brecknockshire, a recognisable unit over almost two thousand years, was swallowed up in a vast sprawling borderland administration that took to itself the old name of Powys. Scotland fared perhaps even worse, where no more exciting name than Highland Region could be found for the whole of the country to the north of the Great Glen. England lost Rutland, a county whose shape had been known since the end of the twelfth century. New names such as Avon and Humberside, lacking historical roots, appeared on the map. For the historian of landscape the only acceptable piece of the 1974 reorganisation, made legal on the first day of April, was the creation of Cumbria. Cumberland, Westmorland and pieces of Lancashire on the northern shore of Morecambe Bay were joined together to give administrative unity to the Lake District and to revive memories of a forgotten Dark Age kingdom of Cumbria. As Professor Hoskins wrote of the series in 1976, 'I had to consider whether we should stick to the old counties as we have known them or adopt the new set-up. As the series was by then so far advanced under the old and well-loved names, we decided to retain them and go on as before.'

The years between the 1950s and the 1980s have seen deeper changes that have influenced our approach to the history of our counties' landscapes. It has been a time of intensive research in several related fields of knowledge where material discoveries and fresh ideas have inevitably influenced the thinking of our several authors. Place-names, their meaning and origins, are fundamental to the work of the local historian. With pleasure one records the debt of the landscape historian to the publications of the English Place-Name Society. One also notes the increasing thoroughness of research in this field. During the years between the 1914 and 1939 wars, when the ground-work of English place-name studies became firmly established, one volume sufficed to analyse the names of a single county. Of late the volumes have multiplied and the letter-press has become smaller and more closely set. Cheshire, still incomplete, runs to five volumes and the fifth volume itself has expanded into three separate parts.

The quantity of material that needs to be considered by anyone who tackles the history of his county has grown immensely. Archaeology has long ceased to be a study only of potsherds and palstaves from centuries long before the Romans. The spade and the far more refined tools and methods of the modern archaeologist have penetrated all the later centuries of history and we have professional journals that report the findings of excavations at medieval sites as well as those that date back only to the eighteenth and nineteenth centuries. Archaeology has something to contribute to every period of landscape history and its findings are frequently set out in immense detail. For instance, the Devon Archaeological Society published in 1982 the results of excavations at Okehampton Castle. The report on the findings in the Bailey alone covers 142 pages. The same journal bears witness to the growth of research into the character of prehistoric landscapes. In a *Review of the Prehistoric and Historic Environment on Dartmoor* the striking results of pollen analysis in unravelling the changes of vegetation in this upland are

19

recorded. By 1981 thirty-four sites had been investigated for their yield of pollen that had been preserved in peat-bogs from the centuries of prehistory. When the first volumes of *The Making of the English Landscape* appeared in the 1950s it seemed reasonable to assume that the continuous history of man's relationship with the countryside began in the depths of a primeval woodland that, it was believed, still covered much of Anglo-Saxon Britain. Over the past two decades evidence has been gathered in abundance to show that prehistory has contributed much to the landscape that lies around us today. Professor Hoskins has argued that many Devon farms are the descendants over a timespan of twenty centuries and more of Iron Age estates and that some of the deep, sunk lanes began as the deliberately hollowed out boundaries of those estates at a time before the Romans knew this land.

In the East Midlands evidence from quite a different source has revealed a fresh prehistoric dimension in the landscapes of Leicestershire and Nottinghamshire. Air surveys made by J. Pickering and D. N. Riley annually through the 1970s have yielded thousands of photographs whose archaeological information, hidden at ground level but visible in crop-marks from the air, has been plotted on maps of a scale of six inches to the mile. The Vale of Belvoir, once believed to have remained heavily forested until after the Saxon settlements because of its heavy clay soils, is now shown 'to have been exploited since Roman times and possibly earlier' and 'the Trent valley shows a density of prehistoric settlement never before suspected'. In his second Introduction, written for this series in 1976, William Hoskins suggested that 'Everything is older than we think.' In so many places local research has come to confirm that belief.

Towns are an important element in the evolution of the English landscape, if not the most important if we judge our society from the places where most people live. Here too the years since the beginning of the series have seen a vast expansion of research. Professor Maurice Beresford's *New Towns of the Middle Ages*, published in 1967, was a landmark in urban studies that presented not only the principles that lay behind the foundation of the medieval new town but also, in its valuable gazetteer outlined the histories of hundreds of

English and Welsh boroughs, both the successful and the failed. Urban History has established itself as an academic discipline in its own right, publishing transactions and organising conferences where the results of research are aired. The volume of publications on urban topics has been immense. Of late, and with a random choice we find a *History of Hull*, from the twelfth century to the present day, and a *History of Modern Leeds*, both published in 1980. That mammoth undertaking, *The Victoria History of the Counties of England*, started almost a century ago, looks towards its completion at some unknown future date. In the eighth volume on *Staffordshire* published in 1979, part of the ambitiously planned twenty volumes that will cover the county, we find ninety closely printed double-column pages on the county town. As one reviewer has written, this is 'the first scholarly account of the county town to cover the whole of its history'.

For each county in the series the authors of *The Making of the English Landscape* have attempted to lay before the general reader the findings or research in a wide variety of related fields, as well as the insights of the 'classic' topographical writings published over the past two hundred years. Even so, as WGH wrote in an earlier Editor's Introduction, 'after so many books and articles and theses have been written, there is so much that remains unknown, and no doubt questions that I and others, have still not perceived . . . in the end, I look upon landscape history as an enlargement of consciousness, a new way of looking at familiar scenes which adds to the enjoyment of life. For those who have eyes to see, the face of Britain will never look the same again.'

Leicester, 1984   Roy Millward

Acknowledgements

The publishers would like to thank the following for
permission to reproduce their photographs:
Aerial Archaeology Foundation: Plate 3
Basilisk Press: Plate 36
Cambridge University Collection: Plates 1, 7, 15, 18, 19, 25,
31,
Cambridge University Library: Plate 24
Colman and Rye Library, Norwich: Plates 17, 26, 37, 44, 45
Crown Copyright Reserved: Plate 20
David Dymond: Plates 10, 23, 39, 46, 47, 49
A. F. Kersting: Plate 29
Norfolk Archaeological Unit: Plates 2, 4, 8, 14, 16, 21, 22 by
Derek A. Edwards; Plate 38 by Colin Shewring; Plate 11
by David Wicks
Norfolk and Norwich Record Office: Plate 27
Graham Pooley: Plates 9, 33, 34, 41, 43, 48, 50, 52, 53
Royal Commission on Historical Monuments (England):
Plates 6, 12, 13, 28, 30, 32, 35, 40, 42, 51
Suffolk Archaeological Unit: Plate 5

1. The land of Norfolk

The sub-regions of Norfolk

OF THE TRADITIONAL counties of England, Norfolk was the
fourth largest with an area of over 1,300,000 acres, or 2,054
square miles. After the reorganisation of local government in
1974, it was slightly expanded to take in about 9,000 acres
from north-east Suffolk. The size of this predominantly rural
county constantly surprises visitors: for instance the distance
from Sutton Bridge on the western boundary to Great Yarmouth in the east is sixty-five miles, while the coastline of
Norfolk, worn smooth by the unpredictable 'rages' of the
North Sea, sweeps on for more than ninety miles.

The shape of Norfolk is probably better known than that of
any other English county. Beginning with the deep indenta-
tion of the Wash, the coast describes a remarkably smooth
curve round to Yarmouth, unbroken by major embayments
or estuaries, and has been aptly described as the 'rounded
shoulder of eastern England'. To south and west the boundary follows major rivers such as the Waveney, Little Ouse and
Nene, and in one part of the fens a dried-up watercourse
which was once the bed of the Great Ouse. As Richard Blome
commented in 1673, this is a county 'which may not improp-
erly be termed an island, as encircled with waters'. Certainly
no assessment of Norfolk's life or landscape should neglect
the North Sea which, in Henry James' words, 'moves for ever,
like a ruminating beast, an insatiable, indefatigable lip'. It not
only provides many fascinating stories of seafaring, piracy,
shipwreck, storm and flood, but helps, more than any other
influence, to give Norfolk a harder, more masculine character
than its sister county to the south.

It is a calumny often repeated by outsiders that Norfolk is
boring and featureless – in Noël Coward's words, 'very flat,
Norfolk'. It certainly contains no mountains or great ranges of

23

hills, and some areas are undeniably flat, for example in the
Peat Fen near Downham Market and on the boulder-clay
plateau of South Norfolk where, as Mosby remarked, the
land 'has the appearance of having been levelled by a gigantic
steamroller'. But for the most part Norfolk is full of subtle
variety and displays a gently undulating countryside articulated by frequent shallow valleys. Indeed in places the relief is
quite dramatic, as at the southern end of the old city of
Norwich, or in the beautiful ravines of the Holt-Cromer
Ridge. In altitude the county ranges from three feet *below*
sea-level in Stow Bardolph Fen to 340 feet on the coastal ridge
at West Runton, but within these apparently narrow limits the
folds of land frequently give an intimate visual scale which is
very different from the 'grander' scenery of, say, Yorkshire or
Devon. One encounters numerous and ever-changing views
across relatively short distances of one to three miles, which
give vertical features, like church towers, windpumps, pylons
or individual trees, a special prominence which is lost elsewhere. Finally, even the most unsympathetic visitor or the
most earthbound East Anglian cannot help noticing the
frequent beauty of the huge sky which forms an almost
complete hemisphere over the softly swelling and richly
productive landscape.

Geologically Norfolk is often said to be one of the youngest
parts of Britain. This is certainly true of the uppermost rocks,
but it must never be forgotten that buried deeper in the
earth's crust are layers of much greater age. For example, at
North Creake in 1946 a deep bore penetrated over 1,500 feet
of rocks laid down in Triassic times about 200 million years
ago. Beneath that again, beginning at a depth of 2,600 feet (or
half a mile below sea-level) the drill encountered a sloping
pavement of pre-Cambrian rocks over 600 million years old.
Nevertheless the rocks which outcrop above sea-level, and
are moulded to make the present landscape, were all formed
'recently' in the last 200 million years. Mostly soft and
sedimentary, they were laid down in great prehistoric seas
which once covered the whole or greater part of East Anglia.
Thus, the fossils of sea creatures such as ammonites, belem-
nites and sea urchins are commonly found well away from the
present coast. Although these rocks were originally laid down

in horizontal bands as sediment of the sea, or of rivers flowing into the sea, they are not horizontal today. Movements in the earth's crust at a later date raised and tipped the whole area, so that the rocks are at their highest in the north-west and at their lowest in the south-east. Put very crudely, East Anglia is a thick flat plate of soft rocks which was raised and slightly tilted towards the Low Countries.

Because of this tilting the oldest rocks appear in west Norfolk as a distinct escarpment overlooking the fens. In a long narrow strip of country from Hunstanton in the north to Southery in the south, various clays, sands and sandstones outcrop to reveal the geological sandwich underlying the rest of the county. The oldest visible stratum rising from under the surface of the fenland is a dark grey-blue clay or compressed mud known as Kimmeridge clay, which accumulated about 160 million years ago. It contains a wide range of fossils including large oyster shells, fish and giant reptiles called pliosaurs. Above this is one of the best known geological formations in Norfolk, a ginger-coloured sandstone called carrstone, which is firm enough to have been used in local buildings; its texture and colour give great character, for example, to the Victorian town of Hunstanton. However the rock which has had the greatest effect on the scenery and human life of Norfolk is the uppermost and latest in this escarpment, the chalk.

Laid down in a Cretaceous sea between 135 and 70 million years ago, the chalk consists primarily of the remains of once living organisms such as algae and foraminifera. It accumulated slowly, probably at the rate of one foot in 30,000 years. In spite of considerable later erosion, it is still up to 1,400 feet thick and underlies the whole county east of the escarpment. Here on the 'East Anglian Heights', where the chalk is highest, we find rolling downland which is reminiscent of Wessex or the Yorkshire Wolds. As one goes east, the chalk gradually descends and is increasingly masked by later deposits. At Yarmouth, in the extreme east of the county, the top of the chalk is 500 feet below the present surface.

Except in the fenland and coastal marshes, virtually every field in Norfolk contains innumerable stones of flint. They have been picked off the arable land for centuries, and since

25

at least Roman times have been used for making roads and buildings. Indeed flint, which can be gathered on the surface or quarried, is the only widespread building stone to be found in East Anglia. Yet ironically this hard and indestructible stone, which can easily draw blood from the hand of a flint-knapper or mason, is derived from delicate sponges which once swayed on the bed of a Cretaceous sea. It was originally formed in the middle and upper levels of the chalk, where it can be found either as bands of irregular nodules or in flat seams suitable for quarrying, as at the famous Neolithic mines of Grimes Graves.

The lower end of the chalk, east of a north-south line from Weybourne to Dickleburgh, was covered in much later Pliocene and Pleistocene times by deposits known as the Crag Series. These shelly sands, clays and gravels, were also laid down beneath the sea, or in freshwater estuaries at its edge, and have memorable names such as the Norwich Crag, Weybourne Crag and Cromer Forest Bed.

In a most graphic way, these deposits remind us of the myriad landscapes and seascapes entombed beneath our feet in the geological record. For example, the famous Cromer Forest Bed can be shown, by an examination of its pollens, to enshrine the record of a whole interglacial period. First came a pine and birch forest typical of a cold climate; this was gradually replaced by a temperate forest dominated by oak, elm and lime. Ultimately, as the climate became cold again, pine and spruce colonised the landscape once more. The catalogue of animal remains is also rich: in the Norwich Crag were the bones of leopard, elephant, hyena and mastodon, while the Forest Bed has yielded the remains of rhinoceros, sabre-toothed tiger and hippopotamus.

Finally, in the Ice Age, huge sheets of ice radiating from the mountains of Scandinavia and northern Britain slowly scraped and gouged their way across East Anglia. They must have greatly altered the relief of the region, planing off higher parts of the sedimentary landscape and creating new lines of drainage when the ice melted. It is thought that the ice advanced and retreated several times over 1½ million years, as it responded to alternating phases of cold and milder weather.

The ice carried before it, and in it, masses of rock and finer debris. When it finally melted, this debris was left behind either in great ridges marking the former limits of ice-sheets (like the well known Holt-Cromer Ridge) or as horizontal layers masking earlier rocks. In areas such as the Breckland, the glaciers left behind light sands and gravels, but elsewhere as in the huge expanse of central and South Norfolk, a layer of heavy clay was plastered over the chalk and crags. As this clay frequently contains fragments of harder rock, often brought considerable distances by the ice, it has been called 'boulder-clay'. Yielding a deep fertile soil, it covers more than half the surface of Norfolk and has had a great effect on local scenery and agricultural history.

It must be emphasised that all the Jurassic, Cretaceous and Pliocene deposits which have been mentioned continue into the areas now covered by the sea. The present county is simply that part of a vast sedimentary landscape which has managed to stay above the sea-levels of the last few thousand years. In geological time the sea-level had fluctuated constantly. For example while a great deal of water was locked up in the form of ice, considerably more dry land must have been revealed. The southern half of the present North Sea was probably exposed marshland and the major eastward-flowing rivers of East Anglia were tributaries of the Rhine. When the sea-level rose again at the end of the Ice Age (about 10,000 – 7,000 B.C.) then Norfolk began, approximately, to take the shape we know today. But that shape too has never been absolutely stable. Between 3,000 and 2,000 B.C. the north coast may have extended as far as the Woolpack Sands; an Early Bronze Age axe/hammer was found about five miles north of the present coastline, and the stumps of a prehistoric forest can still be seen off Holme and Thornham. In spite of modern efforts to combat erosion, the crumbling cliffs between Weybourne and the broads have receded two or three miles since Roman times, and the loss is still said to be between one and five yards a year. Elsewhere, as between Hunstanton and Weybourne, the process of erosion has been reversed in the last 2,000 years or so. An ancient coastline of cliffs is now several miles inland, thanks to the gradual growth of shingle spits and vegetated marshland.

27

Not only did the present coastline take shape at the end of the Ice Age, but also the pattern of hills, valleys and plateaux which are the basis of our modern map. So the county as a whole is the product of ancient sediments accumulating over many millions of years, yet moulded drastically by the ice and water which swept over it in the recent geological past.

The sub-regions of Norfolk

In spite of its lack of dramatic relief, Norfolk has long been noted for its rich variety of soils and land use. In 1676 Thomas Fuller commented that 'all England may be carved out of Norfolk . . . so grateful is this shire with the variety thereof'. But it was not until 1804 that Arthur Young produced the first detailed map of its sub-regions. In the twentieth century several clarifications have appeared, of which A. R. Cartwright's is the most recent and detailed. With one important exception, his regions are basically the same as those of his predecessors, but by using a whole range of criteria in a computerised survey he has drawn the boundaries with far greater intricacy. In this book, thirteen sub-regions have been adopted and are summarised in Fig. 1; they vary considerably in size, and some of the boundaries are far more sharply identifiable than others. The divisions are based primarily on Cartwright's work, though in several cases the earlier, historical names have been preferred.

At its western end, Norfolk includes a substantial part of the flat fenland normally associated with the counties of Cambridgeshire and Lincolnshire. This area is entirely below the twenty-five foot contour, and is now very productive farmland. It has virtually no woodland or heath, and comparatively few trees or hedges. Geologically and historically it should be divided into two parts: to the north and adjacent to the Wash are deep estuarine silts traditionally known as the *Marshland*, while inland to the south is a smaller spread of *Peat Fen* which, because of shrinkage, often lies lower than the silts. The Marshland is conspicuous for its chain of large looseknit villages, winding roads and radiating parishes, whereas the Peat Fen has a much more geometrical appear-

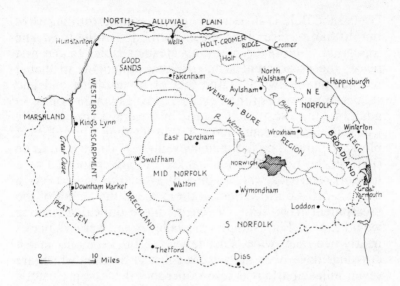

Fig. 1. The sub-regions of Norfolk.

ance, being thinly settled and dominated by long straight man-made drains.

In no other part of Norfolk do we get a clearer impression of man's effect on the environment than in the fens. Even the *terra firma* is artificial, and had to be won from freshwater swamps and muddy salt flats. It is now a strictly utilitarian landscape in which all available land is intensively used, and where little room is left for beauty or sentiment. Yet these vast, open and bleak spaces do have a strange charm. Furthermore, this is a landscape which is still visibly controlled and kept in balance; successive generations of farmers and engineers have built up an intricate system of banks, drains and sluices designed to control the ever-threatening forces of wind, tide and flood. In the winter months, the deliberate flooding of the Ouse Washes near Welney, as a means of accommodating superfluous water, or the sheer weight of water thundering through the sluices at Denver, are unforgettable sights.

The *Western Escarpment*, known traditionally as the

Greensand Belt, is an area of Cretaceous rocks forming a low but distinct terrace along the eastern edge of the fens. The topography, however, is by no means simple. In the first place, the escarpment is tilted along its length, so that it reaches nearly two hundred feet at its northern end and shades to the level of the Peat Fen at Hilgay in the south. In addition, the escarpment is cut by several rivers draining westward into the fens or Wash, thus dividing it into distinct blocks separated by flat, marshy valleys. Villages tend to be sited on the ridges or their flanks, and are connected by a network of roads which similarly avoid the valleys. As a result, north-south communications along the length of the escarpment have always been far more difficult than one would expect. For example, the valley of the Nar is in places nearly two miles wide; since medieval times the only major crossings have been at Narborough and Setchey which are seven miles apart. It is also noticeable that the prehistoric Icknield Way kept to the higher ground beyond the heads of most of these westward-flowing valleys.

Because of the varied geology of the escarpment, land use has been, and is, very mixed. The lighter soils show an abundance of woodland which contrasts strikingly with the openness of the adjacent fenland. Most of these woods were planted in the last two centuries on former commons and warrens. Nevertheless, a considerable acreage of common heathland still exists, particularly north of the Nar, and some of it is still regularly grazed. Better and heavier soils occur at the southern end of the escarpment, particularly between the Nar and Wissey, and this gives rise to good farmland.

The *Good Sands* region was named by Arthur Young in the eighteenth century, and is one of the most famous agricultural regions in Britain. This is because its farming economy was transformed in the late seventeenth and eighteenth centuries by major landowners and their enterprising tenants. The land turned out to be 'good' by the farming standards of the day, and contrasted with the 'bad' sands of the Breckland further south. The region is a large triangular tract of dry, rolling upland with the chalk either at the surface or covered by light glacial soils of a sandy or loamy texture. In the north-western corner of the county, in the vicinity of Docking, the chalk reaches a height of about 290 feet; further to the east and south it dips gently away. Although attractive rounded valleys were long ago moulded by ice and melt-water, little surface water is visible today.

The human landscape is far less intricate than on the Greensand. Villages are normally four to five miles apart – a spacing which is not typical of East Anglia as a whole. The road system is noticeably sparser and more geometrical; in fact the map seems covered by a curious overlapping of rectangles and 'spokes' radiating from the principal villages. The wide spaces between villages are punctuated by isolated farmsteads, often architecturally impressive and supported by large acreages.

On the northern edge of this region, against the sea, is a long thin strip of low land known as the *North Alluvial Plain*. It is about twenty-five miles long running from Holme in the west to Weybourne in the east, yet at its greatest is no more than two miles wide. It accumulated in the last thousand years or so, as fine sediments were deposited at the mouths of rivers or moved from east to west by longshore drift. Since at least the seventeenth century, local farmers have accelerated the process by building walls and digging dykes, in order to convert salt marshes into permanent grazing grounds. Now the area is a fascinating blend of freshwater marshes, mainly grazed by cattle, of salt marshes and winding muddy creeks which are famed for the richness of their birdlife, and subtly curved islands and spits of shingle and sand. Most of the local villages, which lie well behind the alluvial strip, have little harbours or 'staithes' connected by winding channels to the open sea.

To the east the Good Sands merge into a high ridge of gravels, sands and clays known to all geographers as the *Holt-Cromer Ridge*. In origin this is the debris left behind, late in the glacial period, by an ice-sheet which just overlapped the surface of the present county, before melting back to the north. Running approximately east-west, the ridge is one of the most attractive and hilly parts of Norfolk, and reaches a height of about 340 feet on Beacon Hill near West Runton. Its southern face slopes gently towards the interior of the county, and is drained by a network of little streams which eventually feed the river Bure. By contrast, its northern face, overlooking the sea, is an impressive, indented escarpment with outlying spurs and hills bearing fascinating names like Muckleburgh and Gramborough. Much of the escarpment from Cromer to Weybourne is now wooded, but substantial acreages of high sandy heathland still survive. Further inland, the ridge is largely devoted to arable farming.

The lower part of the scenic Glaven valley, between Hunworth and Cley, marks a fairly sharp change in the human landscape. To the west are the widely spaced villages and thin road pattern of the Good Sands; to the east lies the far more intricate landscape of the ridge with its snaking roads, tumulus-haunted heaths, irregular patches of woodland, looseknit villages and modern seaside developments.

The *Breckland* was named as late as 1894 by W. G. Clarke; the 'brecks' were areas of heathland ploughed for a few years and then allowed to revert to the wild. Basically this distinctive region is a tract of very light 'blowing' sands filling a large depression in the chalk. This porous combination, with a rainfall of less than twenty-five inches a year, makes Breckland the driest part of the British Isles. It has always been agriculturally marginal, with its own special patterns of farming and land use.

Of the ancient heaths and commons, some impressive relics still survive in parishes like Brettenham, East Wretham and Foulden, but most of the lonely upland between valleys is now used more productively. It is a geometrical landscape consisting either of large sandy fields, defined by straight tracks and tree-belts but still liable to severe 'blowing', or of huge areas of coniferous woodland planted by the Forestry Commission and private landowners. A noticeable feature of the tree-belts, heaths, and hedges is the warmly tinted and asymmetrical Scots pine, a tree which has been part of the Breckland landscape since prehistoric times.

The Breckland is sparsely inhabited. Settlement mainly consists of nucleated villages sited in westward-flowing valleys or along the edge of the fens. Indeed along certain valleys, villages, though often small, are surprisingly close to each other. For example, a three-mile length of the Wissey valley near Mundford contains no fewer than five parish churches. One of the most unexpected components of the Norfolk Breckland is a so-called 'battle area' used for military training. Its designation in 1940 necessitated the abandonment of thousands of acres of farmland and five complete villages. Now it is a mysterious, wild and lonely tract of country which, uncharacteristically for a progressive agricultural region, is being slowly reclaimed by nature. Already conservationists acknowledge it as a rich reservoir of native plants, animals and birds.

In the centre of Norfolk is a plateau of boulder-clay which yields medium to heavy soils. This is the largest natural region in the county, being about thirty miles across in all directions. It has been called 'high Norfolk' to stress its physical and cultural similarity to the adjoining part of central Suffolk, but the term is misleading: the land is normally no higher than 100 to 200 feet, and only to the west and north of East Dereham does it frequently exceed 200 feet in response to the rising chalk beneath. Because this is a large region and the heaviest soils lie in the south, it can be conveniently divided into *South Norfolk* and *Mid-Norfolk*, using the A 11 from Norwich to Larling as the boundary. In general the topography is softly undulating with frequent small valleys, though the area north of Diss is undeniably flat. Running in an unobtrusive way off the plateau, in all directions, is a dense network of natural streams, many of them nameless; they eventually connect with major rivers like the Waveney to the south, the Wissey to the west and the Yare to the north.

The man-made parts of this landscape are ancient, intricate and irregular. One's eye is immediately taken by the tight informal mesh of local roads which serve a scattered human population. Villages are frequently looseknit and churches often lie isolated in the fields; hamlets abound, and in their names often indicate that they originated around commons or greens; farmsteads are peppered all over the map, and many turn out to be ancient timber-framed buildings standing within water-filled moats. The traditional farming landscape, where it has not been totally obliterated by insensitive modern farmers, contains frequent small patches of deciduous woodland, irregular fields bounded by mixed hedges and ancient pollards, deep man-made ditches and winding lanes.

Cartwright's definition of a new *Wensum-Bure Region* is helpful, although it depends more on topographical features than geology. These two long and meandering rivers dominate and unify the area as they pursue a predominantly south-easterly course towards the sea. Their valleys are, by East Anglian standards, wide and provide lush meadowland; furthermore they introduce the most important changes of relief in an otherwise soft landscape, most of which is below 100 feet. Geologically the region is very mixed. It ranges from heavy boulder-clay at the north-western end, through great spreads of glacial loam which yield fertile light-to-medium soils, to frequent patches of infertile glacial sand and gravel.

Man's use of the fertile loams has produced a landscape similar to South and Mid-Norfolk. Frequent villages, hamlets and farmsteads are served by an irregular network of roads. By contrast, the infertile soils stand out as heathland and modern plantations, especially north of Norwich, or have been absorbed into ornamental parks as at Rackheath.

Two smaller coastal regions are usually distinguished because of their deep and outstandingly fertile soils of light-to-medium loam. The first is only about ten miles across but is normally termed *North-East Norfolk*. From the coast between Mundesley and Sea Palling, it stretches inland as far as North Walsham and Tunstead. It has been referred to as the 'land of Goshen' because it is probably the most fertile part of the entire county. The second district is *Flegg*, just north of Yarmouth, which is even smaller in area but was formerly a distinct 'island' surrounded by sea and marshy valleys. It rises to a maximum height of sixty feet and geologically is a detached part of the loam country. The Muck Fleet is a winding valley, containing several 'broads', which effectively divides Flegg into two halves and two ancient administrative hundreds.

The final region, so well known to holiday-makers and ecologists, is *Broadland*. This is a complicated system of winding alluvial valleys and marshland where the surface water of more than half the county converges, before being funnelled out to sea past Yarmouth. A dense and complicated system of man-made dykes and natural streams feeds three major rivers, the Waveney, Yare and Bure; these in turn converge on Breydon Water which is a natural estuary once connecting directly to the sea but now greatly constricted and deflected by the sandbank on which Yarmouth stands. At intervals along the lower lengths of the major and minor valleys, which are barely above sea-level, are the enigmatic lakes or 'broads' which give their names to the region. Many of these remain as stretches of open water, but unless they are kept clear they become progressively choked by silt, reeds, scrub and trees. For example, Hoveton Broad which covered 130 acres in 1840 is now only 76 acres, while smaller broads at Hickling Priory and Dilham have become completely vegetated. Large acreages of drained grassland between the broads provide rich grazing, especially for cattle.

Between the valleys are fingers of higher ground which are heavily settled and farmed. Above the level of about twenty feet, one finds the familiar patterns of the loam region with closely spaced villages, hamlets and farmsteads. Every minor spur seems occupied by a farm and a network of tracks serving not only upland fields but also the lower grazing grounds. The major roads tend to keep clear of the valleys, but ancient crossings do exist, for example at Ludham bridge or Wey bridge with its mile-long causeway to the island of Flegg.

Broadland is one of the most important 'wetlands' in Europe, supporting an irreplaceable richness of plant and animal life. However, it is also a major agricultural region, both for its arable and pasture, and is under increasing pressure from a growing holiday industry. Here, more than anywhere else in Norfolk, we can see the awesome environmental responsibilities placed on our own generation. The competing claims of agriculture, leisure and sport must be heard, but at the same time the fragile ecological fabric, which is infinitely more precious than any short-term economic gain, has to be maintained for posterity.

SELECT BIBLIOGRAPHY

Blake, P. W., Bull, J., *et al.*, *The Norfolk we live in* (1975).
Chatwin, C. P., *British Regional Geology, East Anglia and adjoining areas* (1961).

Larwood, G. P., and Funnell, B. M., *The Geology of Norfolk* (1970).

Petch, C. P., and Swann, E. L., *Flora of Norfolk* (1968).

West, R. G., *East Anglia* (International Union for Quaternary Research, 1977).

2. Prehistoric landscapes

The first farmers

At about 400,000 B.C., during one of the warmer 'interglacial' periods of the Ice Age, the first human hunters stealthily prospected the northern parts of East Anglia. This was the local beginning of the Old Stone Age or Palaeolithic which lasted forty times longer than the rest of human history. For many thousands of years, small family groups probably moved around seasonally, hunting animals, gathering edible leaves, roots and fruits, and finally retreating southwards again when conditions deteriorated.

Judging from the large number of flint tools which have been found in sedimentary deposits, these groups preferred to hunt and bivouac in river valleys and on the edges of lakes which were then numerous. For example at Whitlingham near Norwich, on the sloping sides of the Yare valley, a concentration of pointed hand axes was found in almost mint condition. Old Stone Age implements have been found in many parts of Norfolk, but particularly in the Breckland. Their frequency has led to East Anglia being called the 'meeting ground of geology and prehistoric archaeology'; they indicate not a large population but the frequent manufacture and discarding of implements, over immensely long and intermittent periods of time. Unfortunately, the effect on the landscape of successive Palaeolithic cultures over nearly 400,000 years was minimal. No doubt these wandering bands of hunters and food gatherers felled saplings, built rough shelters, prised lumps of flint from outcrops and created tracks along the valleys and through the forest, but their efforts were either obliterated by new ice-sheets or have not, so far, been identified by archaeological science.

When the ice finally melted around 10,000 B.C., plants and trees colonised the bare landscape once again – and for the last time – thus introducing a vegetational sequence which has lasted until today. The evidence lies in microscopic pollen which landed on the surface of lakes and fens, and was often preserved in accumulations of mud, silt or peat. For example, by boring into the deep mud of Hockham Mere, a lake on the Breckland which had once covered 280 acres, Harry Godwin in 1939 found the first evidence in Britain for the vegetation of post-glacial times (Fig. 2).

From about 10,000 B.C., while the climate was still cold, the ice swept landscape of Norfolk was slowly colonised by an 'open herbaceous vegetation' with fairly frequent trees of birch, willow and pine. Woodland, predominantly of birch, tended to be denser in river valleys, sheltered hollows and on well drained morainic soils. From about 8,500 B.C. a slow rise in average temperature led to a relatively sharp decline in the pollens of grasses and ferns, as the landscape became increasingly dominated by true forest. This consisted mainly of birch and pine, but gradually new species appeared like hazel, elm, oak and lime. Oliver Rackham has recently suggested that lime, though inconspicuous in pollen diagrams, was 'probably the commonest tree in the prehistoric countryside of Lowland England'.

In the increasingly forested environment of the middle Stone Age or Mesolithic, human technology had to adapt and change. A special kind of flint axe was developed, and various composite tools for catching fish and fowl and for hunting forest animals (such as red and roe deer, cattle and pigs). Scatters of flints and waste flakes have been found on the Breckland, the fen-edge, along the coast and in certain river valleys such as the Waveney and Yare, and show that Mesolithic hunting parties roamed widely over Norfolk, no doubt following seasonal routes. On Kelling Heath is a particularly large site which has produced over a thousand different kinds of tools and 'microliths'. Recently a rich site discovered at Banham has demonstrated that even the forested boulder-clay of South Norfolk was regularly exploited at this time.

One of the imponderables of landscape history is to judge how far Mesolithic man, as a wandering hunter and food gatherer, actually changed his surroundings in his tenure of 5,000 years or so. How effective was his 'tranchet' axe in

Plate 1 Grimes Graves, Weeting: an industrial landscape of shafts and spoil-heaps created by extensive flint-mining in Neolithic times, *c.* 2000 BC. Out of an original 800 pits, 366 are still visible.

Plate 2 Arminghall: a Neolithic temple or 'henge-monument' built *c.* 2600 BC, still a faint circular earthwork with a total diameter of about 260 ft. An entrance and eight central post-holes are visible.

Plate 3 Warham: a fort of the late Iron Age (1st cent. AD or 1st cent. BC). Two ramparts and ditches enclose 3½ acres. The lower end was destroyed *c.* 1780 by landscape gardeners.

Plate 4 Downham West: cropmarks of early fields, roads and settlements, probably Romano-British. To the right, the Fen Causeway, a Roman road following a natural bank of silt.

Plate 5 Gallows Hill, Thetford: a native, Icenian 'enclosure' of 40-60 AD, built at the time of the Roman invasion. Three ditches and lengthy palisades surround a small group of circular buildings. Its purpose is still hotly debated.

Plate 6 Caistor St Edmund: the Roman town of *Venta Icenorum*, with medieval church in one corner, as photographed in 1928. Note the surrounding walls, grid-pattern of streets extending beyond the ramparts, and major public buildings in centre.

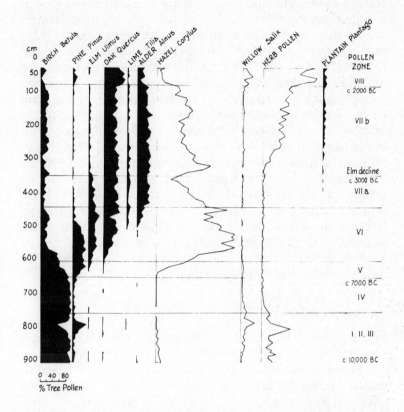

Fig. 2. Hockham Mere: a simplified pollen diagram (after H. Godwin) showing the changing proportions of species. The vertical scale represents the depth of deposit and, therefore, time.

cutting down scrub and trees, and did he use fire to control or modify the natural forest? Although the effects are extremely hard to identify, small human populations surely did cut holes in the forests of Norfolk, by clearing land for seasonal encampments and trackways, and by acquiring fuel and raw materials for dwellings, tools and boats. Even though the forest might have reclaimed what it had temporarily lost, man by his actions may have discouraged some species of plants and encouraged others (hazel was certainly on the increase). Indeed certain areas may have been especially attractive to prehistoric man. For example, the converging valleys of the Norwich area must have provided a rich harvest of animal protein, as well as soils which later proved ideal for cultivation. It is surely not accidental that Mesolithic microliths and flakes were found during the excavation of the Neolithic sanctuary at Arminghall and a nearby round barrow at Trowse. In such areas at least, prehistoric man was probably modifying the world of nature long before 3,500 B.C.

The first farmers

In the fourth millennium B.C., East Anglia was increasingly penetrated by Neolithic people – that is, they were systematic farmers capable of herding domesticated animals and of growing crops. No doubt these new economic ideas were also adopted, sooner or later, by the native Mesolithic population. Settlement sites are gradually being found, usually by chance, which enable us to assess the life of these first farmers of Norfolk five to six thousand years ago. One of the most significant is at Broome Heath, Ditchingham, where an extensive site lies on a gravel terrace close to the river Waveney. Features on the surface include a long burial mound and a mysterious C-shaped earthwork which may have been defensive. Excavation has yielded large quantities of Neolithic pottery and worked flints, as well as bowl-shaped hearths, postholes and fragments of daub.

These settlers were certainly farmers in the true sense. They used saddle-querns for grinding, and lined pits probably for the storage of grain; the impressions of wheat and barley have also been recognised in their pottery. Pollen found under the earthwork suggested that the area had been first cleared about 3,500 B.C.: initially it had been used for pasture, but in about 2,600 B.C. it was ploughed. Then came another phase of pastoralism, before the earthwork itself was erected in *c.* 2,200 B.C. Of course settlement was not necessarily continuous for these 1,500 years, for Broome Heath was probably one of a series of sites occupied in rotation as arable soils became exhausted or grass over-grazed. Nevertheless this clearance survived, be it noted, for many hundreds of years, and may never have been recolonised again by woodland; by the Middle Ages the area had become a common heath belonging to the parish of Ditchingham. Incidentally, that place name may mean 'the village of the dwellers at the dike' which could be an Anglo-Saxon reference to the Neolithic earthwork already more than 2,000 years old. Recently, other settlements of the Neolithic period have been identified in Norfolk: at Eaton near Norwich, where 'deep' shafts have been interpreted as wells or 'ritual' features, at Edingthorpe near North Walsham where traces of Neolithic and later occupation were found sporadically over an area of 150 acres, and at Hunstanton where a group of round houses was found beside a rectangular timber enclosure.

Work at Broome Heath and Old Buckenham Mere suggests that land was certainly being cleared, even on the heavier soils of Mid- and South Norfolk, but it was on the Breckland that these early farmers had the greatest effect on their surroundings. In the 1940s Harry Godwin was able to prove, by pollen analysis, that the Breckland had been substantially and permanently cleared of its natural woodland in Neolithic times, and became an area of grass, heathland and arable with its own very distinctive agricultural history. Not until the early nineteenth century did the Breckland again grow trees in any numbers.

Neolithic farmers developed a considerable armoury of tools and techniques for tackling their forested environment. At Grimes Graves, Whitlingham and several other places in Norfolk, high-quality flint was systematically mined by means of adits, vertical shafts and horizontal tunnels cut into the chalk. It has been estimated that at Grimes Graves itself (Plate 1), a famous site in the Breckland which was extensively developed in late Neolithic times (*c.* 2,000 B.C.), several million axes and other implements must have been fashioned from the black lustrous flint known as 'floor-stone'. Considerable numbers of flint axes were used in Norfolk itself, though certainly a proportion were exported to other parts of the British Isles. By contrast, many implements made of other kinds of stone were brought into the region from surprisingly distant sources such as Cornwall and the Lake District.

Using such tools, Neolithic farmers were cutting clearances like the one at Ditchingham, and winning the timber which was an indispensable raw material for implements and houses. The grazing of domesticated animals and the selective cutting of fodder, such as elm and ash leaves, may also have been altering the botanical composition of the natural 'wild-wood'. Recent research on the prehistoric trackways of Somerset certainly demonstrates that Neolithic man was capable of coppicing, that is, cutting trees and shrubs down to the ground to encourage the growth of multiple straight poles which can be regularly harvested. Coppiced woodland was without doubt a feature of medieval and later Norfolk: it may well represent a form of management which had been going on continuously since prehistoric times.

The most powerful symbol yet found in Norfolk of Neolithic man's increasing control of his environment, as well as of his social organisation and religious beliefs, is the sanctuary or 'henge-monument' at Arminghall just south of Norwich (Plate 2). A large circular bank fifty feet wide, with external and internal ditches, surrounded a central space with a diameter of ninety feet. Here a horseshoe of eight large holes once contained huge timber posts up to three feet in diameter and sunk into the ground to a depth of seven and a half feet. It is not known whether the posts were free-standing 'totems' or actually supported a roofed building. Either way, this technical and symbolic achievement is as impressive for its time as the erection, 3,000 years later and only two miles away in the next valley, of Norwich cathedral.

Metal tools in copper and bronze were available from about 2,500 B.C., and this seems to have led to an increase of human activity over most of the county. In the fenland especially, palaeobotanical evidence points to large-scale clearance of local forests during the second millennium B.C., but settlements of the Bronze Age are unfortunately rare. Where they do exist as at Hockwold-cum-Wilton and Edingthorpe, they are rarely more than a pattern of hearths, scoops and pits. Occasionally, for example at Grimes Graves, Bronze Age settlements are definitely associated with the new working of metals. By contrast, the round barrows or burial mounds of the period are comparatively common field monuments; Norfolk has some 625 recorded examples, of which 228 survive as visible mounds. The majority are on the western side of the county, mainly on the higher ground of the Good Sands and Breckland where large areas of heathland ensured that many barrows were not attacked by the plough until modern times. One of the densest concentrations with about sixty barrows, large and small, can still be seen on the heathland behind Salthouse, associated with evocative names like Three Farthing Hill and Gallow Hill. However, in various parts of the county, but especially on the eastern side, aerial photography has recently revealed nearly a thousand 'ring ditches' which are probably the remains of ploughed-out barrows. Particularly impressive concentrations have been recorded on the gravel terraces of the Bure and, again, in the Norwich area, where the Tas, Yare and Wensum converge. This is a fascinating reminder that landscapes contain 'zones of destruction' where intensive agriculture or urban growth have tended to destroy evidence of early occupation, and 'zones of survival' where traditional grazing and common rights have given earthworks and monuments a much longer lease of life.

A map of both mounds and ring ditches (Fig. 3) shows that the Bronze Age population of Norfolk was widely distributed, at least in death and probably in life. Not only were the western uplands and Breckland well populated, but also the Holt-Cromer Ridge and the valleys of the middle Yare, Wensum and Waveney. Within any locality, round barrows are not likely to have been built on productive farmland in the immediate vicinity of a settlement, but beyond the fields, on the 'waste', or on boundaries between settlements. A good example is that remarkable alignment of barrows at Brettenham, known as the Seven Hills (although originally at least

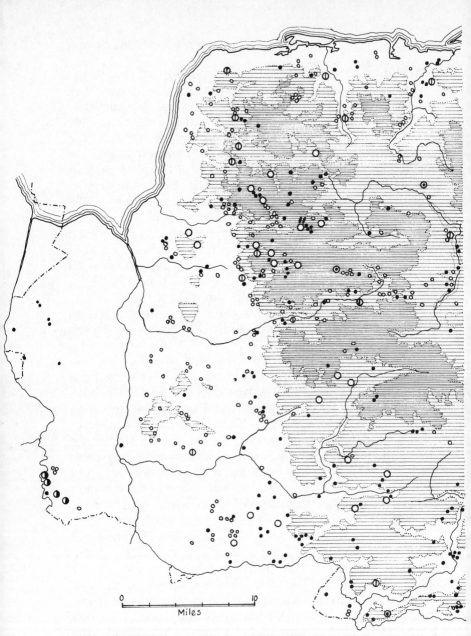

Fig. 3. Barrows and ring-ditches as known in March 1983. This map shows, better than any other evidence, the wide distribution of prehistoric population. Even in Mid and South Norfolk (admittedly the drier parts), 79 new ring-ditches were discovered by aerial photography 1977–83 (based on information supplied by Norfolk Archaeological Unit).

44

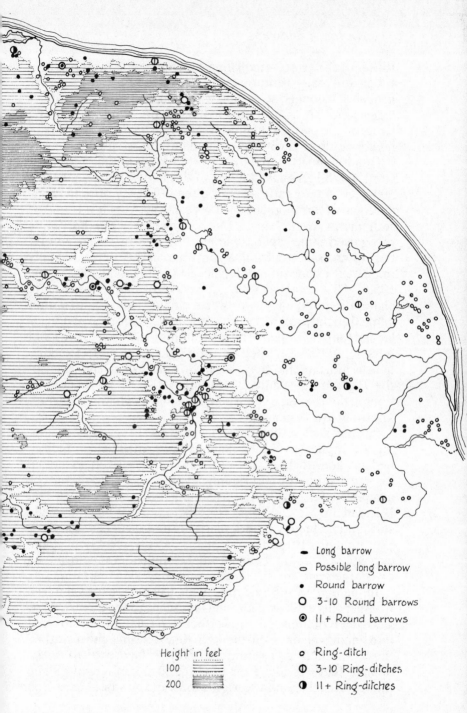

Long barrow
Possible long barrow
Round barrow
3-10 Round barrows
11+ Round barrows

Ring-ditch
3-10 Ring-ditches
11+ Ring-ditches

Height in feet
100
200

45

thirteen). They are sited along a commanding ridge, on land which for many centuries was open sandy heath, but they probably belonged to people who were settled in the valleys on each side. It is interesting that most surviving barrows tend to be 'on the poorest, lightest soil despite the local presence of higher grade soils with better agricultural potential'.

Iron is a much more effective cutting agent than bronze or stone, so the gradual adoption of this harder metal in the last 500 years B.C. greatly increased the efficiency of both clearance and of farming. Until a few years ago, very few Iron Age settlements were known. Now, however, they are being recognised quite regularly in Norfolk by scatters of pottery, very often associated with a later Roman site. One nationally important excavation took place at West Harling in the early 1950s. This revealed a farmstead consisting of three quite elaborate buildings: two were circular and built within banked enclosures, while the third, later in date, was rectangular and timber-framed. The inhabitants bred cattle, sheep and horses, and also hunted to supplement their diet; saddle-querns indicate that they also grew some grain. The valley of the Thet, in the vicinity of Harling, shows that local populations in the Iron Age could be surprisingly high: three sites are known in less than a mile.

Around such settlements, farmers must have been developing a complicated 'Celtic' landscape of small fields, ditches, hedges, and tracks. Little of it has been positively identified by excavation, but intriguing evidence of other kinds is available. For example, palaeobotanists working at Old Buckenham Mere in South Norfolk found that 'the first really substantial clearance took place in the fourth century B.C.'. The pollens of herbaceous plants rapidly increased at the expense of trees, so it appears that woodland was being felled on a large scale and the land largely converted to pasture.

In the light of this scientific evidence, we are forced to ask whether this extensive farming landscape of the Iron Age has since been obliterated, or whether it to some extent survived into medieval or even modern times. Using the so-called 'Essex method' of relating the modern landscape to major datable features like Roman roads, one can already argue that parts of the South Norfolk landscape may be at least Iron

Age in origin. A major Roman road, now the A140, runs up from Scole with an orientation of approximately nineteen degrees east of north. Yet the general alignment or 'grain' of the countryside between Scole and Forncett (taking features like ditches, roads and boundaries) is noticeably different at four degrees *west* of north. Normally one would expect a Roman road to be earlier than local fields and tracks, and to have influenced their layout (probable examples of this can also be seen – for example to the east of Long Stratton). But where a discrepancy exists, we may have a basically prehistoric landscape which has been overlaid by a Roman military road of the first century A.D. It is at least possible that South Norfolk, traditionally regarded as a 'late' landscape cleared in Saxon or medieval times, has considerably more continuity from the prehistoric past than, say, the Breckland where medieval and modern developments have tended to wipe the slate cleaner. This is certainly not to argue that every ditch or track is Iron Age in origin, but that some of the broader alignments and patterns are probably prehistoric and have been repeatedly adapted, ever since, to changing needs and technologies.

The more settled peasant agriculture which is represented at West Harling was the economic base for the emergence of a wealthy aristocratic society, and probably for a rapidly growing population. These people were capable of building strong defensive forts as at South Creake, Narborough and Warham St Mary. At the latter, impressive ramparts and ditches still enclose a circular area of three and a half acres on a slope above the river Stiffkey (Plate 3). This society was also wealthy enough to commission superb ornaments such as the Snettisham torcs and, later on, to strike their own gold and silver coins. By the early first century A.D., all the various ethnic and cultural groups which existed in northern East Anglia had fused to form a tribe and kingdom known as the Iceni. On the basis of their coinage, Derek Allen attempted to reconstruct their fluctuating boundaries and internal organisation: for example, he suggested that the political centre of the kingdom was originally the Breckland of Norfolk and Suffolk. However, shortly before the Roman Conquest of A.D. 43, Belgic immigrants from the south may have pushed the boundary back to the line of the Little Ouse-Waveney valley. The Iron Age fort, which Rainbird Clarke confirmed under the Norman castle at Thetford, deliberately commanded the Icknield Way as it crossed the Little Ouse, and its secondary refurbishing may be connected with this phase of political contraction. The southern boundary of what later became Norfolk (or part of it) may therefore go back to a political and military frontier of the late Iron Age.

SELECT BIBLIOGRAPHY

Clarke, Helen, *East Anglia* (1971)

Clark, J. G. D. and Fell, C. I., 'The Early Iron Age Site at Micklemoor Hill, West Harling . . .', *Proceedings of the Prehistoric Society*, XIX (1953), 1–40.

Mercer, R. J., *Grimes Graves, Norfolk, Excavations 1971–72*, 2 vols (1981).

Rainbird Clarke, R., *East Anglia* (1971).

Wainwright, G. J., 'The excavation of a Neolithic settlement on Broome Heath, Ditchingham . . .', *Proceedings of the Prehistoric Society*, 38 (1972), 1–97.

'The Barrows of East Anglia', *East Anglian Archaeology*, Report No. 12 (1981).

3. Romans and Britons

IN NORFOLK A fair number of Roman sites and roads has been recorded over many generations, and summarised in successive articles and maps. However, it is more than likely that the great mass of evidence for Romano-British life has yet to be found. The sharply accelerating pace of recent discoveries suggests that Romano-British sites are thick on the ground in nearly all parts of the county, and that newer techniques of field archaeology will produce a flood of discoveries in the years ahead.

The political and military fate of the Icenian kingdom is known in some detail, thanks largely to the Roman historian Tacitus. When the Romans conquered Britain in A.D. 43, they made a treaty with the 'brave and warlike' Iceni, and gave them the rare privileged status of client-kingdom. This did not, however, buy peace for long. In A.D. 47, the Iceni rebelled and had to be subdued, with their allies, in a hard-fought battle. Then in A.D. 60, came the famous revolt under Queen Boudicca, when the Iceni organised a strong alliance of native tribes against Roman oppression, and ravaged a large part of the new province including the towns of Colchester, London and St Albans. They were eventually crushed by the legions at a crucial battle, fought somewhere in the east Midlands, after which Icenian territory was firmly and permanently absorbed into the Roman province.

When documentary evidence of this kind is available, one is tempted to make archaeology and history 'fit' each other as neatly as possible. For example, it has been suggested that the first battle, which was fought at a native earthwork difficult of access, took place at a circular fort which can still be seen in the lonely Holkham marshes (though a site in the fens is probably more likely). Another burst of fascinating speculation has followed the recent discoveries at Gallows Hill, Thetford (Plate 5).

This astonishing site, which belongs to the years A.D. 40–60, was accidentally discovered from the air in 1973, and has since been excavated by Tony Gregory. It began as a simple rectangular enclosure, but was rapidly developed into a massive fortress surrounded by three deep ditches and about seventy miles of close-set posts or fencing. So extravagant were the defences that the outer ditch enclosed eleven acres, whereas the inner enclosed only two. In the interior, which could not have held a large garrison, five circular wooden houses have been traced as postholes and gulleys, and a D-shaped structure which could have been a shrine. The strength and scale of the site suggest that it was either a kind of private 'castle' which belonged to someone of importance in Icenian society, or that it was a greatly revered religious centre. The rapidly constructed defences, close to the Icknield Way and overlooking the valley of the Little Ouse, were surely in response to a major Roman threat, but which one? Was it the original invasion of A.D. 43, the revolt of A.D. 47, or Boudicca's frenzied crusade of A.D. 60? Unfortunately no evidence was found for a siege, and the whole site was carefully levelled soon after its construction.

In Roman times engineered roads appeared for the first time and supplemented the informal tracks of the prehistoric period. Certain major lines have survived reasonably well, like the A140 from Scole to Swainsthorpe which was undoubtedly military in origin, and later became the main approach from the south to the cantonal capital at Caistor St Edmund. Elsewhere Roman roads have survived as combinations of secondary roads, green tracks, hedges and parish boundaries. The straight alignment from Holkham to Toftrees is an excellent example. The best known Roman road in Norfolk is undoubtedly the so-called Peddars Way, again probably military in origin, which can be followed for much of its length as an attractive green lane, now rather ironically designated a long-distance footpath. It cleaves a straight line across the high ground of west Norfolk for more than thirty-five miles, keeping to the east of its more sinuous predecessor, the prehistoric Icknield Way, which was itself still used by local farmers and estates. It has been plausibly suggested by C. W. Phillips that the Peddars Way was originally laid out as an approach to a Roman ferry across the Wash.

Recent fieldwork has postulated various new lengths of

Roman road: for example from Barwick to Egmere where a long length of straight trackway leaps to the eye from the Ordnance Survey map; a link road from North Elmham to Toftrees which still survives as an embankment across Brisley Common; and the probable earthen abutment of a timber bridge at Billingford. Many other lines call for investigation, for example a succession of boundaries from Kirby Cane towards Reedham Ferry, and a run of lanes and a boundary from South Creake to Tatterford. A map published in 1973 by J. N. L. Myres and Barbara Green shows that our knowledge of even major roads is still incomplete. As for the minor roads which must once have served numerous local settlements and field systems, only a tiny fraction have been identified. Unfortunately Roman roads in East Anglia generally appear to have been constructed of layers of gravel, which are easily destroyed by ploughing or have been deliberately quarried away. Many minor roads may not have been 'constructed' at all, though they were probably ditched where they ran through fields. Furthermore, they may have been little more than the continuation of long-established prehistoric tracks.

The pattern of Roman settlement ranged from isolated native farmsteads to elaborate towns adorned with baths and temples. The towns of the Roman period are not only the first examples of urban life in Norfolk, but they are the most sophisticated achievements of the period economically, administratively and architecturally. Outstanding are the two walled towns at Caistor St Edmunds and Caister-by-Yarmouth, both of whose names perpetuate the Latin word *castra* meaning a military 'camp' or defended civilian settlement.

Soon after Boudicca's revolt was put down in A.D. 61, the town of *Venta Icenorum* was founded in the parish now known as Caistor St Edmund (Plate 6). As the Latin name implies, it was intended as the main market and administrative centre of the Iceni. It lay among those converging valleys of east Norfolk, an important focus of human activity since Neolithic times – within two miles of the great 'temple' of Arminghall, and three miles from the centre of later Norwich. Today the site is a large field where larks hover over growing crops, but the lines of streets and buildings still show

51

regularly in the corn, and a prominent bank still marks the once-impressive town walls. At first, a rather irregular grid of streets was laid out, surrounded by a defensive bank and ditch, and relatively unsophisticated buildings of timber, wattle and daub were erected. In the second century A.D. the first stone buildings appeared; a market or forum, a public hall or basilica, and public baths. The town was reduced to about thirty-five acres in the third century, and given an elaborate defensive wall (eleven feet thick) to which projecting bastions and gate-towers were later added. One of these bastions can still be found in a thicket near the river. The third century was a period of destruction, neglect and some restoration, but the town probably survived until about A.D. 400. Marketing and retailing were presumably of some importance, but evidence also exists for the manufacture of glass, pottery and cloth. How sad it is that no public right of way has been negotiated around the ramparts of this major site: Norfolk's first real town.

At Caister-by-Yarmouth, an early fort and naval base on the north bank of the Bure (which then connected directly with the North Sea near Caister Point) was later developed into a small but prosperous town and port. It covered only ten acres, yet it was defended by an earthen rampart and ditch. In the late second century a stone wall with internal bastions was provided. Recently the site has been obliterated by suburban development, and few surface traces are visible.

While it remains true that East Anglia was not greatly urbanised (compared to other parts of the civil province) and that planned towns like *Venta* were to some extent alien impositions from the Mediterranean world, archaeologists have recently begun to recognise 'towns' of a more informal and unplanned kind. For example at Brettenham, straddling both the river Thet and the Peddars Way, is a large Roman settlement which has been known for centuries. It is now interpreted as a market town rather than a purely agricultural village. Similarly a spread of pottery, tiles and iron slag recently found over thirty acres at Kempstone, and other sites at Billingford, Saham Toney, Toftrees and Scole, are being put into the same category. At Brampton Keith Knowles has been excavating a remarkable industrial site of twenty acres,

which has already yielded 140 pottery kilns as well as evidence
for a tanning industry. In the later second century a ditch over
twenty feet wide was dug around a hexagonal central area of
fifteen acres.

Substantial Roman farms, or villas, are not common in
Norfolk, but the greatest concentration is in the north-west.
In a strip of country from Snetterton down to Narford, along a
spring-line and adjacent to the Icknield Way, is a striking
series of about twenty Roman farm estates, fairly evenly
spaced. One of them, at Gayton Thorpe, was excavated in the
early 1920s to reveal the plan of a corridor villa. It was over
130 feet long, and had another block, itself 90 feet long,
attached to the south. Structurally it was probably half-
timbered, but had heated rooms and mosaics. The owner
decorated his main hall not only with an elaborate geometrical mosaic, but with marble imported from Italy – just as Sir
Robert Walpole was to do, over 1,500 years later, at nearby
Houghton. The estates of these villas were probably long thin
strips of country running east-west, giving a cross-section
from the high dry downland of the east, through the varied
soils of the escarpment, and down to the valleys and coastal
marshes (like many of the local parishes today, which could
be their actual successors). Certainly the sites at Gayton
Thorpe, Gayton, Grimston and Congham are very evenly
spaced, and may be the result of deliberate land division. This
corner of Norfolk, with its fabulous Iron Age metalwork and
Roman villas (Fig. 4), may have been where the native aristocracy of the Iceni chose to build up their country estates
from the first century B.C. onwards.

But, whoever they were, the owners of villas were not living
in grand isolation, surrounded by a 'natural' countryside; they
clearly exploited their rolling acres, and used tenants and
workers to make their land productive. Modern fieldwork
and aerial photography are now revealing peasant farmsteads
and villages, some quite close to the villas themselves, and
their associated fields. Emphasis was also placed on the
development of local industries. Salt-making was profitable
near the sea and on the fen-edge; clays of the Nar valley were
exploited to make bricks and tiles; and nodules of iron-ore
which naturally occur in the sands and gravels of the escarp-

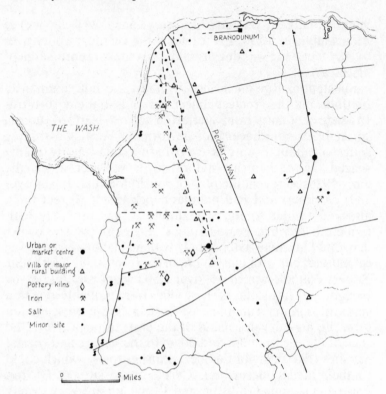

Fig. 4. Roman sites in North-West Norfolk: ranging from towns and sophisticated villas to native farmsteads and industrial sites (after J. Smallwood).

ment were dug and smelted on a considerable scale. Over twenty smelting sites have already been discovered.

A more common form of rural habitation was the humble native farmstead or village. They are best seen in the fenland and on the fen-edge, thanks to aerial photography (Plate 4). In the 1960s Mrs Hallam showed that Romano-British settlement largely ignored the low-lying and wet peat fen, and was concentrated at the northern end of the region where the sea had deposited very rich 'silts' in later prehistoric times. A relatively low sea-level from about A.D. 50 allowed colonisation of the former mud flats at the edge of the sea and up the deeply indented 'Wisbech estuary'. After small beginnings, the area was massively developed in the second century, probably as an imperial estate concentrating on the production of meat, leather, and wool. Soil and crop marks near Upwell form the eastern end of a great spread of Romano-British sites extending right across the Lincolnshire siltland; aerial photographs show an astonishingly complex pattern of natural streams, man-made drains and canals, a major road (the Fen Causeway), a tight system of minor roads and droveways, house sites with small closes, and a bewildering variety of fields defined by drains. In one area south-east of Outwell rectangular or square fields of many different sizes exist (some arranged like a ladder), as well as long strip-like fields. Obviously these features are not all contemporary; at Low Cottage Farm, for instance, two very different patterns must be of different dates within the Roman period.

Another favoured situation for settlement in the fens was along the banks of tidal rivers and streams where bands of silt were drier than the soggy peat all around. Undoubtedly the best example in Norfolk is at Welney, where a string of Roman sites follows the old dry course or 'roddon' of the Great Ouse. Aerial photographs show a complicated pattern of tiny enclosures sandwiched between the two Bedford rivers, created in the seventeenth century, and following the curves of the roddon. This was a native 'village' which had apparently been founded in the second century, was abandoned for at least fifty years when the river flooded, and then redeveloped some time after A.D. 250. Remains of rectangular timber-framed buildings with walls of plastered clay and thatched roofs have been found by excavation. From the sinuous settlement, long ditches extended out into the peat fen, no doubt dividing it into 'fields' or areas for grazing. As this Romano-British village lies just east of modern Welney, some kind of continuous occupation seems highly likely.

Unusually, a peaty area was occupied at Denver, on both sides of the Fen Causeway, and divided into an impressively regular pattern of strips, rectangles and roads. Several fields were subdivided into minute squares eighteen feet across, which look like animal pens. To the east are the remains of a substantial building with hypocausts, roof tiles and bricks. This may be a villa, to which the first site perhaps belonged as a tenant village. Salt-making was certainly part of the economy, and this would have facilitated the storage and export of meat and carcasses.

Although the great prehistoric estuary from Outwell back to Denver is rich in sites, the main block of Norfolk's Marshland has produced very little of the Roman period – certainly nothing to compare with hundreds of sites found in adjacent Lincolnshire. The reason almost certainly lies in the deposition of later layers of silt on this south-eastern edge of the Wash; in other words the Romano-British landscape lies buried a few feet below the modern surface. Occasional finds like the two coin hoards at West Walton and Walsoken prove that the area had indeed been occupied at this time. The so-called Roman Bank (Plate 8), an early line of sea walls which can be traced all round the edge of the Wash, is much more likely to be Anglo-Saxon in date, probably erected between the seventh and ninth centuries when the siltland was recolonised; it is mentioned in local place names like *Wal*ton and *Wal*soken, and is obviously related to the post-Roman pattern of settlement on the uppermost level of the silt.

Although people tended to live on the silts and roddons, they surely used the peat fenland for summer grazing, fuel, thatching materials, fish and fowl. Indeed considerable investment was put into its drainage and the provision of navigable waterways. In prehistoric times, the Great Ouse had captured the waters of several other rivers and entered the sea by a huge natural estuary near present-day Wisbech. It now seems quite possible that Roman engineers made the fundamental decision to divert the Great Ouse from that natural outfall to its present course by Kings Lynn. This was effected by making a new cut of three miles from Littleport to Brandon Creek; at the same time the Little Ouse was also diverted to Brandon Creek, well to the north of its original meandering course. These artificial channels are distinguished by an overall straightness, but with small-scale curves where engineers struggled to keep a line through the uneven peat.

Equally attractive for Romano-British settlement was the upland encircling the fenland. For example, fieldwork by A. J. Orange and W. F. Curtis has revealed dense settlement in the south-western Breckland: on the promontory of land where Blackdyke Farm now sits, Roman sites occur every half-mile or less. Similarly Breckland valleys draining westward towards the fens like the Little Ouse from Hockwold to Santon, or the little valley in which Feltwell lies, were intensively farmed and settled. Because they were founded before a major rise of sea-level in the later Roman period, some settlements were on significantly lower sites than present-day villages and farms. By contrast, the higher sandy tracts of the Breckland were not generally settled, though undoubtedly they were farmed, mainly as pasture.

At Hockwold a large excavated site appears to represent another case where a villa and a native village have an economic and tenurial relationship. It appears on aerial photographs as a tight rectilinear grid of enclosures and drove-roads. Some of the latter penetrate the wet floor of the valley and were obviously linked with meadows, while traces of other roads climb to higher ground. Arable cultivation is attested by the discovery of millstones, but the study of excavated animal bones shows that local farming was based primarily on the breeding of cattle, followed by sheep, goats and horses.

This site, like several other Roman rural settlements, has produced Iron Age pottery. In the south-west corner of the Breckland, in particular, similar coincidences and the regular spacing of sites suggest that Romano-British farming was basically continuous from prehistoric times – although Roman farmsteads do not necessarily overlie the precise sites of their predecessors. Continuity of the same kind has been noted elsewhere in Norfolk, for example at Worthing near Dereham, Shouldham, Caldecote, Warham and Woodcock Hall at Saham Toney. At the last site, not only were Icenian coins found scattered over thirty acres, under a sizeable Roman settlement and probably fort, but also moulds for their making. This surely indicates a native centre whose commercial and political importance goes back deep into the Iron Age: it might even be the Icenian equivalent of *Camulodonum* (Colchester). Only in the fenland can we be sure that Roman farmers created a totally new farming landscape; elsewhere the evidence, fragmentary though it is at present, suggests that Romano-British farming was based on patterns of land use and settlement which had been laid down in Iron Age or earlier times.

Away from the Marshland and Breckland, the known distribution of rural settlements from the Roman period is comparatively thin. To some extent they may be actually fewer on the ground, particularly where soils are very heavy and difficult to drain, but, if field archaeologists have got to work, evidence has usually been found. For example, at Witton in North-East Norfolk, J. E. Owles has found at least four Romano-British sites on one modern farm of about 570 acres. Even on the heavy soils of South Norfolk it is likely that Roman settlement was considerable. For example in the adjacent part of Suffolk, the parish of Mendlesham (3,900 acres) has already produced twelve Roman sites. In a highly productive agricultural region like Norfolk, we must expect some of the highest densities in Britain, though it is important to remember that such sites were not all in existence at the same time. The period lasted nearly 400 years, and some settlements must undoubtedly have replaced others.

So far as Romano-British fields are concerned, it is only in the fenland that we have the chance of seeing really large-scale patterns, but new cropmarks of field systems are being regularly photographed in other parts of the county. Already some Romano-British fields have been subjected to excavation, as at North Elmham and at Eaton near Norwich. At the latter site shallow ditches, up to forty centimetres deep, defined square or rectangular fields which appeared to be forty to fifty metres across, separated by tracks. But all this is a small fraction of the huge acreages which must have existed in all regions of the county. Even on the heavy clays of South Norfolk, the botanical evidence from Old Buckenham Mere suggests 'rapidly extended disforestation' in Iron Age and Romano-British times.

In 1935 Gordon Ward suggested that, in one corner of Norfolk, widespread traces can be seen of a regular form of Roman land division, such as has been found in Italy itself. He pointed out that several parishes along the north-western coast, from Holme-next-the-Sea to Brancaster, display rectangles of roads and hedges – large blocks of 200 to 240 acres containing smaller ones of 25 to 35 acres. In 1967 W. G. Hoskins revived interest in this remarkable landscape, and plumped for a Roman origin. It is certainly undeniable that the pattern incorporates Roman lines (the Peddars Way and a probable east-west road) but this does not of itself date the whole pattern. Since then, other observers have claimed that the present-day landscape incorporates Roman fields, or at least traces of them. For instance, in the Tas valley near Caistor St Edmund, certain hedges, ditches and tracks appear to be aligned on the Roman town and a major road approaching it from the south. They could, therefore, represent genuine survivals. At the other end of the county, around the villa at Gayton Thorpe, rectilinear patterns of hedges, roads and parish boundary seem to incorporate the Roman measurement of 20 *actus* (1 *actus* = 120 Roman feet, or 116 English feet). Such fascinating hypotheses may yet be proved by aerial reconnaissance and detailed excavation.

Select Bibliography

Clarke, Helen, *East Anglia* (1971).
Gregory, T., 'Excavations at Gallows Hill, Thetford', *NARG News*, 27 (1981), 1–4.
Phillips, C. W. (ed.), *The Fenland in Roman Times* (1970).
Rainbird Clarke, R., *East Anglia* (1971).
Rainbird Clarke, R., 'Roman Norfolk since Haverfield', *Norfolk Archaeology*, XXX (1952), 140–55.
Smallwood, J., 'Roman Settlement in North West Norfolk', *NARG News*, 25 (1981), 12–17.

4. A landscape in mist, A.D. 400–650

THE PHRASE 'the end of Roman Britain' is misleading because it implies a total break. Certainly, in the first half of the fifth century A.D., the links with Rome were broken so far as imperial administration and military organisation were concerned. This no doubt led to severe economic difficulties and the disruption of long-distance trade and communications. However, such changes do not necessarily mean that British or Celtic life disappeared at a local level.

Sadly the archaeological evidence for British survival is very thin. The invaluable evidence of coins dries up and we can point to very little of late Roman or sub-Roman character after the early years of the fifth century. This is partly the result of sharply declining standards, culturally and technologically, but partly also a problem of archaeological recognition. Certainly we need the excavation of more Roman sites with well preserved upper levels.

In the meantime our best evidence for British survival may lie in the linear earthworks which are preserved in the west and south of the county. These are the Fossditch, Bichamditch, Launditch, Panworth Ditch and Devil's Ditch at Garboldisham. Although in length and size they vary, these lines of bank and ditch seem to be designed with the same general purpose in mind; they cut off blocks of country with otherwise natural boundaries such as valleys and marshland, and they bar both natural and man-made lines of communication. The five earthworks cross at least three Roman roads and one prehistoric droveway. The attempt to control Roman roads suggests that they were built after A.D. 400 (indeed we know by excavation that the Fossditch must be later than 390) yet they are unlikely to be later than about A.D. 550, by which time Wehha had created the united kingdom of East Anglia.

While one or two of these linear banks may yet turn out to

be pre-Roman, most of them seem to fit the disturbed conditions of the fifth century, when Anglo-Saxon immigrants and perhaps rebellious mercenaries were in conflict with native Britons. They may, therefore, have been deliberate attempts by British groups to maintain their independence. Even if we could prove that all these barriers were constructed by Anglo-Saxons, it would still mean that they were at times on the defensive, and that expansion was slow and intermittent.

The Launditch and Panworth Ditch both face westwards and cut across Roman roads. Peter Wade-Martins suggests that they represent the last-ditch defence of 'the sub-Roman population of central Norfolk, no doubt with the use of *foederati* [mercenaries] to stem the tide of Anglo-Saxon advance into the interior', and surmises that cavalry were still available to patrol the banks effectively. He prefers to see the Fossditch and Bichamditch as built by Anglo-Saxons, because they face eastwards and adjoin the fenland through which many of these invaders entered the region. However, one can argue that they too were constructed by Britons, and may in origin be the boundaries of late Roman estates. Behind the Fossditch are dozens of Roman sites whose population may well have fought for their freedom, especially if their numbers were swollen by immigrants from the silt fenland where drainage was deteriorating. In front of the same earthwork lie several Anglo-Saxon cemeteries. At first sight the Bichamditch (Plate 7) looks different, for it encloses several parishes with English -*ham* names, which some scholars think are early. However, the earthwork is immediately west of, and faces, Swaffham, whose name not only sounds early but also indicates that the higher ground along the Peddars Way had fallen under the control of a Germanic sub-group called Swabians. It therefore seems more plausible that the Bichamditch was constructed by a group of Britons against the newly arrived Swabians, than by one group of Germanic immigrants against another.

'Continuity' is now a popular word, but it needs to be used with caution. The narrow definition implies survival of the same settlement from Roman through to Anglo-Saxon times, but it is almost impossible to prove that a site was not temporarily abandoned between two periods of occupation.

However, other kinds of continuity are historically of greater importance, for example the survival of particular communities who may have moved (or been moved) from one local site to another; or the survival of agricultural estates with a resident work force and more or less stable boundaries; or the survival of recognisable ethnic groups even though they may have been in political and economic subjection.

As more archaeological discoveries are made, the pattern of certain parish boundaries may become increasingly relevant to the debate on British continuity. Can it be, for example, that the total area called Burnham, later subdivided into seven parishes and abnormally large for an East Anglian township, was the remains of a sizeable Romano-British estate? A similar interpretation is tempting in the case of Bradfield near North Walsham. This small parish of 720 acres occupies a natural promontory between two converging valleys. Its traditional boundaries follow streams on three sides, while on the fourth a sinuous line, still partly followed by a lane and hedges, cuts off the neck of the promontory. Although the first documented reference to the parish is in 1212, the place name is Old English in origin and means the 'broad field'. Norman Scarfe has suggested that this place name, which occurs in several parts of England, refers to an area of farmland which the English simply took over as a going concern, with perhaps a native work force. In fact a Roman settlement has already been identified from surface pottery at the southern end of the Bradfield promontory, which makes it virtually certain that the 'field' had been cleared and farmed in Roman times, if not before. With its mainly natural boundaries, the whole unit looks like a small early estate. In East Anglia, as in Wessex, it is surely true that some lengths of boundary, and even complete units, may go back in this way to Roman or prehistoric times.

None of this is to argue that the Romano-British survived always and everywhere. Some were undoubtedly killed, others fled, and populations may have been reduced by natural disasters such as plague. Nevertheless it becomes increasingly difficult to believe that a substantial proportion of the large Romano-British population did not survive to become a subject part of the kingdom of East Anglia; why else was the East Anglian royal house the only one in England to claim descent from Woden *and* Julius Caesar?

On the other side of the equation are the Germanic immigrants themselves, the people who were to call themselves the Northfolk of the East Angles. In the third and fourth centuries, from their homelands in northern Germany and the Danish peninsula, they had menaced the so-called 'Saxon Shore' of the Roman province, and this had necessitated the construction of great fortresses like Brancaster and Burgh Castle. In the last decades of Roman rule, some Anglo-Saxons may have been prepared to fight their own kinsmen, and to have become mercenaries in the pay of the Roman forces at important centres like *Venta*. As soon as the organised defences of the Roman province weakened in the early fifth century, the Anglo-Saxons began to colonise in earnest. Their eventual success, after two centuries or more of immigration, is dramatically shown in the place names of Norfolk. As O. K. Schram wrote, 'The overwhelming majority of the names, both major and minor, is of Anglian origin.' While no doubt a fair number of these were simply new names for surviving British settlements, their sheer numerical superiority shows the political and linguistic domination which the Anglo-Saxons were able to achieve.

Up to the present, the most commonly discovered archaeological sites left by the early Anglo-Saxon inhabitants of Norfolk have been their 'pagan' or pre-Christian cemeteries, where burials are often accompanied by weapons and personal ornaments. In date they fall between the early fifth and early seventh centuries. As early as 1538–43 Leland recorded the discovery of such a site at Kenninghall, and a whole succession of famous antiquaries followed his example elsewhere in the county – Sir Thomas Browne who wrote his famous *Urne Burial* about an Anglo-Saxon cemetery at Walsingham, Henry Spelman, Peter le Neve and William Stukeley. Hitherto unknown cemeteries are still being found, as happened recently at Morning Thorpe, Saxlingham and Swaffham, but many others must have been destroyed altogether by repeated ploughing. Indeed the urns at Kenninghall were only discovered in the sixteenth century because they happened to survive in an unploughed balk of the open field. Altogether about sixty of these cemeteries are known in East Anglia. Their distribution in Norfolk mainly favours the western side of the county, particularly the Breckland and Western Escarpment. This may imply that the main surge of immigration was through the Wash and its river system, but other concentrations in the Norwich area and the Waveney valley highlight the importance of Breydon Water as an entry on the east (Fig. 5).

With their dramatic skeletons, cremations, weapons, ornaments and 'sad sepulchral pitchers' (as Sir Thomas Browne called them), the pagan cemeteries have had a great influence on our thinking about the size of the immigrant population. In fact, at any one time, the size of the community using a large cemetery may not have been very great. For example, although Catherine Hills suggests that her recently excavated site at Spong Hill near North Elmham contained over 4,000 burials (some urns clearly contain the ashes of more than one person), they cover at least 200 years and, moreover, were drawn not just from one local community but from a 'whole region'. Nothing in the archaeological record yet suggests 'massive' immigration, although that kind of assumption was frequently made in the past. The fact that the Anglo-Saxon population was built up over at least two centuries, as successive waves of immigrants came in, makes it even more likely that many Britons managed to survive and find their place in a new order.

Norfolk's pagan cemeteries are frequently on hills and bluffs overlooking rivers, as at Spong Hill and Castle Acre, or in low-lying positions near rivers. Furthermore, they are often on, or close by, Roman habitations which suggests that the immigrants were either taking them over, or living quite close to them. In fact, Anglian settlements are now being found, and therefore our evidence is undergoing an important change of balance. The first pagan settlement in East Anglia was recognised in 1951 by H. Lewton-Brain in the southern part of the parish of Snettisham. Close to a stream called the Ingol he recorded abundant surface remains such as pottery, loom-weights, spindle-whorls, bone combs, mussel and oyster shells, and daub from buildings. Characteristically, this site lies only 200 yards from a Roman settlement, and

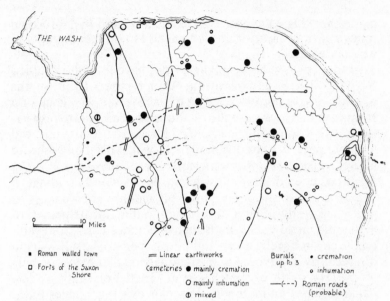

Fig. 5. Early Anglo-Saxon Norfolk: pagan cemeteries and linear earthworks, against the background of Roman roads (after J. N. L. Myres and Barbara Green).

within 700 yards of a supposed Roman villa – an excellent reminder of how the newcomers were tempted to take over existing farmland and estates, if not actual settlements. This Anglo-Saxon site may be the 'village of Snaet' as recorded in the name of the parish; it need not have immediately replaced the Roman settlements, for the latter could have continued, at least for a time, in some tenurial relationship with the newcomers' village.

More recently a pagan village, or at least farmstead, has been excavated by Keith Wade at Witton near North Walsham. Deep ploughing in the 1950s led to the finding of pagan pottery on the surface; excavation has revealed several of the characteristic *grubenhäuser* (wooden buildings below whose floors were rectangular pits of dubious purpose) in close association with a late Roman industrial site. Unfortunately the sandy soil had destroyed all animal bones, but still contained quantities of plain, hand-made pottery, metal slag, spindle-whorls and glass beads. The suggestion has been

65

made that this community grew steadily, and by late Saxon times was farming an arable area nearly four times larger than when it began.

In some places the East Angles may have forcibly occupied Romano-British settlements: at Appleton near Lynn, sherds of early Saxon pottery were found above the wreckage of a Roman villa. Elsewhere the relationship seems more respectful or even cooperative: at Spong Hill pagan burials appeared to avoid part of a late Roman ditch, which itself enclosed an area of considerable Roman occupation; nearby a pagan settlement has been discovered with traces of several buildings.

That comparatively few pagan villages are known must be partly the result of later destruction, but mainly the result of inadequate fieldwork. On the heavy boulder-clays, for example, such sites are virtually unknown. Yet Andrew Rogerson has recently discovered a substantial spread of pagan domestic pottery south of the church at Great Fransham. A few pagan villages undoubtedly lie under existing villages (in at least three Norfolk parishes, their burials have been found closely associated with later Christian churchyards) but most of the others probably lie closer to Roman than to medieval and modern patterns. In spite of the difficulties, we may confidently assert that when parishes or larger areas are *totally* searched, the evidence for pagan occupation in Norfolk will be found much more frequently.

Neither should the value of place names be overlooked. Admittedly the vast majority do not relate to any precise point on the ground, and archaeologists are right to criticise the assumption that a named community has always been on the same site. But examples do exist. At Whitwell near Reepham, a copious spring with a white chalky bed can still be seen beside the remains of a deserted village; at Hoe near East Dereham the present village, certainly in existence by late Saxon times, straggles down a shallow valley but the name (O.E.*hoh*) suggests that the original site was on one of the nearby spurs of higher ground; at (Long) Stratton we can deduce that the village has always been aligned on the Roman road, the A 140 of today; at nearby Mangreen the community must have grown up around a 'common green'.

The dating of English place names is difficult, and in any

case they only suggest the *minimum* age of a community because of the possibility that they replace earlier names. From the 1920s onwards it was believed that the earliest English names were those ending in *-ingas* meaning 'the people of', but now we know that they are unlikely to be earlier than the later sixth or seventh century because their distribution is so different from that of pagan burials. In 1973 Barrie Cox argued that the element *-ham* meaning 'village' may be the earliest, broadly fifth to sixth century in date, representing those areas near Roman sites and roads which would naturally attract the invaders. Over ninety of these names can be found in Norfolk, and they do cluster quite convincingly near the lines of Roman roads; remarkable groups of *-ham* names exist east of Thetford near the Peddars Way, and around Downham Market close to the continuation of the Fen Causeway. Equally we may expect that other place names, particularly topographical ones, denote early, pagan communities: *-ford* is an obvious example, and must be early in places like Thetford and Barford; similarly one suspects that *street* is often early at places like Stradsett and Stratton, and represents early penetration along Roman roads.

Frequently Anglo-Saxon place names include the name of an individual who was the leader or founder of the community. Thus Walsingham means the 'village of Wael's people'. Occasionally we may recognise the person in another source; for example, it is possible that Tittleshall was founded by Tyttla, a sixth century king of East Anglia who is mentioned by Bede. But in general we know nothing of these pioneering English communities and their eponymous heroes – except that they largely created the nomenclature and administrative geography of the modern map, and obscured so much of the achievements of their predecessors. As Christopher Taylor has pointed out, Anglo-Saxon names are only proof of an Anglo-Saxon leader; the rest of the community could be members of an extended family, or of a warband, but they could also be of a different racial origin altogether.

Although *-ingas* names are no longer thought of as particularly early, some of them may have an extra social significance. As the names of later administrative hundreds, they seem to betray tribal groups or even mini-kingdoms which preceded the united kingdom of East Anglia. Good examples are the Loddingas, the 'dwellers by the River Loddon' and the Happingas the 'people of Haep'. The latter not only gave their name to the hundred of Happing, but clearly had an administrative centre or stronghold at Happisburgh. Perhaps an early ditched enclosure covered the hill now crowned so magnificently by Happisburgh church but, if so, it still awaits discovery. The boundaries of later hundreds may approximate to the territory of these 'folk' but are certainly not always identical. The Cnoveringas, who gave their name to the hundred of Clavering (a promontory in the south-east of Norfolk, set within a great loop of the river Waveney), established their stronghold or 'burgh' at Cnobheresburg. This was probably the abandoned Roman fort of Burgh Castle which lies on the far side of the river in the former Suffolk hundred of Lothingland.

SELECT BIBLIOGRAPHY

Hills, Catherine, 'Spong Hill', *East Anglian Archaeology*, Reports No. 6 (1977), No. 11 (1981) and No. 21 (1984).

Lawson, Andrew J., 'The Archaeology of Witton, near North Walsham', *East Anglian Archaeology*, Report No. 18 (1983).

Myres, J. N. L., and Green, B. *The Anglo-Saxon Cemeteries of Caistor-by-Norwich and Markshall, Norfolk* (1973).

Wade-Martins, P., 'The Linear Earthworks of West Norfolk', *Norfolk Archaeology*, XXXVI (1974), 23–38.

5. The Anglian landscape, A.D. 650–1066

FORTUNATELY, FROM ABOUT A.D. 650, the settlement history of Norfolk becomes clearer. In the Launditch area of west Norfolk, Peter Wade-Martins has shown how certain villages evolved physically from middle Anglo-Saxon to medieval times, even though he found no certain trace of preceding pagan or sub-Roman habitations. Perhaps a major shift of settlement in the early seventh century led to the development of many completely new sites which were then occupied until medieval or modern times. One possible reason for a shift at this period is the acceptance of Christianity; a powerful new religion may have impelled local people to form fewer, larger settlements in order to facilitate regular worship. On the other hand, pagan sites may have been deserted for purely social and economic reasons of which we know nothing, and others, as at Witton, may have developed without a shift at all.

Longham (Fig. 6), a parish of 1,248 acres lying about three miles north-west of East Dereham, provides a good example of Wade-Martins' evidence. Most of the present-day inhabitants live in a looseknit straggle of houses in relatively low-lying land on the east side of the parish. By contrast Longham hall and church lie close together, but otherwise isolated, a mile away on high ground near the western boundary. Immediately south-east of the church, fieldwork revealed eight sherds of middle-Saxon pottery (Ipswich ware) spread over 100 yards, thirty sherds of late-Saxon pottery (Thetford ware) spread over 300 yards. Nowhere else, in those parts of the parish which were searched, was either kind of pottery discovered. Small though the number of sherds is, a plausible historical interpretation can be offered: in the seventh or eighth century a small 'community' grew up on this relatively high site, and expanded steadily for several centuries; by the

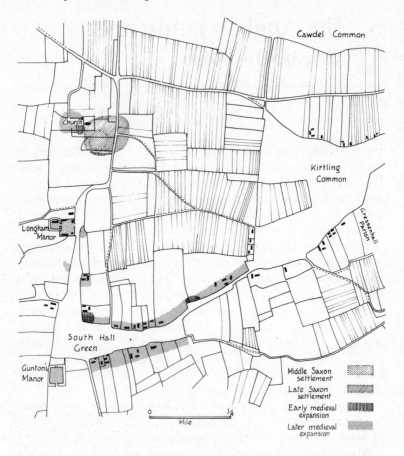

Fig. 6. Longham: the changing pattern of settlement in middle Saxon, late Saxon and medieval times, shown on a map of 1575 (after P. Wade Martins).

twelfth century, judging from the fact that only twelve sherds of early medieval pottery were found, the settlement was probably in decline as the population shifted to other parts of the parish; it was finally abandoned in the fourteenth or fifteenth century.

Although the present fabric of the church is largely fifteenth century, its site appears to mark a 'village' which was

Plate 7 Beachamwell: the Bichamditch or Devil's Dyke, probably early Anglo Saxon, surviving as a linear earthwork and soilmark. It faces east (right) and, beside the wood, cuts across a Roman road. Natural freezing and thawing during the Ice Age 'mottled' local soils.

Plate 8 Terrington St Clements: part of a continuous sea-bank, misleadingly known as the Roman Bank, which kept out the Wash in late Saxon and early medieval times (the sea lay to the right). A breakwater appears to jut out from the largest loop.

Plate 9 Bedingham and Woodton: two Saxo-Norman churches, less than a mile apart, reflect each other across a shallow valley. Bedingham, in the foreground, once had a second church in the same yard.

Plate 10 Stiffkey: the frequent proximity of manor-house and church emphasizes the proprietary origins of local churches. Stiffkey Hall, rebuilt by Sir Nicholas Bacon from 1575, is adjacent to St John's church (tower behind) and St Mary's (now demolished).

Plate 11 Guestwick: a church which moved southwards, leaving behind its central tower. Excavation in 1983 revealed an apsidal chancel aligned with the Saxo-Norman tower – notice the blocked arch and scar of gable. The central wall belongs to a later vestry.

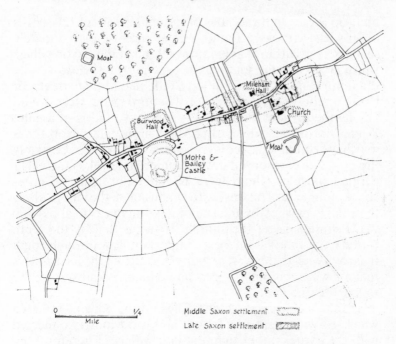

Fig. 7. Mileham: the changing pattern of settlement in middle Saxon and late Saxon times, shown on a map of 1814 (after P. Wade Martins).

founded in mid-Saxon times, and was already in decline soon after the Norman Conquest. Although it was not mentioned in Domesday Book, the first church was surely built before 1066, probably in the tenth or early eleventh century when the village was at its greatest size. Significantly the church appears to have lain on the *edge* of the village: precisely what one would expect if it was added to a community already several centuries old.

At Mileham (Fig. 7), an adjacent parish to the north, the evidence is stronger, and its historical evolution seems different. The present village is a long straggle, well over a mile in length, along a road running approximately south-west to north-east. St John's church lies at the eastern end of the village, 100 yards south of the road and just clear of the

71

built-up area. On three sides of the church, about 120 sherds of Ipswich ware were found over an area of approximately seven acres. This probably represents a middle-Saxon village which lay well to the south of the present street. However, by the tenth century it had shifted to the line of that street, for approximately sixty sherds of Thetford ware were found among the present buildings for about two-thirds of a mile. Wade-Martins calculates that Mileham in late Saxon times may have contained over forty separate properties. Certainly the population recorded in the Domesday Book is high (111 people, most of whom were undoubtedly heads of unrecorded families). The westward expansion of the village along the road is marked by the site of a Norman castle about 700 yards south-west of the church. It seems that by the tenth century the road had become important as a through route from Norwich to the west of Norfolk, and that the lord and his tenants were tempted by certain commercial advantages to re-site their houses.

St John's church at Mileham lies on the edge of the area where Ipswich ware was found, and is obviously connected with the earlier rather than the later village. Therefore, the church must have been in existence by *c.* 850, before the Danish invasions, in spite of the fact that it too is not mentioned in Domesday Book.

It should not be thought that all the 'middle-Saxon' villages found by Wade-Martins were subsequently deserted. Wellingham for example, in spite of periods of growth and decline, still lies close to its church – around which the usual scatter of Ipswich sherds was found. At Weasenham All Saints, a small gappy village still partially occupies the site of a very large late-Saxon settlement built around an extensive chequerboard of streets. The outline of this road system, 500 yards across, can still be seen on the ground; it may have been a planned expansion in the ninth and tenth centuries around an original middle-Saxon nucleus just east of the church.

This impressive and original campaign of fieldwork emphasises that churches mark the sites of Anglo-Saxon villages (whether or not they were subsequently deserted), and that early settlement was often very fluid. The further we go back in time, the less likely are we to find settlement matching the modern pattern. Villages have frequently shifted their centres of gravity or shifted their sites altogether; deserted villages were even more common in the Anglo-Saxon and Norman periods than they were in the later Middle Ages. It is of great interest that middle-Saxon settlement was apparently more nucleated than in Roman or pagan-Saxon times; instead of fairly frequent single farmsteads and small hamlets, there emerged a widespread pattern of spaced villages which is particularly clear in areas like west Norfolk and the Breckland.

However, Wade-Martins' fieldwork was selective and until Norfolk parishes have been submitted to total archaeological exploration, we are likely to underestimate the extent to which settlement was scattered. Indeed, Wade-Martins found a site at Weasenham St Peter which may represent quite a common phenomenon: a small area half a mile from the village yielded late-Saxon pottery and was interpreted as an outlying manor. In the heavier soils of South and Mid-Norfolk, a considerable degree of dispersal existed long before the Norman Conquest. In fact, Domesday Book makes it clear that settlement was denser in that area than anywhere else in the county, ranging no doubt from proper villages down to tiny hamlets and isolated farmsteads. Although some of the minor settlements (for example, those bearing names ending in *-ton*, *-thwaite* and *-thorp*) may have been created in late Saxon times when population was again rising, others could be genuine survivals of the much more looseknit patterns of Roman and sub-Roman times. After all, we have already argued for the survival of substantial numbers of Britons in the Dark Ages, particularly in the interior of the county.

One of the major historical themes of this period must be the steady rise of population. The first towns that Norfolk had seen since Roman times were beginning to emerge at key sites like Thetford and Norwich, and rural communities were also expanding. We have already seen how Weasenham All Saints and Mileham developed into comparatively large villages before the Norman Conquest. Place names ending with, for example, *-wic*, *-set*, *-worth* and *-thorp* confirm that villages which had some importance in Domesday Book had begun life as no more than farmsteads, or outbuildings, or even as enclosures for animals. Keswick near Norwich had been a dairy farm specialising in cheese, Hardwick a sheep farm, Barton and Barwick outlying farms where corn was grown, Caldecote began simply as a shelter for wayfarers or animals (and a cold one at that) while Hethersett was perhaps no more than a fold for deer. Yet, by 1066, all these were true communities with modest populations.

Another probable manifestation of growth is the way estates were breaking down into smaller units, thus creating secondary or daughter communities. For example the three Wrethams in the Breckland were all in existence by 1086, also the two Dunhams (both of which have already produced middle-Saxon pottery). But the process is most clear in the north and north-west of the county where many groups of parishes have the same basic name, in twos, threes and even, in the case of the Burnhams, in a group of seven. This sometimes produces a pattern where related villages are noticeably close-set, with their churches frequently less than a mile apart. The three Birchams and the three Barshams are good examples, and all were in existence by the end of the eleventh century. In each group we must assume that one village was the original parent. For example, place names and topography suggest that Great Bircham preceded the other two villages of that name and, conveniently, middle-Saxon pottery has turned up beside its church. The process cannot be wholly explained as the result of rising population; it must also be connected with the development of local estates and manors, and particularly with the division of estates among co-heirs. Twenty years before the Norman Conquest, Should-ham already had a north hall, a middle hall and, by implication, a south hall.

Sometimes an early economic relationship between adjacent townships is suggested more directly. For example Sandringham was simply the 'sandy part of Dersingham'; at first it was probably heathland used for grazing, but subsequently became a separate community in its own right. Even more striking is the example of Somerton and Winterton in Flegg, to which W. G. Hoskins has drawn attention. He suggested that East Somerton was the original parent community in a relatively sheltered inland position, and that Winterton, on the coast, began as a collection of temporary huts used in the winter when abundant shoals of codling tempted local farmers to take to their boats. By Norman times this temporary encampment had certainly become a permanent and sizeable village.

Occasionally place names suggest an economic relationship between two communities which were miles apart. In the opinion of Eilert Ekwall, for example, Guestwick was a woodland clearing belonging to Guist four miles away. Originally Guist may have acquired this outlying possession because it lacked sufficient woodland in the valley of the Wensum. At the very least, it seems likely that Guestwick was settled by men from Guist. Similarly, Dickleburgh may have begun as the 'forest belonging to Diss' which lies three miles off. Such names may mark a stage in the economic development of parts of the interior, particularly the heavier plateaux; by something akin to Scandinavian transhumance, people from a certain village or estate may have travelled several miles to obtain an important economic resource. In the course of time, what began as a group of temporary huts could become an independent and permanent community.

When the Anglo-Saxon Chronicle says that the Danish army in A.D. 870 'took possession of the land [of East Anglia] and divided it', we must imagine yet another military aristocracy taking political control of the region and its native population. They certainly influenced local place names in various ways. For example, the island of Flegg is dominated by Danish names ending in -*by* meaning 'village'. These could be new Danish foundations in a district where English villages are widely spaced; on the other hand the Danes may simply have re-named earlier Anglian communities as they took over seigneurial control. More than forty places in Norfolk are called -*thorp*, generally accepted as a Danish word meaning an outlying, dependent hamlet or farm. They are particularly common in a broad band across the centre of the county, and a quarter of them still show the English village in whose territory they were established, for example Gayton Thorpe and Honingham Thorpe. 'Thorpes' which are mentioned in Domesday Book may well have been founded by small groups of immigrants in the late ninth or tenth centuries, who established some tenurial relationship with the natives but preferred to live slightly apart.

An added complication is that neighbouring villages were sometimes founded so close to each other that they later fused. Paradoxically, this seems particularly characteristic of poorer farming areas where suitable sites were in short supply. For example in the Breckland valley of the Little Ouse, the churches of Wilton and Hockwold are only 1,100 yards apart. Although the two villages have merged into one continuous built-up area, the two names have survived. At Beechamwell near Swaffham, not only did two settlements fuse, but also their names; Domesday Book refers to two separate vills, *Bycham* and *Welle*. Because of later decay, the two nuclei can still be identified on the ground today.

Beside the village of North Elmham, in an area which was emparked in the early nineteenth century, Peter Wade-Martins uncovered, between 1967 and '72, a substantial part of the Anglo-Saxon and medieval community, thereby reminding us of the rich archaeological legacy which lies sealed, but frequently unobtainable, under living villages. A complicated and tangled pattern of features was investigated, consisting mainly of slots, postholes, pits and ditches. Interpretation was difficult and inevitably contains a degree of conjecture and subjectivity, but nevertheless the ground plans of forty-six structures were postulated, ranging in date from the seventh to twelfth centuries.

The earliest evidence came from the middle-Saxon period (A.D. *c.* 650–*c.*850). A length of ditched street with property boundaries was found to contain a bakehouse, a lined well nearly forty feet deep, a cistern twenty-one feet deep and three sizeable 'halls', with walls of upright posts set in continuous trenches. In the late-Saxon period (*c.* 850–1100), the area appears to have been laid out anew and was more heavily built-up. Over twenty buildings were found. The method of construction still involved the use of trenches, but narrower and shallower than before – perhaps because of better bracing above ground. One L-shaped structure was extraordinarily large, and had a width of thirty feet. From roughly the late tenth century onwards, walls tended to be built with individual postholes rather than in a continuous trench. A hundred years later again, by the end of the eleventh century, buildings appear for the first time to have been supported by widely spaced trusses of principal timbers; this presumably represents the local start of the medieval style of timber-framing.

The interpretation of this important excavation is made more difficult by Elmham's undoubted role as an ecclesiastical centre. At the highest point of the village lie the stone ruins of an unusual church with transepts and an eastern apse. These are now interpreted as the chapel of an early Norman bishop, but it lies on the site of an earlier wooden church which was almost certainly an Anglo-Saxon cathedral. On its southern side lay a large contemporary cemetery, of which about 200 graves were recently excavated. Against this background Wade-Martins is tempted to interpret the large L-shaped building which he excavated as 'the bishop's palace of the early tenth century'. Indeed he argues strongly that Elmham was the seat of a bishop from the mid-seventh century, when for the first time two bishops were consecrated in East Anglia. He therefore sees the middle-Saxon halls as 'almost certainly ecclesiastical in function'. However, this part of the case is not proven for South Elmham in Suffolk also has a claim to be the seat of the second East Anglian bishop from A.D. 673 – at least for a time, if not down to the middle of the ninth century when life was disrupted by the Danish invasions. Until other extensive middle Saxon sites are excavated in this region, we shall not know for certain the extent to which Elmham was a typical agricultural village, and the extent to which it was a special ecclesiastical community.

For the appearance of the countryside in Anglo-Saxon times, we are dependent on miscellaneous and disconnected scraps of evidence. The few pre-Conquest charters which survive for Norfolk carefully specify arable land, meadows, commons, woodland, fisheries and mills. All were clearly regarded as complementary economic assets of considerable value to the owners of estates. Domesday Book confirms that, by the time of the Norman Conquest, East Anglia was one of the most populous regions of England, and indubitably the richest. The vast majority of parishes which we see on the map

today were already in existence as named communities, and
had all the possessions which we could expect of a manorial-
ised agricultural society. The inhabitants of the region, whatever their mixed racial origins and however controlled by
successive lords, had undoubtedly developed a prosperous
pattern of farming.

In spite of the economic value of well managed grassland
and woodland, the balance of land use was undoubtedly
tilting towards arable farming because this was the quickest
way of feeding a growing population. As in the prehistoric
and Roman periods, the best evidence has come from the
work of palaeobotanists. From the pollens at Old Buckenham
Mere, Harry Godwin discovered a slight increase of clearance
in early Anglo-Saxon times followed by 'a great extension of
arable cultivation' at the expense of both existing woodland
and pasture. While the proportion of tree pollens continued
to decline, particularly such species as oak and hazel, those of
cultivated crops and their associated weeds increased. By
1086, parts of East Anglia shared with the Sussex coast and
certain Midland districts the highest density of plough teams
in England, three and a half to the square mile.

But what of the actual fields and other topographical
features which made up the countryside? Up to the present
nobody has positively identified fields created by Anglo-
Saxons or Danes, or Romano-British fields still being farmed.
Nevertheless, by the end of the Saxon period, we can be sure
that considerable acreages of small intermixed parcels lay
around settlements, and that the open fields which feature so
strongly on Norfolk maps in the sixteenth and seventeenth
centuries were already in the making. Charters and wills of
the tenth and eleventh centuries suggest that land in Norfolk
was becoming increasingly subdivided. One reason for this is
undoubtedly the splitting of inheritances among heirs: for
example, Thurketel of Palgrave whose will dates from before
1038 left twenty acres of land at Roydon near Diss to four
named men. The same document speaks of the 'middle
furlong' at Roydon Hill. At Brandon just over the Little Ouse
in Suffolk the *Liber Eliensis* refers to the sale of 'every eighth
acre' which suggests regular allotment (or re-allotment) in a
pattern of strips.

No longer do we suppose that the open-field system of arable farming was introduced fully formed by Anglo-Saxon immigrants from the fifth century onwards. Archaeological research in Germany and Denmark has shown that, in the migration period, small rectangular fields were at first normal but then were progressively adapted into long thin strips. Similar developments surely occurred in East Anglia. Christopher Taylor has suggested that Romano-British agriculture involved the use of a permanently tilled 'infield' around settlements and an 'outfield' which was cultivated for a few seasons and then abandoned. He goes on to argue that open fields may have developed in the Saxon period under the pressure of growing population, as the permanent infield was extended outwards to recolonise land abandoned at the end of the Roman period. This might have had two effects. First, as the amount of grazing land shrank, so commoning rights over both the waste and arable had to be defined and elaborated. Secondly, as population grew, so physically the older patterns of fields had to be subdivided, adapted or even drastically re-designed.

It has been suggested that the frequent 'town fields' are original nuclei of arable farming which may go back to Anglo-Saxon times or earlier. Similarly Peter Wade-Martins has pointed out an area at Stansfield where the existing fields are smaller, narrower and more compact than elsewhere. It is surrounded on three sides by common land and on the fourth by the village street. 'One is tempted,' he writes, 'to conclude that this was the original late Saxon assart for the Stanfield settlement'. However if Taylor's hypothesis is correct, this area may, in its outline and perhaps some of its divisions, be much older than late Saxon. David Yaxley has already made the fascinating suggestion that a group of small furlongs which he reconstructed from documentary and landscape evidence, in the south-east corner of one of North Elmham's open fields, could have originally been the arable surrounding the 'pagan' settlement at Spong Hill (Fig. 10). In such places, aerial photography may reveal even earlier fields underneath the strips and furlongs of open fields, yet somehow physically related to them, as at Great Bourton in Oxfordshire. Nor should we forget that in areas like South Norfolk some

hedged and ditched fields may prove to have survived un-
changed from Roman or prehistoric times.

Recent excavations at North Elmham have thrown considerable light on the pastoral side of Anglo-Saxon farming.
Nearly 3,000 fragments of animal bone, which came from a
single ditch of middle-Saxon date, have been expertly analy-
sed by Barbara Noddle. For every cattle bone she found three
of pig and five of sheep. The sheep were mainly over six years
old, with an estimated weight of ninety pounds, so the main
emphasis was clearly on the production of wool and mutton.
Rams' horns showed that the sheep were by no means primitive but 'of the modern duplex black-faced type', and therefore related to the extinct Norfolk Horned sheep and the
modern Scottish Black-face. Cattle were also surprisingly
large, in fact equal in size to some modern beasts. By the ninth
century, therefore, the breeding of farm animals was already
highly developed in this region. The fact that many animals
were not slaughtered at the onset of winter surely indicates
that grazing was already carefully organised, and that quantities of hay were harvested from regulated meadows.
Although land was increasingly brought under the plough in
this period, Domesday Book underlines the immense importance of naturally watered meadowland where hay could be
systematically harvested. And although it is not usually mentioned in Domesday or in early charters, we must not forget
the substantial acreage of permanent pasture or 'waste' which
must also have made an important contribution to animal
husbandry.

SELECT BIBLIOGRAPHY

Hart, C. R., *The Early Charters of Eastern England* (1966).
Heywood, Stephen, 'The ruined church at North Elmham', *Journal
of the British Archaeological Association*, CXXXV (1982), 1–10.
Smith, A. H., *English Place-name Elements*, 2 vols (1956).
Wade-Martins, P., 'North Elmham', *East Anglian Archaeology*,
Report No. 9, 2 vols (1980).
Wade-Martins, P., 'The origins of rural settlement in East Anglia'
in Fowler P. J. (ed.), *Recent Work in Rural Archaeology* (1975),
137–57.
Wade-Martins, P., 'Village sites in Launditch Hundred', *East
Anglian Archaeology*, Report No. 10 (1980).

6. The church in its setting

IN NO OTHER region of Britain is the antiquity of the parish church so convincingly revealed as in East Anglia. This is primarily due to the evidence of Domesday Book. In Volume Two ('The Little Domesday') which covers the three eastern counties of Norfolk, Suffolk and Essex, we are given more references to churches, their patrons and endowments than in any other early source. From it Norman Scarfe has already demonstrated that no fewer than 418 out of the eventual 520 medieval churches of Suffolk were in existence by 1086. For Norfolk, in spite of its larger size, only 217 rural churches were mentioned, some twenty-nine per cent of the 750 listed in the mid-thirteenth century. This lower proportion is probably due to the differing priorities of local assessors; it is inconceivable that this county had a significantly lower *proportion* of early churches than Suffolk, for East Anglia was one of the most densely inhabited parts of England in the eleventh century, and the settlement histories of the two counties are broadly similar.

We know from other kinds of evidence that certain Norfolk churches, which the compilers of Domesday Book ignored, were nevertheless in existence. Thus, early churches are implied in some place names (for example, Colkirk), and by some dedications (for example, St Botolph or St Ethelbert). Furthermore, the architectural historians, Harold and Joan Taylor, have identified at least fifty-four churches which still possess fabric of the eleventh century or earlier – more than in any other English county. Of these, twenty-eight were omitted by the Domesday assessors. Simon Cotton's map shows all the rural churches which are known to have been in existence by *c.* 1100, some 286, but it is almost certainly incomplete. It is interesting to note that Domesday also mentioned about sixty other churches in the three major towns of Norwich, Thetford and Yarmouth – a far higher *urban* proportion than in neighbouring Suffolk.

Visitors from other parts of England are inevitably surprised by the close spacing of medieval churches in Norfolk. Not only is the general density high, but the county has frequent examples of villages with two churches, often no more than a few hundred yards apart (witness Feltwell, Wood Norton, North Burlingham and Swainsthorpe). In fewer cases, three churches were built (for example, at Warham, Barton Bendish and Congham) and sometimes four (as at Shotesham and Ormesby). In the extreme case of the Burnhams, nine churches existed in the thirteenth century, of which seven were within one and a half miles of each other. As an extra complication, we meet the phenomenon of two churches in the same graveyard, as at Antingham, Great Melton and South Walsham. The tightest concentration of all was at Reepham which had, until the sixteenth century, three functioning churches in one yard (Fig. 15).

Some of these churches, individually, may have been founded as late as the twelfth or thirteenth centuries, but nevertheless the provision of multiple churches was commonplace before the Norman Conquest. Of thirty-seven pairs of churches in Norfolk, twenty-two were already mentioned in Domesday Book. In other words, this practice seems to be the rural equivalent of the numerous closely spaced churches which appeared in late-Saxon towns, such as Thetford and Norwich. The actual reasons for such 'over-provision' are harder to identify. It may have to do with the splitting of estates and manors or, as W. G. Hoskins suggested, with the competing claims of English and Danish inhabitants. Certainly these churches represent the fiercest competition among landowners, anywhere in England, to provide places of worship for local communities.

Discounting the fact that several medieval churches were swallowed by the North Sea (for example, Snitterley off Blakeney, Whimpwell and Keswick), the sites of churches, once established, seem to have remained remarkably stable. Even though villages expanded, contracted, shifted their centres of gravity and jumped to new sites, churches almost invariably stayed put. This is why they are such good guides to patterns of early settlement. Very occasionally, however, it can be shown that a church was shifted for some pressing reason. For example, the medieval churches of Overstrand

and Sidestrand were moved inland and rebuilt, the first in
1399 and the second in 1880, when the cliffs on which they
stood threatened to collapse. In the thirteenth century, St
Peter's at West Lynn was destroyed by the tidal river Ouse,
and a new safer site was provided by a landowner in 1270–1;
the present building contains Norman arches which must have
been salvaged from the old building.

Only very occasionally, as at Cringleford, do early stone
churches survive substantially complete. Normally we only
see fragments (such as a tower or length of walling) embedded
in later rebuildings. Although the Taylors offered approximate dates, and sometimes even postulated more than one
Saxon phase of building (for example at Haddiscoe Thorpe
and Houghton-on-the-Hill), it remains difficult to distinguish
late Saxon from early Norman and we therefore fall back on
the convenient term, Saxo-Norman.

In spite of their fragmentary survival and the difficulties of
dating, certain generalisations can be made about Saxo-
Norman churches. They were mainly built of local flints and in
plan usually consisted of a rectangular nave and apsidal or
square chancel. Variants included central towers, as at
Weybourne, and even transepts, as at Newton by Castle
Acre. Among the detailed characteristics of Saxo-Norman
architecture are long-and-short work, walls thinner than
three feet and double-splayed windows, including circular
ones. Out of fifty-four early churches recognised by the
Taylors, twenty-nine had round towers which still survive at
the west end; in many cases this is the only early feature to
survive. The theory that round towers were defensive is surely
untenable because of their small internal size and wooden
floors. More plausible is the suggestion that an early lack of
easily cut freestone encouraged masons to build round rather
than square (though squared corners of flint and glacial
boulders can be found in Norfolk). Whatever the original
explanation of the form, it certainly became an architectural
fashion adopted widely in eastern Norfolk and Suffolk.

Yet paradoxically these towers and stone buildings, though
they are the earliest pieces of ecclesiastical architecture to
survive above ground, were probably part of a 'great *re*building' in the eleventh to twelfth centuries, when earlier and

83

more primitive churches were demolished and replaced. The excavation of St Michael's at Thetford revealed a sequence of three churches from the twelfth century back to the tenth, and reminds us that the earliest East Anglian churches were of wood and comparatively tiny. Postholes and foundation trenches showed that the first nave, of the tenth century, had been a timber rectangle measuring only twenty-three by seventeen feet, and the chancel a near-square of ten by nine feet. More recently, a similar timber church of the tenth or early eleventh century has been excavated in the centre of Norwich.

Of course, Christian worship may have had an even earlier stage. Before building its first church, a local community may have worshipped in the open air, beside a cross of stone or, more likely, of wood. The names Crostwick and Crostwight both refer to clearings with crosses in them, while at Whissonsett a wheel-headed stone cross still survives – in the church which probably replaced it.

So we may suppose that, as in Suffolk, the majority of parish churches were in existence by 1066, or at the latest by 1086 when the Domesday survey was probably completed. As we study the impressive frequency of churches on the Ordnance Survey map, or survey the dark silhouettes of their towers from some vantage point like the Cromer Ridge, we glimpse something of the distribution and density of population in later Anglo-Saxon times (Plate 9). Although the kingdom had been nominally Christian since the early seventh century, the majority of churches were probably first built in the tenth and early eleventh centuries after East Anglia had emerged from the fearful shadow of the Danish invasions. The reconquest of the region by Edward the Elder, and the conversion of the Danes to Christianity, had led to a remarkable Christian renaissance. From the mid-tenth century bishops of East Anglia were once again appointed, existing churches were no doubt restored and, most important of all, a great impetus was given to the building of new churches.

They were founded to serve individual estates and communities which already had recognised secular boundaries. So the ecclesiastical parish referred to in Domesday Book was not just the area served by a particular church and priest, and from which tithe was levied; it was an earlier, perhaps already ancient, unit of secular ownership and local government, taken over by the church as a matter of convenience, and thereby fossilised. This is why parish boundaries are much more obviously related to economic than religious considerations; take for example the radiating parishes of Marshland which were clearly designed to give each community access to the fabulously rich grazing of the Smeeth, or the general way in which the size of Norfolk parishes varies in response to soils, topography and density of population.

Domesday Book also reveals the owner of the estate within which each church fell, its monetary value and the land with which it was endowed. At this period churches were regarded as private property which belonged exclusively to the founder, or to the founder's successor as owner of the estate. Thus Siflaed who died between 990 and 1066 referred to 'my' church at Marlingford and 'my' priest Wulfmaer. As time went on, the original endowments were extended by other benefactors, such as Edwin, who in his will of 1040–57 left at least seventy-five acres to eleven or more churches in east Norfolk. By 1086 the recorded churches of Norfolk had an average endowment of about twenty-two acres of land; they ranged from Witchingham with no land at all to St Michael's at Tombland, Norwich, with 112 acres. Finally, Domesday gives us a rare glimpse of the actual process of founding and endowing a new parish church. In the hundred of Humbleyard, a priest named Colbern had just built a new church, and was awaiting the king's permission to endow it with twenty acres of land. Unfortunately the parish is not named.

In spite of all this activity in the tenth and eleventh centuries, it is clear that some churches were founded before the Danish invasions. Reedham for example is mentioned in the *Liber Eliensis* as having been created in the early seventh century by St Felix, the first bishop of East Anglia. Dedications to such saints as Felix, Botolph, Ethelbert, Withburga and Helen also suggest a pre-Danish origin for a score or more of churches. At Larling in South Norfolk an isolated church, which probably marks an original focus of Anglo-Saxon settlement, is dedicated to St Ethelbert, an East Anglian king martyred by the Mercians in A.D. 794. In 1970, a beautiful bone panel dating from the ninth century was found beside it. According to the monks of Ely, St Withburga, the daughter of an East Anglian king, was buried in 743 beside a religious house which she had founded, probably at West Dereham. Holkham, where this saint is said to have lived, was formerly known as 'Withburgstowe' and its church, still dedicated to her, may have been founded in her lifetime, or shortly after her death.

Before the Danish invasion Norfolk probably had a number of special churches called 'minsters'. These were missionary centres each staffed by a community of priests who served and proselytised a large rural area, at a stage when comparatively few local or parish churches had been established. Dickleburgh certainly had an early minster, if not two, and was well placed on a major Roman road. References in Domesday Book to exceptionally large endowments of land, as at West Barsham and Langley (100 acres each), and particularly imposing later buildings such as Weybourne and Dunham, could well indicate other churches which had this special early status.

A glance at the Ordnance Survey map will confirm that many churches are close to halls or manor houses – whether or not there is, or was, a village as well. Normally it was lords or owners of early estates who founded, endowed and actually owned the early church. Therefore the site which they provided was often close to their own residence. In these cases, the site of the hall must be regarded as the primary feature, regardless of the date of the present buildings (Plate 10). Subsequently the shrinkage, desertion or movement of many villages has left this early association even more conspicuous than it originally was; good examples can be seen at Sculthorpe, Kirby Cane and Scottow.

Finally, we should not overlook the possibility that some churches reflect much earlier patterns of settlement and worship altogether. The last shattered remnants of the church tower on the beach at Eccles (Latin *ecclesia* meaning a church) may mark the site of a Roman Christian church of the fourth century, founded soon after the Emperor Constantine promulgated his famous Edict of Toleration. The same place name occurs on the eastern edge of the Breckland, in an area

thick with Roman sites and finds. Other churches may have
been sited in a deliberate attempt to 'christen' places of pagan
worship. The Taylors observed that the Anglo-Saxon church
at Morton-on-the-Hill is on 'an interesting circular mound'
which may have been a pagan barrow, and that Cranwich has
a round churchyard which could mark an early sanctuary.
Several other Norfolk churches, like Fersfield, Wereham and
Shadwell, are closely associated with 'holy wells'. It would
certainly be foolish to overlook the possibility that pagan
features from the dim prehistoric past may have been adopted
for Christian worship – precisely what Pope Gregory in A.D.
601 encouraged his English followers to do.

SELECT BIBLIOGRAPHY

Cotton, Simon, 'Domesday revisited – where were the eleventh
century churches?' *NARG News*, 21 (1980), 11–17.
Lunt, W. E., *Valuation of Norwich, 1254* (1926).
Record Commissioners, *Taxatio Ecclesiastica, 1291* (1802), 78–114.
Taylor, H. M. and J., *Anglo-Saxon Architecture*, 3 vols (1965,
1978).
Victoria County History of Norfolk, Vol. 2 (1906), 1–203 (text of
Domesday Book).

7. Origins of urban life

IN LATER ANGLO-SAXON times, the most significant economic development was the emergence of towns and markets from a background of steadily recovering population and agricultural prosperity. By 1066 we may guess that minor markets were appearing in most parts of Norfolk, but strangely only three were specifically mentioned in Domesday Book – at Holt, Dunham and Litcham. The last two, in Launditch hundred, are only two miles apart, and must have been in commercial competition.

Three places in Norfolk are of outstanding importance as examples of early economic growth. They are Thetford, Norwich and Great Yarmouth, each of which had an established merchant community by the time of the Norman Conquest. Unlike their Roman predecessors, these new towns of the ninth and eleventh centuries were not deliberately planned with an elaborate paraphernalia of walls, gates and large public buildings. They were agricultural or fishing communities which, in a period of commercial and industrial expansion, happened to be in the right places and responded by a combination of organic and planned growth.

Thetford (Fig. 8), from the ninth to the twelfth centuries, was one of the largest and most important towns in England – it had industrial, military and ecclesiastical significance – yet thereafter it seems to have lost status rapidly. Since 1947 a considerable amount of archaeological excavation, necessitated by the economic revival of the town, has made the evolution of the place clearer. The 'public ford' which carried the prehistoric Icknield Way over the rivers Little Ouse and Thet, and which gave its name to the town, was obviously a focus of settlement from a very early date. A ramparted fortress commanded the ford in the later Iron Age, and the south bank was occupied in both Roman and early Saxon times. However, Thetford emerged as an undoubted 'town' in the ninth and tenth centuries, probably through the fairly rapid amalgamation of two or more agricultural hamlets. By

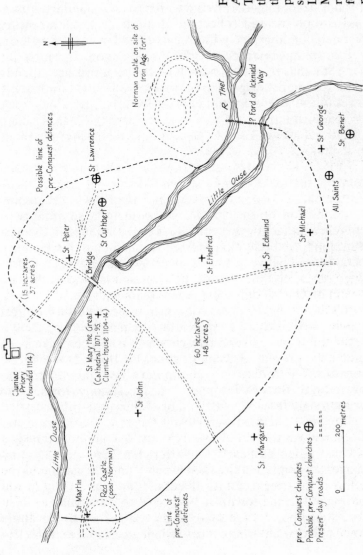

Fig. 8.
Anglo-Danish Thetford: showing the great extent of the early town, particularly on the south bank of the Little Ouse. Modern main roads are shown for the sake of reference.

N

Norman castle on site of Iron Age fort

R Thet

? Ford of Icknield Way

St George
St Benet

All Saints

St Michael

St Edmund

St Ethelred

Little Ouse

Possible line of pre-Conquest defences

St Lawrence

St Cuthbert

St Peter

Bridge

(15 hectares 37 acres)

Cluniac Priory (founded 1114)

Little Ouse

St Mary the Great (Cathedral 1071-95) (Cluniac house 1104-14)

St John

(60 hectares 148 acres)

St Margaret

St Martin

Red Castle (post-Norman)

Line of pre-Conquest defences

pre-Conquest churches   +
Probable pre-Conquest churches   ⊕
Present day roads   =====

0   200 metres

about A.D. 1000 it had a population of several thousands and occupied about a mile of the south bank; it produced industrial goods such as cloth, metalwork and pottery, minted its own coins, and was defended on its southern, landward side by a curving rampart and ditch. Within the ramparts an area of three acres was completely excavated by Brian Davison in 1964–6. It contained well engineered roads, boundary ditches and a sophisticated collection of ninth-to-eleventh-century wooden buildings, including an aisled hall over 110 feet long. A fascinating reference in the Anglo-Saxon Chronicle for A.D. 869 makes one wonder how far Thetford had already emerged as an Anglo-Saxon town (if at all), and how much it owes to the attentions of the great Danish army which 'took up winter quarters' there. From this base the Danes sallied out to defeat the East Angles and kill their king, the pious Edmund.

In 1066 Thetford boasted 943 privileged 'burgesses' and a total population of over 4,000, which put it in the same league as Lincoln, York and Norwich. Like other towns developing in late Saxon times, it had a surprisingly large number of churches; in fact twelve and a half are mentioned in Domesday Book, and one monastery. (The half-church must have been shared between two or more owners or estates.) Most were on the Suffolk side of the river and lay within the late Saxon or Danish defences. A few years later, in 1072, Thetford's importance seemed confirmed when the bishop of East Anglia moved there from North Elmham, and created his cathedral in an existing church which is said to have been under the present Grammar School for Boys. However, he regarded Thetford as only a temporary base and soon tried to move on to Bury St Edmunds – unsuccessfully, for his plan was strongly resisted by the abbot of Bury.

By 1086, Thetford's greatest days were over. Domesday Book records that, after twenty years, the number of burgesses had fallen by nearly a quarter. Furthermore, 224 messuages lay empty – a situation which cannot be blamed on the effect of clearing a site for the castle, because the latter was peripheral to the town. In 1096, as if to acknowledge Thetford's decline, Bishop Losinga moved his see to the larger town of Norwich, where it has remained ever since. It is clear that future research must attempt to explain not only the heyday of Thetford, which lingered for many centuries in local memory and legend, but also its striking decline; how and why did one of the most important urban communities of Anglo-Danish England sink to the status of a mere market town? (One major factor may have been the rise of King's Lynn, lower down the same river system.)

On the eve of the Norman Conquest, the most important town in Norfolk, as now, was Norwich. Fortunately its early growth (Fig. 9) has recently been the subject of a special survey by both archaeologists and historians, and the results have been usefully summarised in several publications.

The river valleys of eastern Norfolk had been a major focus of settlement and communication from prehistoric times, and they marked the intersection of several rich and diverse regions. By the time of the Norman Conquest, seven of the local hundreds had populations of more than twenty per square mile; only three other hundreds in the whole of England could equal this density. Norwich grew up where two probable Roman roads crossed, and at the lowest bridging point of the navigable river Wensum. Although the area was occupied in prehistoric, Roman and early Saxon times, settlement was scattered, small-scale and purely agricultural. By A.D. 650–850 several separate 'villages' were in existence where the city stands today. An early settlement called Needham occupied the higher ground later covered by the Norman castle. Further north, in the vicinity of the later cathedral, was Conesford ('the King's ford', probably near the later Bishop bridge) which became the real 'germ' of the later city. About three-quarters of a mile west again, at a point where a small tributary valley approaches the Wensum, a third community called Westwic had developed. Finally on the north side of the river was Coslany ('Cost's long island') which probably occupied a narrow spur of dry ground among marshes.

Alan Carter persuasively argues that Conesford developed, in the tenth century, into a small but real town called Northwic ('the trading settlement north of Needham'?), which can be reconstructed from the street pattern of today. He suggests a roughly rectangular area of forty-five acres,

91

defended by a rampart and ditch, and containing two possible market places, seven churches and a grid of streets which may have been planned deliberately. This little urban community of English or Danish origin may well have had the status of 'burgh' from about A.D. 917 when Edward the Elder regained East Anglia from Danish rule. Certainly coins bearing the name of Northwic were being produced in the reign of Athelstan (A.D. 925–40).

The space between the original nuclei filled up rapidly. For example an industrial suburb, which specialised in the making of pottery and iron goods, was taking shape by the end of the tenth century on the lower ground between Northwic and Westwic. Similarly a major new quarter sprang up on the north bank beside the original village of Coslany, and was also enclosed by defences. This phase of rapid expansion in late Saxon and Norman times is also reflected in the distribution of churches. They occupy sites within the original nuclei, and also mark the ribbon and suburban development which linked them into a large sprawling conurbation with a population of at least 5,000. Domesday Book mentions twenty-four churches in 1066; by 1086 the number had risen to forty-six. Seventeen of this total were on the north side of the river, but the most remarkable density of all is in St Benedict's Street where seven churches were founded in just over a quarter of a mile. St Gregory's, which has a Saxon tower under nineteenth-century refacing, is likely to be the original parent church of Westwic; out of the parish others were later carved.

By the time of the Norman Conquest, the nuclei on the southern bank had fused to form an L-shaped band of continuous development following the great river bend. The Normans took advantage of this shape by planting two powerful new institutions which squeezed and dominated the centre of the town.

First, before 1075, a formidable royal castle was built on the end of a spur overlooking the valley. According to Domesday Book, the raising of its motte and ramparts necessitated the destruction of ninety-eight properties. The present stone keep was added in the twelfth century. About 400 yards away on the edge of the river meadows, Bishop Losinga began, in

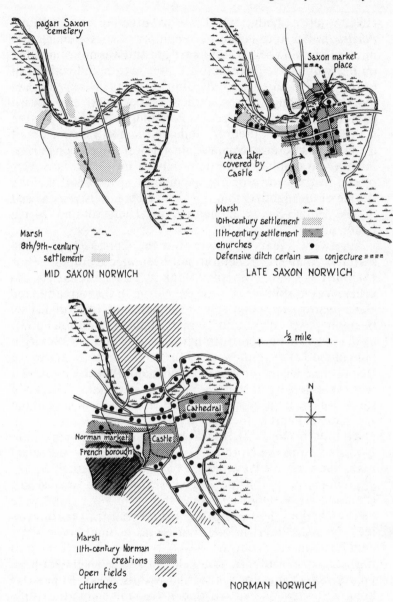

Fig. 9. Saxo-Norman Norwich: the emergence of a great city
(after A. Carter).

1096, a new cathedral which was to serve the whole of East Anglia, and also to house a community of sixty Benedictine monks. Building began at the east end and was not completed until about 1145. To establish a precinct for the cathedral-priory, the greater part of old Northwic had to be de-molished – many houses, streets and at least two parish churches. The monks lived in conventual buildings on the south side of the cathedral, while on the north Losinga built for himself a defensive palace, the earliest stone keep in East Anglia. To emphasise the antiquity of his office, he wisely placed in the centre of his magnificent apsed choir a stone throne of the eighth century, which had previously been used in the Anglo-Saxon cathedrals of Thetford and North Elmham.

For twenty years or more after the Conquest, Norwich suffered from fire, rebellion and economic disruption. For example, in 1086, Domesday Book records 295 empty prop-erties. Yet in spite of all this, the Normans had already – by 1075 – shown their faith in the importance of Norwich by beginning to create a major, largely planned extension known as the New or French Borough. This was laid out on virgin land immediately to the west of the castle, and was to survive as a distinct legal entity until about 1200. Already by 1086 it was inhabited by at least 125 French burgesses. The main focus was a large sloping market place which is still the commercial heart of the city.

Yarmouth (Fig. 17), the third major town to appear in Norfolk before the Norman Conquest, is a highly individual place. Not only did it evolve one of the most remarkable town plans in medieval Europe, but its very site was a freakish gift of nature. In Roman times, an estuary over two miles wide had discharged the freshwater of three major rivers directly into the sea. Later, a long thin island of sand and shingle began to emerge from the waves, dividing the estuary into northern and southern channels. In the elegant words of Henry Manship, a local historian writing in 1619, the sand bank 'did growe to be drye' and 'waxed in height and also in greatness'. Quite early in the Middle Ages, the northern channel which had served the Roman port of Caister became blocked and unnavigable, and the 'island' continued to grow southwards as a long spit deflecting the river for as much as eight miles.

Local tradition, as expressed in the well known 'hutch map' of Elizabethan times, states that the sand bank was first inhabited soon after the year A.D. 1000. But the town's origins are surely earlier, for by 1066 Yarmouth was a small but established trading community with seventy burgesses and a total population of over four hundred. Tradition also states, more credibly, that the island in the Yare-mouth was first occupied seasonally by local fishermen who built temporary huts when the herring shoaled in the autumn. This estuarine site gave fishermen the advantages of a sheltered shore for beaching boats, plenty of space for spreading nets and handling catches, quick access to both sea and estuary, and perhaps, initially at least, freedom from manorial interference. A Saxo-Norman site recently excavated in the centre of the town has yielded quantities of iron fish hooks and skeletal remains of no fewer than nineteen species of fish. Domesday Book specifically mentions twenty-four fishermen at Yarmouth in 1066, who belonged to the manor of Gorleston on the Suffolk side of the Yare.

The plan of the medieval town must have been substantially complete when the defensive walls were begun in the late thirteenth century. The built-up area was then long and thin, hugging the river side of the sand bank, and turning its back on the sea. The major north-south streets pursued roughly parallel S-like curves, sometimes converging slightly and sometimes diverging. Forming east-west connections between these main streets were about 150 narrower lanes and alleys, the famous 'rows'. But how and why did this unusual plan evolve?

The original focus of settlement was probably on the highest ground of Fuller's Hill. Here, in 1974, excavations have suggested that the line of George Street (one of the three main streets) was already established in the eleventh century. Of the two rows which crossed the site, one appears to have been created by 1200 and the other in the thirteenth century. A remarkable feature was the amount of blown sand between the remains of buildings; strong onshore winds must have constantly threatened the efforts of early inhabitants, and increased the height of the sand bank. Could the east-west 'rows', therefore, be a deliberate attempt to combat the effects of winds and sand storms?

The main north-south streets must have developed south-wards from Fuller's Hill, as the population grew. In 1963 A. P. Baggs suggested that they represent successive beach-lines as the level of the estuary fell: when a new strip of dry land became available, a new road was created just out of reach of high tides, and new properties were laid out on its uphill side. But Andrew Rogerson raises the objection that George Street, as found in his excavations of 1974, is too high to mark an early beach-line, especially as sea-level in Norman times was lower than it is today. Nevertheless, a connection must surely exist between these gently curving streets and the river bank at different periods. While some lengths of streets may represent early beach-lines, others may have been laid out at a higher level but roughly parallel with developments at the water's edge.

An Anglo-Saxon church dedicated to St Benet disappeared at an early date, but soon after 1100 Bishop Losinga of Norwich was given permission by Henry I to found a new church, dedicated to St Nicholas. It lies significantly on the north-eastern edge of the town, is now claimed as the largest parish church in England, and was the only church in the town until the building of St George's in 1714. This imposing building which then had transepts, central tower and three eastern apses, demonstrates the interest which the Normans had in Yarmouth, as a town and riverside port, and its role as a gateway to the inland port of Norwich.

SELECT BIBLIOGRAPHY

Carter, Alan, 'Great Yarmouth – an Introduction', *Archaeological Journal*, 137 (1980), 300–303.
Carter, A., 'The Anglo-Saxon origins of Norwich: the problems and approaches', *Anglo-Saxon England*, 7 (1978), 175–204.
Dunmore, Stephen and Carr, Robert, 'The Late Saxon Town of Thetford', *East Anglian Archaeology*, Report No. 4 (1976).
Rogerson, A., 'Excavations on Fuller's Hill, Gt Yarmouth', *East Anglian Archaeology*, Report No. 2 (1976), 131–246.

8. The medieval scene

Peopling the land.   Farming the land.
Common land.   Woodland.   Parks.
Broadland.   Roads, bridges and waterways.

Peopling the land

OF THE 726 'vills' or townships which the Domesday scribes listed in Norfolk, the vast majority can still be equated with names on the modern map. For example, *Methelwalde* is clearly the predecessor of Methwold, while *Scotohou* has now become Scottow. In most cases the modern version of the ancient name applies to some human settlement – a village or hamlet or just an isolated farm. However, because settlements have frequently changed their shapes or even their sites, the Domesday name stands less for a precise spot on the map than for a human community or estate which has had a continuous history since at least Anglo-Saxon times. If it was the achievement of our Anglo-Danish and earlier ancestors to have created this vigorous pattern of life and administration, it was the achievement of Norman bureaucrats to have recorded it in unprecedented detail.

H. C. Darby's map of Domesday Norfolk shows interesting regional differences. Settlements lay close together on the Western Escarpment, and in the eastern half of the county where soils were fertile and a water supply was not difficult to find. On the other hand, settlement was noticeably less dense and populations smaller on the lighter and drier lands of the Good Sands and Breckland. The Peat Fen was virtually empty, except for islands like Southery and Hilgay. These regional differences have persisted ever since; in spite of recent changes, the *comparative* distribution of rural populations is much as it was in Norman times.

In the countryside south of Norwich and in the North-East loam region was the greatest concentration of vills and rural population in Norman England. Over a wide area, Domesday scribes recorded more than twenty heads of household per square mile, which implies (with women and children) a total population four or five times greater. Although this is not high by modern standards, the landscape of these areas has had a crowded appearance ever since: close-set villages and hamlets, churches frequently less than a mile apart and parishes of a remarkably small size. For example, three parishes in South Norfolk were each less than 800 acres, yet by 1086 at least one of them had a church, and all three, even Holverton with an area of only 331 acres, were reckoned as distinct townships.

The modern parishes of Forncett provide a detailed example of both the density and dispersal of this remarkable human landscape. Here in a later manor of about 1,500 acres, were no fewer than four Domesday vills: *Kekelingtuna* which lay at the western end of the modern parish, near Forncett End; *Fornesseta* itself which probably centred on modern Forncett St Mary; *Tuantuna* which later became Twanton Green half-a-mile from St Mary's, and on the east side of the Tas valley; and *Middeltuna*, now known as Bustard's Green, half a mile to the south of the last. Place names suggest that these communities may have originated as single farms, but by 1086 they had moderate populations and were fully independent.

Some Domesday vills were subsequently deserted. For example, Shipden near Cromer and Snitterley near Blakeney were both destroyed by the sea. A few others have never been identified, such as *Letha* in the Hundred of Blofield or *Narvestuna* in Clavering. However, new evidence can turn up at any time. For instance, by using medieval court rolls, Paul Rutledge was recently able to show that a lost vill called *Mora* lay in the parish of Freethorpe.

On the other hand, a few medieval communities were not mentioned at all in Domesday Book. For example, Irstead nestling in the marshes of the river Ant was first recorded in 1140, and Needham in the Waveney valley in 1352. However, we should never assume that such places did not exist in Norman times. Worthing, for instance, does not feature in Domesday Book, yet archaeological evidence shows that a late-Saxon settlement lay around the church. Some communities may also have been included by Domesday scribes in their description of a neighbouring vill. For example, Stinton is now a hall and farm but it had a large recorded population of sixty-five in 1086: it is therefore possible that Heydon, which was not mentioned, was lumped together with Stinton.

An even better example is provided by *Helmingham* which, according to Domesday Book, had two churches. This name cannot be found on the modern map of Norfolk, but it was nevertheless recorded in the Middle Ages as an alternative for Morton-on-the-Hill. Morton is not mentioned in historical sources until 1196; thereafter it appears as a hamlet of Helmingham. So, without doubt, one of the Domesday churches was at the parent village of Helmingham, and the other at a daughter settlement called Morton. As a place name Morton means 'village by the fen', a description which fits the site of present-day Morton reasonably well, set in the Wensum valley at the south end of the medieval Attlebridge. The original focus of settlement is probably marked by the site of St Mary's church, just west of the bridge. What we *now* call Morton church, a half-mile away on the hill overlooking the valley, is almost certainly Helmingham's. The parent village must have lain beside it in the grounds of present-day Morton Hall.

Recent archaeological research has proved that local settlement has always tended to be fluid. In the medieval period, no less than the Anglo-Saxon, villages were regularly expanding, contracting or shifting their sites. For example, scatters of pottery have shown that the village of Longham, having moved from its original high site beside the church to a large irregular green three-quarters of a mile to the south, later still drifted eastwards to the margins of another green. Similarly West Dereham on the Western Escarpment appears to have spread down the hill to a green, eventually leaving the church quite isolated on its Saxon site. At Caldecote on the Breckland the church had become isolated by the thirteenth century, because the village had also moved down hill to the edges of a green. Many early village sites, founded in Saxon or earlier times, were abandoned, leaving the church behind as a marker of the former layout. Whereas older sites had tended to centre on streets and cross-roads, on comparatively high land, the newer medieval sites were frequently around greens or commons, often in the lower and wetter parts of their parishes. Most greens are likely to have been communally grazed for centuries, if not millenia, but some may have been new creations. At North Elmham, for example, a green was laid out in the twelfth or thirteenth century where houses had stood in Saxon times.

Wade-Martins argues that greens, whatever their origins, did not usually become the focus of settlement (and therefore 'village greens') until the twelfth century and later. He calculates that, by the end of the thirteenth century, roughly twice as many villages or hamlets were grouped around greens as were built along streets. Scatters of surface pottery indicate that most of these movements were gradual, as individual families decided to move, or were moved by their landlords. But while archaeological evidence proves that movements occurred, it does not explain them. It may be that wet commons were becoming better drained by means of open ditches, aided by a drier phase in the climate. Another attraction of common land was that families could often appropriate areas, officially or unofficially, as farmland or building plots. For example, the north side of Brisley Common shows three successive lines of encroachment, which helped to reduce an area of about 300 acres to the present 130. At Diss tenants were positively allowed by manorial custom to make steps and seats in front of their doors, stairs down to cellars, and props under projecting windows – with protective bollards! In such a climate, the ancient East Anglian sport of appropriating common land would have flourished. But the most important reason for living around greens was probably the increasing importance of common grazing, when the population was booming and ever more land was falling under the plough. This may be the period when communal grazing was first regulated or 'stinted' according to the size or position of each holding. Certainly the fluidity of settlement in the early Middle Ages argues that people moved their houses and tofts from one part of a manor to another with a freedom which would be inconceivable under modern planning.

The evolution of local settlement could take many forms. At Kempstone, for example, a completely new community sprang up around a green, whilst at the same time the old nucleus near the church was actually enlarged. Weasenham All Saints, which had been a particularly large village in late Saxon times, may have expanded slightly on its margins but abandoned a large central area. At Beetley the village migrated not to a green but to a cross-roads. The village of Horningtoft slowly expanded from an old nucleus near the church along a road for three-quarters of a mile, until it reached a green. Wellingham also maintained its Saxon site, but at the same time grew southwards to the edges of Whin Common. At Mileham the village continued to expand east and west along its main street. Similarly Pudding Norton expanded in a systematic, almost planned, manner on each side of its original, irregular core. Sometimes, as at Tittleshall and Sutton, one large sprawling village resulted from the fusion of two smaller nuclei. One method of increasing the size of a village, which is shown on later maps of Cawston, Tittleshall and elsewhere, was to take over the ends of arable strips and to convert them quite simply into tofts for new houses. But not only did settlements move and expand, they also became denser by subdividing existing properties. For example at South Creake in the thirteenth century each holding or 'tenement' was officially subdivided into six newer and smaller units. The variations are endless, but the theme is undeniable: medieval settlement was dense, flexible and highly mobile.

In many parts of Norfolk the population is not so much concentrated in compact villages as scattered in small clusters of buildings, or in a sprinkling of isolated farmsteads. Darby went so far as to say that the 'dispersed' village is 'ubiquitous in Norfolk'. Certainly it is very common in South and Mid-Norfolk, the Wensum-Bure region, the North-East and Marshland. Only in the Breckland and Good Sands does the nucleated village seem normal.

Like villages, the numerous hamlets of Norfolk show a strong connection with common land. Many of them bear in their names the words 'green', 'common' or 'moor' (meaning a wet, fenny place). Other names include 'street', 'end' (an outlying place), 'row' (a line of dwellings) and 'gate' (which probably refers to a gateway leading to a common, but may simply mean 'street'). Although they often expanded again in the late eighteenth and nineteenth centuries, most of these fascinating clusters and straggles of buildings are at least medieval in origin. Moreover, archaeological evidence now shows many more hamlets than exist today, especially in the centre and south of the county where they were frequently abandoned in the later Middle Ages.

Just as important are isolated farmsteads. Whether they are early timber-framed survivals, or rebuilt in the eighteenth or nineteenth centuries, they often overlie sites which have been occupied continuously since at least the early Middle Ages. The best evidence that this kind of dispersal is ancient is the fact that many isolated farmsteads are moated.

Whether or not they are empty today, nearly all moats enclosed domestic or agricultural buildings, and were probably dug in the twelfth–thirteenth centuries (Plate 14). They certainly had practical uses. For example they drained the sites of houses, yielded clay for buildings, supplied water for humans and animals, provided fresh fish and were a way of impounding stock at night. Nevertheless, they are best regarded as a fashionable status symbol in a desperately competitive age. While some moats may have been contemporary with the first farm on the site, others were surely dug around sites already occupied, or already ancient. The possibility seems increasingly strong that some medieval moats mark sites genuinely surviving from the dispersed patterns of pagan-Saxon, Roman or prehistoric times.

Moats are often found within villages or on their edges, but are even more common in isolated positions or as parts of looseknit hamlets. Their distribution is particularly dense on the heavier lands of South and Mid-Norfolk. For example, at the north end of the parish of Diss is a fascinating area called Heywood; it was felled and converted into farmland by the thirteenth century at the latest, and contains the remains of at least six moats. In the parishes of East and West Bradenham, near East Dereham, are nine moats; most of them lie towards the parish boundaries and may mark the relatively 'late' colonisation of waste and woodland. Three of them are associated with farms called 'manor' and two with halls, so they mark the proliferation of manors and sub-manors in the early Middle Ages. Sometimes, indeed, old moated farm-

Plate 12 Hales: a small but near-perfect Norman church with rectangular nave and apsidal chancel. The round tower is probably earlier and contains re-used Roman tiles. Gothic windows were inserted *c.* 1300.

Plate 13 Salle: one of the great Perpendicular churches of Norfolk, rebuilt 1400-50 with wide aisles and transepts. It contains good medieval fittings such as a suspended font-cover, rood-screen, pulpit, misericords and brasses.

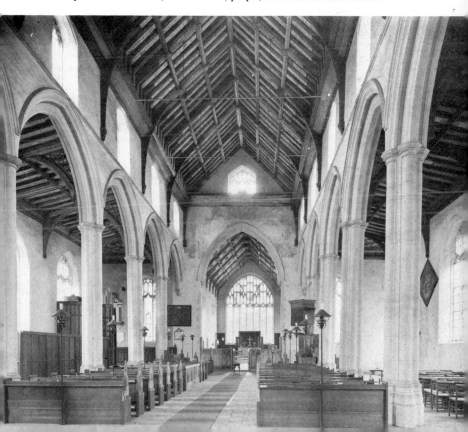

Plate 14 Mannington: a turreted flint hall of 1450-70, inside a fine broad moat which may be earlier. Cropmarks of other buildings have been seen on the 'island'. In the 19th century, the house was greatly extended and an ornamental lake dug.

Plate 15 Halvergate Marshes: a magical wilderness of grassland and water, improved over the centuries by embanking, dredging, cutting dykes and pumping, but now threatened with ploughing. Many old windpumps have now lost their sails. Breydon Water and Gt Yarmouth are visible in the distance.

Plate 16 West Dereham: the site of an important Premonstratensian abbey, founded in 1188 and dissolved 1539. The ruins (centre) are part of Sir Thomas Dereham's house, *c.* 1695. These remarkable cropmarks, photographed in 1976, showed in barley and sugar-beet.

Plate 17 Gasthorpe: one of many ruined and isolated churches in Breckland, drawn by Robert Ladbrooke (he published over 700 engravings of Norfolk churches in 1843). These ruins, now buried in a wood, probably mark the site of an early village.

Plate 18 Godwick: a
deserted village. Notice
the church tower, hollow
roads and earthworks
of former houses and
boundaries. The ruinous
Godwick Hall (centre),
Elizabethan home of the
Coke family, has since
been demolished.

Plate 19 Grenstein:
one end of a deserted
medieval village, showing
as cropmarks in plough-
land. A line of ditched
properties can be seen on
one edge of a long, tri-
angular green; they were
abandoned by 1596.

steads still bear the names of early manorial lords; witness Channonz Hall in Tibenham which was held by the Chauns family in the early 1200s, or Bainard Hall in Fincham which may hark back to Ralph Bainard, the Domesday tenant.

Farming the land

The farming landscape of medieval Norfolk was a vastly complicated patchwork which, in the absence of maps, we can never fully reconstruct. In the thirteenth century most people lived wholly or partly by farming, and the countryside was used intensively and with an ecological sensitivity which makes twentieth-century farming look like open-cast mining.

Open fields were certainly an important part of the scene. They were depicted on scores of maps for Norfolk parishes from the sixteenth century onwards, though by that time the pattern was probably less complex than it had been. Indeed they survived over huge acreages on the lighter soils of west Norfolk until the late eighteenth and early nineteenth centuries; in 1764 John Kirby talked of the 'most delicious Champaign Fields', extending from the Little Ouse to Lynn. Here the older style of farming still made economic sense, and enclosure had therefore, not been attempted on a large scale. However, in the thirteenth century, open fields were probably common in *all* parts of the county. In East Norfolk, for example, Bruce Campbell has found evidence for extensive open fields with 'a degree of fragmentation which was nothing less than extreme'. The same applies to the heavier land of South Norfolk. At Pulham in 1222 the lord's demesne included 724 acres of arable scattered in twenty-nine different parts of the parish.

Open fields were large areas of arable land, divided into furlongs or blocks of various sizes, which in turn were subdivided into small parcels, usually in the form of strips. The lands of individual owners and tenants were normally scattered and intermixed. Although individual strips were hedgeless, open fields were not featureless; they were an intricate patchwork of small pieces of land, ridges and headlands left by the plough, tracks of varying width, ditches for drainage, balks of grass and occasional features like marl-pits and

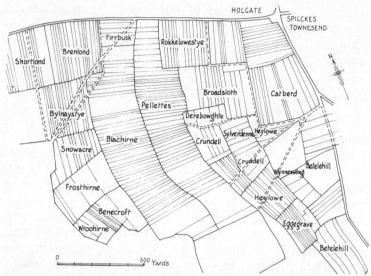

Fig. 10. North Elmham: a reconstruction of Burgrave Field, 568 acres of arable strips and furlongs, in 1454. The smaller furlongs in the south-east corner may be the earliest, perhaps associated with an early Anglo-Saxon village on Spong Hill (after D. Yaxley).

windmill mounds. Because of their complexity, they carried an equally intricate pattern of names. For example, in and around one area of open field at Ashill the following features were recorded in the fifteenth century: Bury Way, Westgate Stokes, Caldewell Sprynge, Caldewell Stye, Goose Meere, Collardez Woode, Wormell More, Rydgate and many others. The vast majority have now disappeared from the map and, more sadly, from human consciousness.

On the whole, the open fields of East Anglia were more individual and flexible than the Midland kind. Instead of two or three fields, Wymondham for example, had eight in the fourteenth century, and the number may not have remained constant. Indeed 'fields' usually appeared to have no real agricultural significance, and were little more than topographical zones used as a convenience in manorial surveys. Similarly, the furlongs or blocks of strips within 'fields' were very numerous. North Elmham, in the fifteenth century, had over 150 furlongs which themselves varied greatly in size from a few acres up to fifty. As for the individual strips, they were often tiny. In 1292 the prior of Norwich's manor at Martham had over 2,000 individual parcels; ninety-four per cent were smaller than one acre and sixty-six per cent smaller than half an acre. Medieval ploughing usually built up long broad ridges, one or more per strip, but most of them have been destroyed by more recent agriculture. However, broad 'ridge-and-furrow' is sometimes noticed on aerial photographs, and occasionally recorded on the ground, as at Babingley and Oxborough.

Important variations existed within the county. On the Breckland, for example, a distinction was made between 'infield' which was regularly cultivated near the village, and 'outfield' or 'brecks' which were taken from the heath, cultivated for a few years and then allowed to revert to waste until their turn came again. Variable areas called 'shifts' were defined for the cultivation of particular crops, so that some kind of agreed rotation could be imposed on a rather haphazard distribution of strips. By contrast North-East Norfolk had no shifts or common rotations at all. Cultivation, in Bruce Campbell's words, 'seems to have been left to the initiative of the individual farmer'. Here the keynote was personal freedom, and the only significant communal arrangements related to grazing after harvest.

In the north and west of Norfolk, early farmers had realised, probably long before the earliest documentary references in the twelfth century, that these lighter and hungrier soils could only be made productive by regular 'tathing' or dunging. Thus the growing of corn in open fields and the grazing of sheep had become essentially complementary, and this association survived until the eighteenth and nineteenth centuries. The Norfolk sheep was a distinct breed, now (alas) extinct, which had evolved on the local heaths since prehistoric times: it had a black face and legs, a short but fine fleece and was horned in both sexes. A 'foldcourse' was an area designed to give a particular flock grazing for a whole year: each consisted of pasture and waste, largely for the summer months, as well as arable which was used after harvest and during fallows. This was the system whereby, in Eileen Power's famous words, 'the little golden hoof turned sand into rich soil'; more prosaically Eric Kerridge referred to

Norfolk sheep as 'mobile fertiliser works and animated muck-spreaders'.

Traces of deliberate planning were sometimes visible in Norfolk's open fields. For example, in the thirteenth century Cawston had twenty-four holdings of eighteen acres, fifteen of four acres and four of two acres, while at Rougham one man's lands were said to abut the same neighbour at least ten times. Topographically, too, regularities appeared which do not look accidental. The inner and presumably earliest open fields at Coltishall, for example, were noticeably regular in lay-out. At Weasenham, strips west of the village ran east-west and others south of the village ran north-south.

A major factor, however, in the development of open fields was the increasing pressure of population. This was at its greatest in the late thirteenth and early fourteenth centuries, but had been building up since long before the Norman Conquest. Campbell calculates that the number of tenants at Martham increased fivefold in the twelfth and thirteenth centuries. By the early fourteenth century, the vast majority were 'near landless small-holders', and the average size of holdings was between two and five acres. In this situation, tenements were subdivided and fragmented, until there was 'a chaotic intermixture of holdings in the fields'. Customs of inheritance which nearly all led to the increasing subdivision of land among heirs, and a buoyant market in free land, both supported the same trend. Topographically, the result was twofold; existing fields were subdivided and, wherever possible, new land was broken in from woodland or rough pasture by the process of 'assarting'. At Horstead in the mid-twelfth century, 35 assarts are mentioned totalling 170 acres; individually the pieces varied from 24 acres to half an acre. At Martham new assarts were quickly broken down into smaller pieces and thereby incorporated into the open fields.

Whereas parishes on the lighter soils tended to refer to furlongs as 'wongs', those on the heavier soils frequently refer to 'crofts' and 'tofts' as major subdivisions of the open fields. This probably means that they had originally been simple enclosures, later subdivided. Their frequency suggests that they are part of much older field systems which were breaking down under the pressure of population. The relationship,

therefore, between open fields and 'closes' is complex. Enclosed fields could break down to become open fields; open
fields could be enclosed at a later date; and some closes,
particularly near houses or on lords' demesnes, may have
survived from early times without major fragmentation.

Permanent grassland was another vital component of the
farming scene. Meadows, particularly, may not have covered
large acreages but they produced the hay which was a vital
fuel for the medieval economy. They too were often minutely
divided into strips or 'doles' and had been valued highly since
Saxon times. In 1251 hay meadows at East Dereham were
worth four shillings an acre, whereas arable rarely exceeded
twelve pence. On each manor the lord was also likely to have
'several' or private pasture for his horses and oxen. At
Pulham in the thirteenth century some of this private grassland was reclaimed alder-carr and some was in the form of
'ways' or green lanes.

Common land

'Commons' of various kinds, including 'greens' which have
already been discussed as focuses of settlement, are still one
of Norfolk's most attractive features. No discerning person
can fail to be impressed by Kelling Heath with its superb views
of the north coast, Flordon Common with its wealth of wild
plants, or Fritton Common with its towering trees and timbered houses. Today Norfolk has only 8,339 acres of common
land (0.64% of its total area) but as recently as 1808 it was
calculated that it had 143,346 acres of 'waste', and the
medieval acreage must have been larger still. The names of
former commons and greens are still used in everyday par-
lance, and their outlines can often be reconstructed (Fig. 21).

Faden's map, published in 1797 before the main spate of
parliamentary enclosures, shows a huge acreage of common
land, named variously as heaths, commons, warrens, fens,
moors, or greens. Some villages and towns like Wymondham,
Thetford and Methwold were almost surrounded by common
land. Furthermore the commons of adjacent parishes often
abutted: for example, the commons of Guist, Stibbard and
Ryburgh were contiguous and connected with those of Wood

Norton and Fulmodeston. Although the greater acreage lay on the lighter soils of West Norfolk, large numbers of commons and greens existed in the centre, south and east. Some were quite sizeable, like Badley Moor near East Dereham or Mousehold Heath which extended almost to the river Bure at Hoveton, but the majority were small, irregular patches where local roads tended to converge.

Two kinds of common seem especially characteristic of Norfolk. The first, a very numerous group, occupied valleys and other low areas. They ranged from large common fens in major valleys, as at South Lopham and Wormegay, to quite small and narrow blocks occurring at frequent intervals along most minor streams. Five such commons formed an almost continuous chain down a little tributary of the Bure which runs from Gunton to Oxnead. These 'low' commons, as they were often called, were obviously of considerable economic value for they often became the focus of medieval and later settlement. The other sort of common, aptly described by Christopher Barringer as 'linear', was characteristic of the south and south-east; Faden shows excellent examples in the vicinity of the Pulhams and Denton. These were long thin greens or wide grassy roads connecting villages, farms and markets in a pastoral area which was enclosed early. The valuable common grazing along these features was sometimes known, picturesquely, as the 'long meadow'.

Some commons were created in the Middle Ages; for example the prior of Westacre in 1343 was given licence to enclose two acres of a common, so long as he provided another area of similar size elsewhere; similarly a Great Common was laid out at Fersfield *c.* 1500 to compensate for an area lost when Kenninghall Park was extended. But these are exceptional, and the majority of commons had evolved long before. After all, they are patches of largely unimproved and primeval 'waste', left primarily for grazing after other areas were more intensively developed. Several characteristics point to a pre-Norman origin: for example the existence of 'intercommons' which were shared by two or more parishes; Banham and Winfarthing shared a large common of 1,200 acres, and a marsh was common to the inhabitants of Stoke Ferry, Wretton and Wereham. In one remarkable case, a thirteenth-century common was recorded as belonging to the whole *hundred* of Taverham. This is surely a primitive form of commoning which pre-dates the highly organised usages of medieval manors. The frequent proximity of woodland, and the 'woodland' names of some commons, suggest that grass-covered commons sometimes evolved from areas of woodland or wood-pasture. For example, two of the commons of Briningham in the eighteenth century were called Burgh *Stubbs* and *Stock* Heath, names which imply that they once bore trees.

Rarely did commons remain stable in size or outline. Abundant documentary evidence from the thirteenth century onwards shows that local people frequently enclosed or encroached on commons, usually by taking long and thin strips from their edges. For example, in the thirteenth century, Nicholas de Ripton encroached on the common of Wimbotsham by putting a ditch around a strip four rods long and twelve feet wide. Where commons were depicted on maps, one often sees indented edges and islands resulting from such piecemeal erosion. For instance, Blofield Heath contained a mass of small islands, while the eastern edge of West Winch Common looked positively battlemented.

In spite of their diversity of soils and siting, commons share certain characteristics. Generally a clear boundary prevents animals from wandering off into adjoining fields. On the heavier land especially, commons are bounded by very large earthworks, particularly deep ditches and thick hedges containing many species of shrub. These may be among the most ancient landscape features still in regular use, and they desperately need some protection. Entries to commons were often controlled by gates, which are still frequently referred to in local place names. Pits were regularly dug on common land, with and without manorial consent, to extract sand, gravel, clay and other materials. At Aldeby for example, the prior of Norwich was allowed in 1310 to take marl out of a common called *Mekylheyth*. In some cases, commons were dug over so much, that they became pock-marked with 'hills and holes', as can still be seen at Stow Bedon and Caston. Pits often filled with water but, in the form of ponds, were useful for watering stock and for fishing, and might occasionally

109

have industrial significance as at Diss where tenants were able, in certain places, to soak their hemp.

By the thirteenth century at the latest, commons of various kinds were subjected to careful rules of management. An example can be drawn from the Ely Coucher Book of 1251. On the manor of East Dereham as many as nine commons were listed. Four of them were described as 'turbaries' in which the township of Dereham and the tenants of certain other local lords were allowed to common 'horn underhorn', but nobody was to cut wood or dig peat without the bishops' licence. The names of two turbaries suggest that, in their natural state, they had been alder carr, but that by the thirteenth century they were chiefly valued for their grazing and peat. (In 1797, these turbaries were represented by Badley Moor, a very large area of wet marshland shared by Dereham, Yaxham and Mattishall.) The five other areas were described as 'common pastures'; three of them bore the name 'grene'. One of these, *Northalegrene* was already in the thirteenth century a focus of settlement, and several tenants bore the surname 'de Northal'; it was commoned by the township of Dereham and thirteen specified tenants of two other lords who lived 'next that pasture'. This deliberate stinting, whereby the right of grazing was attached to the possession of specific tenements, was becoming normal at this period.

Woodland

No longer can we regard medieval villages as 'islands of cultivation in a sea of primeval forest'. Most of the landscape of Norfolk had been cleared long before, and in certain parts of the county (like Flegg, the Good Sands, Breckland and Marshland) practically all woodland had disappeared by the time of the Norman Conquest. Even on the heavier land of South Norfolk, pollen analysis attests that steady clearance had been resumed in later Anglo-Saxon times. Therefore, in the medieval landscape, we are concerned with 'islands of woodland' which were allowed to survive in certain parts of the county, given defined outlines and carefully managed as an economic resource. It is a miracle of medieval economics

110

that huge quantities of wood and timber were grown from relatively small acreages of woodland. The fifteenth-century roofs of Norwich cathedral alone demanded 680 oak trees with basal diameters of fifteen inches, and we must allow for thousands of timber-framed houses, farm buildings, implements and hand tools, as well as fuel for hearths and ovens, all of which made the medieval period a veritable 'Wood Age'. Nevertheless, in spite of the high productivity of local woods, Yarmouth and Lynn were importing soft-wood from Scandinavia and the Baltic at least as early as the thirteenth century.

Domesday Book lists a large number of woods in Norfolk, but they were relatively small. The greatest concentration was in what Oliver Rackham calls 'the wooded crescent' which started on the north-east coast and continued through the centre of the county to the south. This is an area of medium to heavy soils, in which place names implying woodland clearance, such as -*ley* and -*feld*, also tend to cluster. The Domesday woods of Norfolk were measured by their capacity to feed so many swine, whether real or conjectural, and only rarely was the capacity said to be over 1,000. The largest of local woods lay north-west and west of Norwich, where parishes tended to be larger and population was less dense. Conversely, the many woods of South Norfolk were small, probably because parishes were small, had comparatively dense populations and carried a high proportion of plough-teams. In many vills, the number of swine was reduced in the twenty years between 1066 and 1086. This probably represented not a new cycle of clearance, but a change in management away from grazing and towards the growing of more coppice-wood.

The medieval woods of Norfolk were destroyed in large numbers between 1500 and 1800, but fortunately some good examples survive. Wayland Wood, south of Watton, where the ancient story of the 'Babes in the wood' had its setting, is a coppice in which the underwood, unusually, is bird-cherry. It bears a Norse name and was the meeting place for an Anglo-Saxon hundred; Rackham suggests that it was a 'grove of assembly, perhaps even of heathen worship, long before the Norman Conquest'. He sees it as a surviving fragment of the primeval forest or 'wildwood' which once covered the greater part of the county. Great Wood at Swanton Novers is excep-

111

tionally rich, and is said to be one of the finest examples of ancient woodland in East Anglia. Hockering Wood is one of the largest lime woods left in England; this gives it a special historical and botanical significance, because lime is now regarded as one of the dominant species of the 'wildwood'. These ancient manorial woods tend to be sited towards the edges of parishes, if not actually against the boundary, often on relatively high ground and in areas which could locally be regarded as marginal. They often carry the names of the manors or parishes to which they belonged.

Generally, manorial woods were managed to produce two kinds of wood: large timber from mature trees or 'standards', and small straight poles grown from many-stemmed clumps or 'stools'. Stools were cut to the ground regularly, which encouraged them to shoot again and grow vigorously. So, in the early fifteenth century at Bunwell, large numbers of oaks and, to a lesser extent, ash and maple were being sold as mature trees; at the same time considerable quantities of coppice-poles, thorn and bark (for tanning) were being produced. Rackham quotes examples of coppiced shrubs growing seven–eleven feet in the first year, and in certain favoured spots as much as two inches a day. As this rigorous form of management was quite incompatible with grazing, coppiced woodland was protected by a strong earthwork, ditch and bank surmounted by a fence or hedge. Often it was the task of manorial tenants, as at Blickling and Bunwell, to mend the hedge and keep the ditch clean. Conversely, the existence of moats and other earthworks inside some woods in South Norfolk suggests that some secondary woodland was being deliberately created on land formerly cleared.

Parks

Where animals were still allowed to browse, woods might in the course of time develop into pasture or open common, or they may have been formally converted into hunting parks. For example, Rackham has described how Thorpe Wood just outside Norwich turned, from the twelfth century onwards, into the treeless Mousehold Heath. The bishop, who owned the wood, could not, it seems, control or extinguish commoners' rights of grazing. A similar example probably exists at Toftwood near East Dereham. The interlocking plan of a former wood and common suggests that they originated as an area of wood pasture which was, before the mid-thirteenth century, deliberately partitioned: 70 acres were defined and enclosed as a permanent wood, the bank of which was maintained by manorial tenants, and 130 acres were given over to common grazing and in time became the treeless common which is depicted on Faden's map. At North Elmham, an abnormally large area of woodland seems to have been divided four ways: into a permanent coppice-wood of about 145 acres (which was recently saved from extinction), a large hunting park which had appeared by the early thirteenth century, an extensive common and a block of 'assarted' farmland.

Over sixty medieval parks have now been identified in Norfolk by a combination of fieldwork and documentary research. These areas of wood and grassland, on average about 200 acres, were set aside for the hunting and breeding of deer – though they might also contain other kinds of domesticated and wild animals. A park should be distinguished from the right of 'chace', as at Castle Rising, which enabled a landowner to pursue large game animals such as deer and foxes over open country, and also from the right of 'free warren' which was a commonplace licence to hunt small animals such as hares, rabbits and pheasants over any kind of land in a particular manor. Although medieval parks were mainly intended to give good sport to manorial lords and their guests, they also produced timber, fish, fowl, bedding for animals and, above all, venison.

To keep deer in and poachers out, parks were normally given a strong boundary consisting of ditch and bank surmounted by a pale or hedge. This had to be regularly maintained: for example, certain free tenants at East Dereham were each responsible for twenty-four perches of the lord's park boundary. Internally parks often contained smaller enclosures, presumably for breeding deer, gathering hay and grazing horses. A sixteenth-century map of Haveringland shows five such internal compartments, some of which were certainly meadows. The largest parks also had lodges in them.

113

The ruins of one still survive at Drayton, while a circular moat beside the river Bure at Burgh-by-Aylsham is known to have contained an elaborate royal lodge. In 1313 this building included a great hall, chapels, a chamber for the queen, and a chamber for the knights; it also had two watch-towers and two bridges.

Though one already existed in 1066 at Costessey, the great majority of Norfolk's hunting parks were created between 1100 and 1350. They appeared in the north-east, centre and south of the county and were virtually non-existent in the Breckland, Good Sands, Marshland and Flegg. In other words, they occur in areas where ancient woods existed, and indeed appear to have developed out of woods. Some manors, such as Winfarthing, even had two parks. A few examples survive today because they were later absorbed into ornamental parks as at Kimberley or Old Hunstanton, or into woods as at Haveringland. The vast majority, however, were 'disparked' and converted into farmland during the sixteenth and seventeenth centuries, leaving only traces in the landscape of today. For example at Silfield (Plate 21), the outline of a 750-acre park has survived on modern maps as a continuous hedge-line, enclosing two small valleys, a small block of ancient woodland and two farms. The southern farm is called Lowerpark and, being moated, almost certainly marks the site of a medieval hunting lodge.

A rather different kind of park was the rabbit warren, in which rabbits were deliberately bred for their 'hollow meat' and skins. Such warrens existed in various parts of the county where the land was suitably light, but are particularly associated with the Breckland. It has been calculated that by the end of the thirteenth century, over 10,000 acres in thirty-five parishes of the Norfolk and Suffolk Breckland had been set aside as warrens. Generally they occupied the higher and more remote parts of their parishes, and were defined by high banks of turf topped by growing vegetation such as furze. Many of these banks, now eroded, can still be seen in the Breckland among the Forestry Commission's trees, and particularly where the edge of a warren coincided with a parish boundary. Internally a lodge was often built for the accommodation of a warrener and his family. An excellent example survives almost intact at Thetford; it is a small defensive tower dating from the fifteenth century, with living accommodation above a storeroom. Maps of Methwold in the sixteenth century show a huge warren of 1,500 acres, extending into six parishes, which was criss-crossed by roads and had a lodge at its northern end. It was well known for its 'Muel' rabbits which fetched high prices in the London market.

Broadland

The winding alluvial valleys of east Norfolk are distinguished by two fascinating features largely developed in the medieval period. First, as the three rivers of Waveney, Yare and Bure converge on Breydon Water behind Yarmouth, they meander across the vast expanse of the Halvergate marshes, which have provided rich grazing for a thousand years and more (Plate 15). Here Domesday Book recorded Norfolk's largest concentration of 'meadow' belonging to villages on the surrounding upland. Because it was economically valuable, the area was divided between individual parishes, to form a complicated patchwork of interlocking territories and detached portions. In general, these boundaries followed natural winding streams and tidal creeks; internally, however, each parish strove to improve its marsh, lying at or just above sea-level, by digging straighter artificial drains. Some villages which were not adjacent to the marshes, but sited higher up the valleys or on upland ridges, nevertheless acquired an interest in this grazing, usually in the more distant marshes nearer Breydon Water. By means of drove-roads, causeways and even boats, they conveyed their stock over long distances. Thus Langley somehow acquired a marsh seven miles away on a lonely peninsula between the converging Yare and Waveney, while South Walsham similarly owned a marsh over seven miles away near the Fleet Dike.

Upsteam, in the middle reaches of the same valleys, are the lakes known since the later Middle Ages as 'broads' (Plate 20). Over thirty of these irregularly shaped sheets of water survive, amounting to about 2,600 acres. For several generations writers and artists have been intrigued by the gentle beauty of the broads, and by the richness of their wildlife, but nobody could adequately explain them. It was widely assumed that they were natural in origin, and this seemed confirmed in 1952 when a geomorphologist published a monograph arguing that the broads were natural lakes, held back by lips of natural clay deposited in Roman times. Then new research was begun by a team of specialists which included a botanist, geomorphologist, historical geographer and archaeologist. Their report, published in 1960, is an impressive example of interdisciplinary research. First, over 2,000 borings were made at regular intervals across the valleys to see how layers of soil and vegetation changed. This simple but laborious technique soon showed startling results. A clean break was found between natural deposits in valley floors and deep mud on the beds of broads. The sides of the broads turned out to be vertical faces of undisturbed peat or clay, and their bottoms were generally horizontal; within the broads were peninsulas of solid, steep-sided peat with the same natural stratigraphy as the sides. Thus, it was no longer possible to think of the broads as natural lakes: they were large 'holes' from which huge quantities of natural material had been removed. And they were indisputably man-made.

It was also possible to prove that the physical plan of the broads was dictated by man-made boundaries and allotments of land. Detailed maps of the nineteenth century depicted a complicated pattern of strip-like holdings imposed, rather improbably, on the waters of the broads and their vegetated fringes. Some strips corresponded exactly with peninsulas or islands of peat; in other cases the edges of strips corresponded with narrow balks left between adjoining holdings. These later maps also indicated the original size of the broads before vegetation started to encroach, and their boundaries agreed with the evidence obtained by boring.

But precisely why and when were the broads dug? Maps of the sixteenth century show that they were already filled with water, so they had been dug long before. On the other hand, they were partly cut through the Upper Clay which had been laid down in Romano-British times. The great depth of mud on the bed of the broads (on average between nine and twelve feet) might suggest that they were dug well back in the medieval or Anglo-Saxon periods, yet mud may have accumulated rapidly because of the lime-richness and abundant biological life of the broads, and because of silting caused by the rivers and nearby arable farming.

The essential fact is that huge quantities of peat had been removed from these holes: one estimate suggested about 900 million cubic feet. The broads were therefore holes from which peat had been quarried. This was a valuable fuel for domestic and industrial purposes in an area where the medieval population was high (including the towns of Yarmouth and Norwich) and woodland was scarce. Scattered historical sources revealed that local parishes did indeed have 'turbaries' which were producing peat from the twelfth to fourteenth centuries, if not earlier, and that religious houses were heavily involved in the exploitation of this natural resource. The peat must have been dug from open pits, at a time when sea-level was lower and the risk of flooding was not so great. Even so, the excavators must have been faced with many practical problems. They wanted to dig as deeply as possible to get the best and most combustible peat, yet the danger of seepage and flooding must always have been present. The deepest pits are in fact in the side-valleys, and no doubt attempts were made to lead water away from the workings, or to dam it. Some of the balks may have been deliberately left to delay flooding. Conditions must have deteriorated sharply after 1300 when the climate worsened and sea-level rose; by the fifteenth century these open pits had become, or were becoming, the water-filled lakes we know today, and local records referred less to turbaries and more often to fens, waters and fisheries.

Roads, bridges and waterways

The nature of local communications also deserves attention. During the Middle Ages, Norfolk was covered by a tight network of roads, tracks and paths which were sometimes mentioned in contemporary charters and surveys. That network is of course related to the history of local settlement, farming and land use, and also helps us to understand how each community developed its links with the outside world. Unfortunately, we are faced with two difficulties. First, our present-day mileage is only a fraction of what once existed because, in the last two centuries, so many rights of way have been abandoned or destroyed. Second, local roads and tracks normally precede the earliest surviving documents and are therefore impossible to date with precision. Of course we can usually recognise a Roman road or those created by parliamentary enclosure, but the great majority of 'organic' and unplanned roads are virtually timeless.

A few roads must always have been used as through routes, even in prehistory, and many others must have acquired that significance in later-Saxon and medieval times. By the thirteenth century most of our 'A' roads were already accepted as *viae regiae* or 'King's highway', and many others which are now no more than by-roads. They were vital for the development of towns, markets, fairs and pilgrimages, for the running of great estates, and for the carrying out of justice and administration. Indeed, the road system must have been reasonably efficient for, in March 1256, King Henry III and his household did a circular tour of Norfolk in only eleven days – calling at East Dereham, Castle Acre, Gayton, Walsingham, Thornage, Gimingham, Broomholm, St Benet's and Norwich.

Roads were given many local improvements in the Middle Ages, especially where they crossed valleys and marshes. Artificial raised causeways were certainly in existence by the thirteenth century at places like Setchey, Fakenham 'Dam' and Haddiscoe. The latter pursues a sinuous course over the Waveney marshes for two miles, and is as impressive as the causeways linking the Isle of Ely to the southern uplands of Cambridgeshire. Bridges were certainly another major form of investment. For example, Wiveton and Wroxham had bridges by the thirteenth century, while the vital Wey Bridge which connects the island of Flegg to Acle and Norwich was there by 1101 (an earlier stone causeway lies upstream). Indeed the building and repair of bridges had been accepted as a charitable obligation since Anglo-Saxon times. Thus the bridge at Stoke Ferry lay derelict in 1291, precisely because it was first built by public alms and nobody knew who was responsible for it. Wayside crosses of stone and timber also appeared in large numbers, to give direction and spiritual comfort to travellers. In the mid-fifteenth century, for example, pilgrims along one of the many 'Walsingham Ways' would have passed five crosses in the parish of North Elmham alone. Some stone crosses have survived to this day, as at Aylmerton, Langley and Pentney, but in most cases they are commemorated, if at all, by a name.

Although the medieval road pattern was not normally planned, and was subjected to constant encroachment, roads were sometimes deliberately diverted by individuals or for the public good. For example, the Paston Letters mention disputes where the family was accused of diverting public roads for their own convenience. At Little Walsingham, one can still see where a road was diverted in 1351 when the Dominican friary was increased in size, while the enlargement of parish churches and graveyards not infrequently caused roads to curve around them – as at Titchwell and Weston Longville.

In the later Middle Ages, local people increasingly used the profits of farming and commerce for the upkeep of roads and bridges, and left specific bequests in their wills. In 1432 John Spendlove left one mark to the 'Brygg in Wroxham', while John Prikke in 1505 left money to repair 'le fowle slowthe' between Diss and Roydon. During the Reformation, too, money received from the sale of church goods was often spent in maintaining roads, bridges, causeways and a system of beacons. For example, Foulsham in 1547, having sold off unwanted plate and vestments, decided to repair two furlongs of a 'noysum drove way' which was used daily by the poor to drive their dairy cows to the local common.

Water transport was also important, especially for the carriage of heavy materials. Thus, oaks which were sent from Sherwood Forest to Norfolk in 1229 were to be carried *per aquam*. A fascinating series of small ports grew up around the coast, especially from Cromer westwards. Here, at places like Blakeney, Wells, Burnham Overy and Thornham, nature provided sheltered inlets and estuaries at frequent intervals. Inland, staithes or 'hithes' were in existence before the Norman Conquest and have left their mark on place names like Rackheath, Setchey and 'Otringheia' (Methwold Hythe). The channel from the Wensum into the Close at Norwich is

119

thought to be Norman, constructed so that Caen stone could be landed for the new cathedral; other navigable cuts served the town of Castle Rising and the abbey at Langley. Under the south-west wing of Fastolf's castle at Caister, a canal of the fifteenth century runs into an internal 'Barge Yard'.

SELECT BIBLIOGRAPHY

Darby, H. C., *The Domesday Geography of Eastern England* (1971).

Davenport, F. G., *The economic development of a Norfolk Manor, 1086–1565* (1906).

Lambert, J. M. and Smith, J. N., *et al.*, *The making of the Broads*, Royal Geographical Society Memoir, No. 3 (1960).

Rackham, Oliver, *Ancient Woodland* (1980).

David Yaxley on the topography and agrarian economy of North Elmham, in *East Anglian Archaeology*, Report No. 9, Vol. 2 (1980), 517–96.

9. The Marshland

AT THE WEST end of the county is a landscape of special distinction. Known as the Marshland since at least the thirteenth century, it occupies the greater part of Norfolk's fenland. Nowhere higher than twenty feet above sea-level, it consists of a broad curving band of fertile silt, red in colour as local field names suggest, and surrounded by lower areas of salt marsh and peat fen. This is probably the only part of Norfolk which is entirely medieval in origin, (that is, post-Roman) simply because the remains of Roman and prehistoric occupation had been covered by later water-borne deposits. Here, if anywhere, lords and peasants started afresh in the Anglo-Saxon period, in a natural wilderness which was never easy to exploit or control. At about A.D. 700, the fenland was described as 'a very long tract, now consisting of marshes, now of bogs, sometimes of black waters overhung by fog, sometimes studded with wooded islands and traversed by the windings of tortuous streams'. By 1300, Marshland had a prosperous, communally organised landscape of great complexity, which even today is a lasting monument to medieval society, agriculture and technology.

Domesday Book reveals that a chain of agricultural communities had long been established along the silt ridge. Proportionally less land was ploughed than in any other part of Norfolk, but no woodland was mentioned and the main emphasis was on the grazing of pastures and meadows. For example, West Walton had 1,300 sheep, by far the largest number recorded in Norfolk. Had the Domesday scribes recorded pasture more systematically, particularly common marsh and fen, then the Marshland would undoubtedly have appeared richer. Already place names like Walton, Walsoken and Walpole show that these communities had invested heavily in the building of sea-banks, which probably linked to form a continuous defence against the surges of the North Sea.

From the twelfth century onwards, the increasing survival

of documents suggests how this difficult landscape was made more productive. For example, in 1166 the bishop of Ely claimed that in the previous thirty years he had created two knights' fees out of marsh. Thirteenth-century surveys of property belonging to Ely record such names as *Newelond* and *Newecroft* (in West Walton), *Rednewelond* (in Terrington) and *Newefeld* (in Walpole). The reclamation was probably no more than the continuation of work which had been going on for centuries, since long before the Norman Conquest, but reaching a crescendo in the thirteenth century when the population was at its highest.

One of the best examples of medieval reclamation was recorded at Wiggenhall in the early fourteenth century. A large area 'from Busterdesdole unto the south side of the same town' had all been waste or fenland. It contained no inhabitants except the small nunnery of Crabhouse, and was said to have no value. Between 1181 and 1223, however, the inhabitants of Wiggenhall and other places 'with draining and banking won as much thereof, by their industry, as they could'. The land was divided by sinuous dykes running south-west to north-east, and part of it undoubtedly became open field. This phase of reclamation was connected with the digging, in 1223, of a major drain called Old Podike. Several townships were involved in this major project and in its continued maintenance. Its purpose was to drain a large area of fenland and to head off freshwater flooding from the south. This was the southern defence of a highly populated and intensively farmed Marshland, and just as important as the northern line of defence provided by the earlier Roman Bank.

However, natural disasters occurred from time to time, and particularly in the period 1250 to 1350 when, it has been estimated, Marshland was flooded twelve times. For example, a chronicler reported that, after a violent gale in January 1287, the 'part of England known as the Marshland . . . became a lake and innumerable people were cut off by the water and drowned'. Special commissions of sewers were often appointed to cope with flooding, and taxes remitted when townships were damaged. Trouble sometimes occurred around Upwell and Outwell, along the old silting course of

the Nene, as in 1301, but the main threats were around Stow
Bardolph Fen to the south and in the winding lower course of
the Great Ouse to the east. In 1338 the river bank between
Clenchwarton and Wiggenhall was broken in five places: £300
worth of damage was done at Tilney where pastures were
flooded, corn and hay destroyed, and 160 sheep drowned. In
1362 it was said that the Great Ouse, which used to run
between banks twelve perches apart, was 'a full mile in
breadth'. The special danger of freshwater flooding from the
south led to the construction of the New Podike in 1422–3,
with the help of all the landowners in Marshland and Wiggenhall. It ran from west to east, about three miles south of
the Old Podike which was described as quite ruinous; its
purpose was to improve the natural Well Creek by leading
water eastwards into the Great Ouse at Salter's Lode.

Expansion over several centuries created a landscape
which in plan resembled a spoked wheel (Plate 24). Individual
townships and parishes tended to be wedge-shaped, with their
thicker ends against the Wash or the vast estuary which
originally lay north of Wisbech, and their thin ends resting on
a central area of common fen.

The salt marshes against the sea provided valuable grazing,
as well as fowling, fishing and sites for boiling salt. Their inner
edge was defined by the 'Old Roman Sea Bank' which
pursued a sinuous, sometimes jagged, course from West Lynn
round to Wisbech (Plate 8). It survives as a broad, high bank,
but was probably not all built at the same time. In places the
bank is followed by modern metalled roads. An exciting
example is the by-road from Walpole St Andrew to the
hamlet of Cross Keys, which is raised high above surrounding
fields and still has the feel of an ancient barrier between the
inhabited silt ridge and the salt marshes of the former estuary.
For centuries local people were obliged to maintain this bank:
for example, in 1348, inhabitants of West Walton repaired six
feet two inches of sea bank for every acre they held (also one
foot of the Podike). Aerial photography has recently revealed
that 'spurs' were built outside the main bank, at right angles
to it, as a means of combating the erosive power of tides and
floods.

Inside the Roman Bank are the main settlements and fine

churches of medieval Marshland. As villages they are mainly large and sprawling, and follow a dense, irregular pattern of lanes, greens and droves. Further inland still, descending towards the fens, the landscape becomes much more regular in layout. Each township had a long, wide drove-road leading from the inhabited area to the fen. This drove-road was extended southwards as new blocks of land were reclaimed, and often itself became the focus of later settlement as new houses were built along its edges. In some places this process resulted in totally new villages, served by their own chapels, as at Terrington St John or Kenwick. The outlines of these great droves are still to be seen in several parishes, and sometimes survive as broad bands of permanent grassland bounded by deep ditches. Here, if anywhere in Norfolk, are ancient landscape features worthy of protection, yet they are being rubbed out yearly by modern agricultural methods.

On modern Ordnance Survey maps, many of these rectangular blocks of land still bear the hallmarks of former open fields. Some of the old names are still current, and until at least the 1950s the area was minutely subdivided into long, thin strips, sometimes straight and sometimes curved, defined by miles of small drainage ditches. Some strips, for example at Wiggenhall St Germans, were over half a mile long. In several townships, a complete succession of open fields is visible. They begin with relatively small and irregular fields close to the main village, such as Cranny Hill field (Walpole) and South Croft (Terrington); some of these look as if they were enclosed at an early date. Beyond is a succession of more geometric fields with such names as Red Newland and New Sibley fields (both in Terrington) and Great West New field (in Walpole). Each of the latter is defined by an obvious southern boundary, usually a lane today but originally a bank and ditch. Thus the inner group of fields at Terrington is separated from Red Newland and Church fields by Fenditch Lane, which in 1591 was called the New Fendyke. In fact it was already old: the medieval chapel of St John 'against the Marsh', founded by the middle of the thirteenth century, lies *outside* this bank, so it must have been built in the twelfth century or even earlier. It is noticeable that successive intakes remained roughly in step, as the banks often line up across township boundaries. Furthermore the boundaries themselves, often dead straight for miles, were presumably defined by mutual agreement between townships at, or before, the time of reclamation.

Finally, the hub on which most of these townships converged was a large, circular common called West Fen and The Smeeth (an Old English word meaning 'level' or 'smooth'). In the eighteenth century Blomefield called it 'a famous common', so fertile that if a stick were left overnight on the ground, it would 'be covered with grass of that night's growth'. Technically this fen was an 'intercommon' because it was used jointly by seven adjacent townships for digging turf and grazing their cattle and sheep. For access, each township had a 'gate' at the end of its drove.

The full extent of the fen, now enclosed, can be seen on Faden's map of Norfolk, published in 1797. It was described verbally in the famous Ely Coucher Book of 1251:

> It begins at Walsokensuthdrove [Walsoken South Drove, at TF 508080] and extends as far as Cancelresdichesende on the east [the end of Chancellor's Dike, probably the northern end, at either TF 552112 or 556100], as far as Pokedich [the Old Podike], and then by Pokedich as far as the fen of Thomas son of Ralph of Wells [Well Moor on Faden's map], and by the fen of the same Thomas as far as Bucrofteshende [probably near Titkill Bridge], and from Bucrofteshende as far as Walsokensuthdrove.

The best symbol of Marshland's medieval wealth is undoubtedly the architecture of its parish churches. Here, though often surrounded by mean modern developments, are some of the most memorable churches in Britain: large, sumptuous and varied, they range in date from the twelfth to the fifteenth centuries. Even the earliest are on an impressive scale, such as Walsoken and Tilney All Saints with their long Norman naves and arcades, or West Walton which is one of the noblest examples anywhere of the Early English style of *c.* 1240. Later came the cathedral-like masterpieces of Walpole St Peter (1350–1400) and Terrington St Clement (largely fifteenth century).

It will be noted that townships tended to subdivide into smaller ecclesiastical parishes, as population grew and settlements proliferated. Thus all four Wiggenhalls were in existence as independent parishes by 1254. Sometimes an original mother church can be identified, and the newer places of worship to which it gave birth. At Terrington, for example, St John's began in the thirteenth century as no more than a chapel dependent on St Clements, and serving a new settlement growing up along the edges of a drove. In spite of subdivision the value of ecclesiastical livings in Marshland was unusually high. For example, Walpole, Tilney and, above all, Terrington were worth more than any other Norfolk livings mentioned in the Ecclesiastical Taxation of 1291.

The Lay Subsidy of 1334 reveals that six townships in Marshland paid more than any other rural community in Norfolk, on average £29-4-0 as compared with an average for the county of £4-18-7. However, it is possible to exaggerate the comparative prosperity of this area. When allowance is made for acreages, Marshland was no more remarkable in 1334 than certain other prosperous parts of the county, for example, the North-East, Flegg and Henstead hundred south of Norwich. The real distinction of Marshland is that the combined efforts of lords, especially ecclesiastical ones, and a numerous peasantry, created a thriving agricultural economy, beautifully attuned to a difficult but potentially rich environment.

SELECT BIBLIOGRAPHY

Darby, H. C., *The Medieval Fenland* (1940, 1974).
Glasscock, R. E., 'The distribution of wealth in East Anglia in the early 14th century', *Transactions & Papers, Institute of British Geographers*, XXXII (1963), 113–23.
Hallam, H. E., *The new lands of Elloe*, Occasional Papers No. 6, Dept. of English Local History, University of Leicester (1954).
Miller, Edward, *The Abbey and Bishopric of Ely* (1951).
Owen, A. E. B. (ed.), 'The Records of a Commission of Sewers for Wiggenhall, 1319–24', *Norfolk Record Society*, XLVIII (1981).

10. Medieval builders

Religious houses.   Parish churches.

FROM NORMAN TIMES onwards, the architectural legacy becomes more important. Most of the early survivals, reflecting both practical and spiritual needs, are either castles or religious institutions. The new Norman overlords quickly consolidated their control of the county and its native inhabitants by building about ten castles at carefully chosen strategic points, or at the centres of their estates. At one end of the scale were small motte-and-baileys built by local lords and consisting of earth and timber; well preserved examples have survived at Horsford and Denton. At the other extreme are massive fortresses built to control towns and major routes, where early timber buildings and defences were usually rebuilt in stone. At Castle Acre, the Warenne family first built — an elaborate stone country house and then in the mid-twelfth century converted it into 'one of the grandest motte-and-bailey castles in England', controlling the Peddars Way and the Nar valley. At Norwich, Henry II in about 1160 built a rectangular keep, decorated with blank arcading, which was almost as large as the White Tower in London, and placed on probably the largest motte in England. But after 1200, the emphasis in Norfolk swings from military control to economic development; most castles were still maintained and occasionally modernised, as when the inner ramparts at New Buckenham were raised in the thirteenth century, but no new castles were built until the fifteenth century and some of the existing examples, as at Thetford, were abandoned.

In the fifteenth century an important group of large defended houses was built in Norfolk. They expressed the growing ambitions and factionalism of local gentry and nobility, at a time when central government was weak. Quarrels and threats sometimes erupted into violence, as when the Paston family were attacked at Gresham Castle in 1450 and at

Hellesdon manor in 1465. So, while they were comfortable and up-to-date as residences, major houses still needed to be defensible: they lie, as it were, halfway between the medieval castle and the Tudor country mansion. In most places, we are able to see only fragments today: at Middleton and Bacons-thorpe a gatehouse is the principal survival, while at Hales it is an outer courtyard and barn; at Kimberley Old Hall and Shelton, a few mounds of stone inside a moat are the only remains of large quadrangular houses. Two examples, however, are much better preserved. Caister Castle (Plate 28) was built for Sir John Fastolf in 1432–5, and is a recognisable castle with moat, machicolations, arrow slits, gunports and a dramatic circular tower ninety-eight feet high which recalls castles of the Lower Rhineland. Later in the century, in 1482, Edmund Bedingfield was licensed to crenellate his house at Oxborough, where his descendants still live. This is a more obviously domestic building of red brick, built around a courtyard and inside a broad moat. Its finest feature is a soaring gatehouse, seven storeys high, which still retains the military conventions of battlements, machicolations and gun-ports but was principally intended to express the wealth and taste of its owners.

Lower down the social scale, we only have a few precious survivals from the early Middle Ages. For example, a ruined manor house of the twelfth century, with an aisled hall, masquerades under the name of Weeting Castle, while a few stone-built houses of the same period have been identified recently in the towns of Lynn (Plate 38) and Norwich. Manor houses of the later Middle Ages, as one would expect, survive more often. Two excellent moated examples, built of flint and stone, are Elsing Hall (*c.* 1460) which still has a hall with open timber roof and large window lighting the high table, and Mannington Hall which was licensed in 1451 and still preserves a simple medieval core of hall, private apartments and service rooms, embedded in nineteenth-century additions.

Religious houses

Norfolk has been described as 'astonishingly rich' in religious houses, with a total of about seventy abbeys, priories and friaries. Although St Benet Hulme may have been founded as early as *c*. 800, most of these institutions were established by local magnates between the eleventh and thirteenth centuries. They occurred in most parts of the county, except for the Marshland and South Norfolk which had comparatively few. The actual sites ranged from lonely spots, deliberately chosen, like Crabhouse and Slevesholm in the fens, or St Benet's among the marshes and rivers of Broadland, to clusters of priories and friaries in major towns. An interesting rural concentration is in the Nar valley, from Castle Acre down to Wormegay, which Augustus Jessopp called 'Norfolk's Holy Land'. Nearly all the known religious orders were represented in the county, though the most important were undoubtedly Benedictines and Augustinian canons. The size of communities varied from sixty monks at the cathedral-priory of Norwich in 1101, to tiny establishments like Mullicourt which only had one monk in 1381, or Toft Monks whose only inmate in the fourteenth century was the prior.

Although the destruction of monastic buildings was enormous after the Reformation, it is still possible to reconstruct the plans of some houses from ruins and excavated foundations. Thus one sees the layout of a small Benedictine house at Binham, where the nave of the monks' church is still used by the parish, an extensive Cluniac plan at Castle Acre, and a compact fourteenth-century Franciscan friary at Little Walsingham. Aerial photography can also make an impressive contribution. In 1976–7, for example, Derek Edwards was able to reconstruct most of the plan of West Dereham abbey, covering three and a half acres, from cropmarks in corn and sugar-beet (Plate 16).

Two religious houses in Norfolk achieved a national reputation as centres of pilgrimage. At Broomholm, on a bare clifftop overlooking the sea, a small Cluniac community was established in 1113 as an offshoot or 'cell' of Castle Acre. In about 1205, its fortunes were transformed when an East Anglian priest, who had visited Constantinople, gave the monks two small pieces of wood which he claimed to be parts of the True Cross. By 1223 miracles were being talked of; in 1226 Henry III paid the first royal visit to this obscure corner of North-East Norfolk, and the monks began a new campaign of building (parts of which can still be seen). In the fifteenth century one chronicler wrote that nineteen people had had their sight restored, and that no fewer than thirty-nine had been raised from the dead. Sadly, this potent relic disappeared in 1537, after it had been sent to Thomas Cromwell in London. Today, a gatehouse and a few jagged pieces of masonry do little to convey the wonder and hope which must once have suffused this place – when so many people prayed, as did Chaucer's Norfolk-born reeve, 'Helpe, Holy cross of Bromholm'.

Even more famous was Walsingham where the attractions included three curative wells, a finger joint of St Peter, milk of the Virgin Mary and, of course, the Holy House. This last was a wooden building modelled on the house of the Holy Family at Nazareth; it was built in the twelfth century by Richelde de Fervaques after she had received a visitation from the Virgin Mary. It contained the celebrated figure of 'Our Lady' which, according to Erasmus, glittered with silver, gold and jewels. The wooden house lay immediately north of the priory church and, in spite of later claims, well within the precinct wall; in the fifteenth century it was surrounded by a protective stone building, the plan of which was uncovered in Victorian times. Today, virtually all the priory buildings have disappeared, except for part of the church's eastern end and the refectory. The walled precinct, which attracted many thousands of medieval pilgrims, has now become a quiet English garden of grass and trees.

Several pilgrim routes converged on Walsingham, through Lynn and Coxford, for example, or through North Elmham, but the most important came from the south, and was marked on the so-called 'Gough Map' of about 1350. It entered Norfolk opposite the small Suffolk town of Brandon Ferry, and ran up through the Pickenhams, Litcham and Fakenham. It still shows on the modern map as a fairly direct line of minor roads crossing the river Wensum by an ancient ford west of Fakenham, and was probably, partly at least, an adaptation of a Roman road. Just over a mile south of the shrine, at Houghton St Giles, a wayside chapel was provided in the mid-fourteenth century and is still used by modern pilgrims. Although the medieval figure of Our Lady was burnt at

Chelsea in 1538, it is worth remembering that earlier in his reign Henry VIII had walked barefoot from Barsham, in order to place a circlet of gold around Our Lady's neck.

Parish churches

The strong dark silhouettes of church towers dominate the Norfolk landscape (Plate 9). On Anglo-Saxon or Norman sites, the majority of these parish churches are medieval structures modified by centuries of repair and restoration. Close-up, they are often subtle patchworks of black and grey flint, creamy limestone and mortar, relieved by the warmer tones of brick and shot through by shafts of light. They are more inspiring than any other human contribution to the landscape because they express the highest aspirations of local people, and symbolise the lives of whole communities. Around each church, in peace, lie hundreds and thousands of people who once worshipped there and played out the ritual of their lives. Here, better than anywhere else, we realise that the landscape is merely held in trust; we pass it on after a short stewardship, and are accountable to posterity for what we do.

After the Norman Conquest a large number of parish churches of Saxon foundation were rebuilt in the simple, powerful style of the new overlords. Large aisled naves of the Norman period still survive in the prosperous Marshland, but usually the plan was more simple: an aisleless nave and smaller chancel of rectangular or apsidal shape. Hales has one of the most perfect examples in England of a small Norman church (Plate 12). Later rebuilding has destroyed much of the county's Norman architecture, but many fragments survive and are often unrecognised because of the misleading insertion of later windows and doors. At South Pickenham, for example, the thick tapering walls of the nave are almost certainly Norman in spite of fifteenth-century windows; at Hunworth a blocked-up window of Norman date was accidentally discovered in 1960. Norman churches tend to survive best where parishes never had sufficient wealth thereafter to replace them, as in the Breckland which has always been comparatively poor.

The last great period of ecclesiastical rebuilding began in

131

the thirteenth century and reached its peak in the fifteenth. Some examples are nationally famous and have been frequently described, such as the thirteenth-century splendours of West Walton, the deeply moulded elegance of Snettisham and Cley, the vast and beautifully textured interior of Salle (Plate 13). Yet all over the county one can find less famous churches of great fascination and interest: witness the atmospheric interiors of Banningham, Wilby and Scottow, or the external perfection of Shelton and Stody. The whole collection is an astonishingly rich and varied legacy from the medieval world.

The church can be interpreted in human terms better than most components of the medieval landscape. Thus, Sir Hugh Hastings rebuilt the church at Elsing about 1330, with one of the widest naves known. He was buried under a magnificent brass in the middle of the chancel. In 1978 his skeleton was recorded in an iron-bound wooden coffin, set in a brick cist and beneath a marble slab bearing the brass; he was wearing a hat or wig of cow-hair. At Bixley, a foundation stone of 1272 commemorates the rebuilding of the church by William of Dunwich, while at Trowse an inscription of 1271–88 marks the provision of a fine east window by a prior called William of Kirkly. But large numbers of humbler people were also involved in the building and furnishing of medieval churches. For example, the Black Book of Swaffham lists the names of 123 benefactors and gives the names of fifty-two people who had promised sums of money, ranging from twopence to six shillings and eight pence, for the repair of the tower.

Other fascinating links between churches and their medieval benefactors are provided by wills, because it was then normal to leave bequests for repairs, new building or furnishings. For instance, John Hacon in 1437 gave forty pounds, to 'the makyng of a newe churche' at Wiveton; Geoffrey Boleyn, ancestor of Henry VIII's queen, left twenty pounds in 1463 to 'the werk of the bodie of the churche' at Blickling; and William Smyth in 1469 gave ten shillings for battlements on the tower of Burlingham St Andrew. Simon Cotton's work on wills has revealed a widespread building of towers in the fifteenth century, with a climax in the 1480s. All over Norfolk, the clink of metal tools on flint must have been heard as towers slowly rose, year by year, and permanently altered the skyline of the county. The work could go on for forty to fifty years, as can be proved by wills for Bradfield and Wood Dalling. By the 1540s, when Protestant ideas were taking root, the great period of church building was over. A few towers, as at Felmingham and Toftrees, were never finished.

In the main, the contribution of individual craftsmen is hard to identify. A few names are known, like John Auntell who was working on the chancel of Worstead in the 1480s and had previously been connected with King's College chapel, Cambridge. Very occasionally building contracts have survived, for example for the rebuilding of Trowse church in 1283 and for making the roof at Norton Subcourse in 1319 –20. Nevertheless, the hand of individuals is often discernible, even if we cannot attribute names to them. A good example is provided by masons' marks at New Buckenham and Weasenham St Peter. Recently Richard Fawcett has made a major contribution to the techniques of architectural history by showing that the same decorative features can be found in more than one church, and therefore reveal the work of 'schools' of masons, or even of individuals. Thus, he has demonstrated that Hockwold, Larling and Croxton have the same simple tracery of the early fourteenth century; that a particular kind of elongated quatrefoil was used in the Attleborough area after 1320, and has links with Norwich Cathedral; that the towers of Blofield, Brisley, Fakenham, Foulsham, Heydon, Ingham and Southrepps were all the work of one man in the mid-fifteenth century; and that a mason who designed Wiveton St Mary worked elsewhere in Norfolk and north Suffolk in the second quarter of the fifteenth century, and must have used the same templates repeatedly.

After the Reformation, Norfolk churches suffered greatly from the deliberate destruction of 'Popish relics' (a campaign which Augustus Jessopp called 'The Great Pillage'), and also from neglect, changing taste and over-enthusiastic restoration. Therefore, very little survives of their rich and colourful medieval fittings and furnishings. This makes rare survivals particularly precious – like the screens at Ranworth, the Easter Sepulchre at Northwold, the roodloft at Sheringham,

the Dance of Death at Sparham, and the painted rood at
Ludham. We also have to rely heavily on surviving documents. For example no Norfolk church should be visited
without consulting its list of church goods in 1368. In this way
we re-imagine the medieval church as the setting for rituals
and a liturgy which were constantly evolving. As chancels
grew longer, so they were increasingly provided with sedilia,
piscinae, sepulchres, tabernacles and lights; new fashions
become detectable such as the provision of processional
doorways at the west end, or the installation of ever more
elaborate screens, known locally as 'perks'. Nor should we
forget the relics which were so much revered, such as the
alleged head of St John the Baptist at Trimingham, or the
Good Sword of Winfarthing which was regarded as especially
useful for recovering stolen goods and for shortening the life
of a married man.

SELECT BIBLIOGRAPHY

Cathcart King, D. J., *Castellarium Anglicanum*, II (1983).
Coad, J. G. and Streeter, A. D. F., 'Excavations at Castle Acre
   castle, 1972–77 . . .', *Archaeological Journal*, 139 (1982), 138
   –301.
Cotton, Simon, 'Building the late medieval church', *NARG News*,
   16 (1979), 10–16.
Cotton, Simon and Fawcett, Richard, 'Further aspects of medieval
   churchbuilding', *NARG News*, 28 (1982), 5–14.
Fawcett, Richard, *The Architecture and Furnishings of Norfolk
   Churches* (1974).
Knowles, D. and Hadcock, R. N., *Medieval religious houses,
   England & Wales* (1971).
Pevsner, Nikolaus, *Buildings of England, Norfolk*, 2 vols (1962).
Spelman, H., *History of Sacrilege* (finished 1632, published 1846),
   Chapter VI (a Norfolk man's view of the Dissolution of local
   religious houses).
Watkin, A., 'Inventory of Church Goods, *temp*. Edward III',
   Norfolk Record Society, XIX, Parts I and II, 1947–48.

11. Fewer people, more space

THE BLACK DEATH of 1349 ushered in a period when the population fell dramatically and when important changes overtook farming and rural life. Norfolk did not immediately lose its position as one of the wealthiest counties of England because all regions were affected, to some extent or other, by the events of the fourteenth century. In fact it stayed high in the league until about 1500 when the centre of economic power began to shift southwards to a broad belt of counties from Kent to Somerset. Even then, agricultural and industrial enterprise remained a feature of Norfolk life until at least the eighteenth century.

Today the most eloquent reminder of these demographic changes is the remarkably high number of medieval settlements which shrank or were abandoned. The decline of population in almost all parts of the county is as obvious as its earlier density. Faden's well known map of 1797, although it coincided with a new spate of rural building, shows the effect particularly well: empty-looking parishes, many small villages, others which were gappy and looseknit, yet others which had virtually shrunk to the status of single farms, and many isolated churches. It portrays the remnants of a once densely populated landscape which had reached its peak around 1300, and had then been thinned by centuries of economic change and declining population. Indeed, the effect is still obvious on the modern map, and some parishes have continued to shrink until the present day (Fig. 11). Of course, the experience was not new. Settlements had been regularly abandoned or moved since prehistoric times, and the local population had fallen drastically at earlier periods, perhaps above all in the Dark Ages. From the later fourteenth century, however, the consequences of depopulation are more obvious above ground, and affect the pattern of settlement which is still in use today.

Villages which were totally deserted, or almost totally except for one or two buildings, are a major feature of the

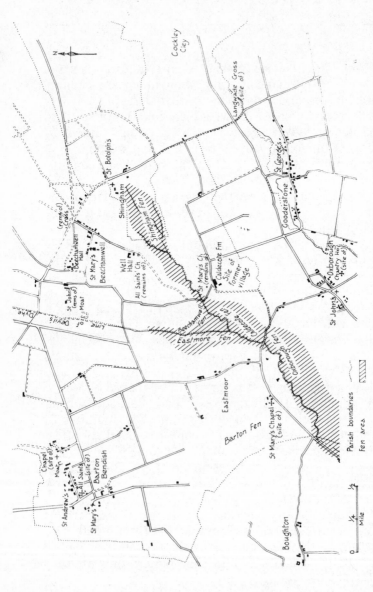

Fig. 11. The advance and retreat of rural populations: a sandy but well-watered area of west Norfolk which proclaims an eventful history. Notice the high density of villages, the remarkable number of medieval churches and the effects of shrinkage and desertion after 1350 (ruinous churches, abandoned sites and streets with gaps).

Norfolk scene and have attracted comment for generations. In 1637 Archbishop Laud wrote a lament on the ruinous churches of Norfolk. He commented that frequently nothing was left standing except a manor house and parish church, 'and that turned to the lord's barn, or worse use'. Dr Price in the late eighteenth century mistakenly used Norfolk to argue that the population of England was *then* declining, but correctly interpreted the signs of earlier decline such as isolated churches and tracks which seem to lead nowhere. In 1940 John Saltmarsh was the first historian to document the 'economic decline' of the later Middle Ages. He was particularly moved by the Breckland 'where I have visited five ruined churches in a single afternoon' (Plate 17). The first systematic survey of Norfolk's deserted medieval villages (DMVs as they are often called) was produced in 1957 by Keith Allison. He listed 130 sites, mainly on the lighter soils of the Breckland, Good Sands, and Western Escarpment. From a variety of documents, he showed that some villages had been deserted before 1349, but that the majority disappeared between the fifteenth and eighteenth centuries, and that generally their decline was long and slow. In recent years, Peter Wade-Martins has investigated the subject archaeologically: in the hundred of Launditch, he found that forty per cent of the medieval villages were subsequently deserted, especially on heavy, ill-drained plateaux where it had always been more difficult to build up populations than in the valleys. If this proportion applies to the county as a whole, then the true total of DMVs will be much higher than Allison originally suggested.

On the modern map, deserted villages show as a combination of features. The Anglo-Saxon or Danish name of a parish may be written across a rather empty-looking piece of countryside, as at Babingley near King's Lynn, Illington near Thetford or Sisland near Loddon. A more powerful clue, as Dr Price realised, is the existence of a ruined church. A new survey by Neil Batcock reveals that Norfolk has 261 disused or ruined churches, which represents more than a quarter of the medieval total. They can be found in various stages of physical decay: for example Mintlyn still has the recognisable shell of its church on a bare hilltop, Rockland St Andrew has

137

the dramatically cleft ruin of a western tower, Bickerston has a small mound of rubble, Pattesley has fragments of a church built into a later farmhouse, and Shouldham St Margaret has no more than a discoloured patch of soil. Like the last, no fewer than 138 Norfolk churches have utterly vanished, and can only be studied therefore as archaeological sites. At Barton Bendish, Andrew Rogerson recently excavated the site of All Saints church, whose ruins were finally demolished in 1788, and recovered the plan of a simple Norman church with apsidal chancel.

Most abandoned villages have a single farm surviving on them, usually a 'hall' or manor house close to the church, as can be seen at Appleton or Threxton. If the house became the centre of a gentleman's estate in the seventeenth or eighteenth centuries, then it, the church and remains of the village may be embedded in a landscaped park, as at Raveningham and Gunton. A parsonage may also have been allowed to survive, and one or two cottages. Finally, a convergence of footpaths, roads or drives across a park may represent the skeleton of a former village as at Ashwicken or Ketteringham. All this means that so-called 'desertion' is hardly ever total. Indeed, in the eighteenth and nineteenth centuries, the place may actually have grown again, as new cottages were built for a population which was once more rising.

Compared with the 'grassy' shires of England, Norfolk is not well endowed with earthworks because they have been eroded by centuries of ploughing. Nevertheless, where permanent grassland does survive, for example in closes around farmhouses or in parks, the mounds and hollows of former villages can still be seen. Good examples survive at Egmere, Pudding Norton and Roudham, and new sites are still being found. In detail, the best preserved features are usually the long hollows of former streets, ponds and the banks, scarps or ditches which once bounded individual properties (Plate 18). Generally the sites of houses and farm buildings are not easily recognisable, probably because they were made of perishable materials like clay and timber, or were systematically dismantled. But occasionally, as at Babingley or beside Hales Hall, one can still see the low outlines of the 'voyd' tenements which were frequently mentioned in manorial surveys from the fifteenth century onwards. Regrettably, some earthworks are being destroyed before they can be protected. For instance, two well preserved sites at Caldecote and Letton were obliterated in the 1970s by bulldozing and ploughing.

Where DMVs have been ploughed (Plate 19), systematic fieldwalking can recover important evidence from the topsoil, mainly in the form of datable pottery. For example, Alan Davison and colleagues found 300 sherds in one season's work at Rougham, while at Middle Harling, around the site of a demolished church, they found pottery ranging from mid-Saxon to late seventeenth century. A recent report on several of Norfolk's DMVs has shown the value of combining such fieldwork with documentary research, to give an outline history of each community's rise and fall.

For every place which was substantially deserted, at least two others merely shrank. All over Norfolk it can be seen that existing villages had larger populations in the early Middle Ages. For example, Weasenham St Peter, Stratton St Michael and Beechamwell all have earthworks outside their present built-up areas. The effect of this contraction has sometimes been to leave the church rather isolated, or at least to one side of the village. Elsewhere, gaps have appeared in village streets themselves, making the place more looseknit than it was. Good examples can be found at Sporle, Hindringham and North Tuddenham. Similar effects can be seen in hamlets. For instance, scatters of medieval pottery mark the site of an abandoned hamlet called Cotes, which was built around a common in the parish of Sporle, while at Hall Green in Longham and Ramsgate Street in Edgefield surviving clusters of buildings show evidence of having been thinned out.

In the south and east of Norfolk where settlement was more widely dispersed, the effects of depopulation are less easy to measure. Villages and major nucleations, where they existed, certainly contracted and were sometimes abandoned, but we also have evidence of deserted farms and small clusters of buildings scattered widely over the landscape. For example, dozens of medieval sites are now being found around the edges of the large Hales Green, where only a few inhabited buildings now exist. 'Voyd' sites are frequently mentioned in manorial surveys, while court rolls give numerous examples of tenants neglecting or abandoning houses and farm buildings. Indeed the customs of some manors positively encouraged the trend, as at Bressingham and Fersfield, where tenants had the 'liberty to pull down' unwanted buildings. The total effect of this thinning could be quite dramatic. At Forncett, for example, out of a total of 135 bond tenements which existed before 1350, seventy-eight had been deserted by 1565 and the total population had probably been halved (Fig. 12). By contrast the number of freehold tenements was only slightly reduced. The abandoned sites opened up gaps in the main village street which straggled between two churches, and punched holes in some, but not all, of the outlying hamlets. For example, at Twanton Green a small hamlet of nine fourteenth-century tenements was reduced to five. Finally, a handful of isolated farmsteads disappeared in Forncett. Related to this decline are the hundreds of empty moats to be found on the heavier land of Norfolk, though in some cases the inhabitants were probably shifting to less restricted sites nearby.

Norfolk was without doubt gravely affected by the Black Death of 1349. For example, court rolls at Snetterton and Tibenham give poignant lists of dead tenants, and the diocesan authorities recorded heavy mortality among the clergy. Nevertheless a large number of local deaths did not necessarily lead to the immediate shrinkage of a built-up area. The only village which may have died in 1349–50 was Little Ringstead. In the majority of cases, heirs came forward and took up empty tenements; if not sons, then daughters, nephews or cousins. It was the continuing erosion of population in the later fourteenth and fifteenth centuries which led to shrinkage. For this we can suggest several reasons. Plague tended to recur at fairly frequent intervals, as a study of local wills has recently proved. Meanwhile the fertility of local communities was declining: for example at Northwold from 1414–59, forty-three per cent of tenants died childless and forty-seven per cent left no sons. In addition, some people were leaving the manors of their birth, usually to seek employment in local towns: thus in the later fourteenth century

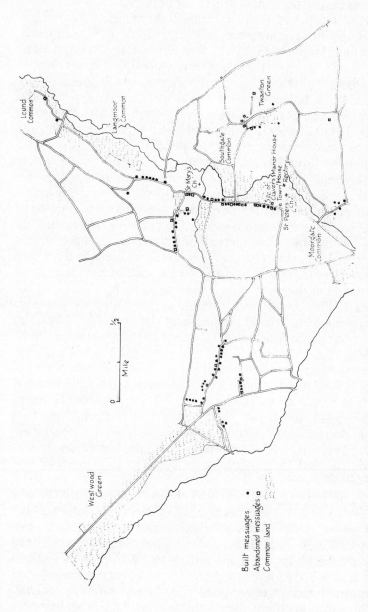

Built messuages •
Abandoned messuages ▫
Common land

Fig. 12. Forncett: showing houses still occupied in 1565, and sites already abandoned (after F. G. Davenport).

Blickling lost six men of villein status in this way.

Another major factor leading to shrinkage and depopulation was the farming policy of landlords. As in the Midlands, the increasing profitability of sheep-farming induced some landlords to convert as much land as possible to grass, including former arable fields and the sites on which houses stood. In 1517, a commission of enquiry revealed that 'Thomas Thurysby, senior, who lately died, destroyed a whole hamlet called Holt hamlet [near Bawsey], with all its tenements, and turned land which had been ploughed into sheep pasture . . .' But in an area like western and northern Norfolk, where sheep and corn had been essentially complementary for centuries, other options existed. Instead of converting arable into sheep pasture, landlords were more likely to enclose or empark commons and wastes, to increase and overload their own foldcourses while restricting the grazing and common rights of tenants. This enabled them to augment their own flocks, reduce their tenants' flocks, and at the same time maintain arable fields which were essential for the survival of sheep. The threat was different but, if ruthlessly pursued, could also lead to shrinkage and depopulation. Thus, at Sturston in the Breckland, Edward Jermyn absorbed as much arable land as he could, including the parson's glebe, ploughed up former boundaries, seized a foldcourse belonging to the rectory, converted the commons to his own use and finally pulled down houses in the village. Thomas Thursby, mentioned above, was also accused of enclosing areas of common land, and of having dwellings pulled down and their occupants ejected, at Ashwicken, Leziate, Bawsey and Mintlyn. The last three of those villages are now more or less deserted.

A declining population and shrinking settlement did not leave the countryside derelict. On the contrary, the relative plenty of land gave new economic opportunities to those who remained. In the fifteenth and sixteenth centuries trends were established which led ultimately to the highly productive agriculture of today. For example, farmland increasingly fell into the hands of fewer people, whether owners or tenants. Bruce Campbell has shown that by 1497 Martham had only seventy-seven holders of land compared with 376 in 1292.

Moreover, forty-three per cent of the land was held by only eleven men and, at the other end of the scale, only six holdings were less than one acre in size, compared with 153 in 1292. These trends were accelerated by poor harvests, periods when agricultural prices were low, and the raising of rents and entry fines.

As the size of holdings tended to grow, so did the size of individual fields and parcels of land. For example at Rushworth in 1441–2, open fields amounting to 856 acres contained only 556 separate pieces, some as large as nine acres. At Congham a croft of nineteen acres was created by Thomas Lawes in the later fifteenth century: it took in parts of four different furlongs of the Westfield. At Martham in the fifteenth century, the general impression was that 'subdivision was nowhere near as acute as in 1300'. Campbell calculates that by the sixteenth century, a third of the arable of east Norfolk was in blocks of five acres or more. Inevitably this kind of consolidation also gave the opportunity to enclose, that is to say, to put a ditch and hedge around a viable piece of land, so that it could be farmed with less dependence on communal decisions.

Large acreages of open field continued to be farmed for centuries on the lighter soils, particularly on the Good Sands and Breckland, and in places where the population was particularly dense (like Marshland), but elsewhere, on medium and heavy soils, lords and tenants were increasingly tempted to enclose in a piecemeal, cumulative fashion. Thus, maps of the 1580s for Cawston and Lessingham show enclosure nibbling into the edges of open fields, particularly behind houses, while other Elizabethan maps for Longham and Tittleshall reveal that enclosure was well advanced in central Norfolk. Typically, the accounts of Caister Castle in 1433–4 refer to the making of new ditches and the planting of hawthorn and other shrubs, in an area where twenty-five per cent of the arable was enclosed in most townships by 1600.

But early enclosure is most evident in South Norfolk. At Bressingham and Shelfanger, court rolls of 1416–54 reveal that live and dead hedges were being planted, ditches dug, commons encroached upon, footpaths obstructed, roads narrowed, and thorns stolen to make dead hedges. Thus, in 1416

Thomas Drew was accused of narrowing 'Chyrche Way' at Shelfanger with newly created hedges and ditches. In 1454 John Lancaster Esq. made an encroachment of six perches on 'Thweytgrene' in Bressingham by putting up a new hedge. In both cases the individual was fined and ordered to remove the obstruction – which he almost certainly did not! By the end of the fifteenth century, such cases were even more common as lords levied fines, not to stop enclosure but to get some return from it. By 1565, it was calculated that between a third and a half of the fields of Forncett were in closes of three to fifteen acres; the process doubtless continued.

Although a proportion of South Norfolk had probably been enclosed for many centuries, and never broken down into strips and furlongs, the existence of numerous open fields, of a small and irregular kind, is not in doubt. Gradually from the fifteenth century onwards they, with commons and road verges, were transformed into a tightly enclosed bosky landscape which gave the traveller the impression of being 'on the verge of a forest which is never reached'. These changes are also confirmed by botanical evidence. A rise in the proportion of oak pollen in Old Buckenham Mere reflects not only the less frequent felling of large trees for timber but also the increase of oaks in new hedgerows. Similarly, it has been suggested that most hedges in Tasburgh are between 400 and 800 years old, because they contain an average of four to eight species in every length of thirty yards. The average count falls to four species or less in the south and west of the parish, where large commons were not enclosed until *c*. 1818. A total of thirty-four different species was recorded in the survey; some were particularly associated with older hedges, such as hazel, maple, spindle and dogwood.

This strong trend towards enclosure in South Norfolk is connected with changes in land use. The new hedged and ditched enclosures were increasingly likely to contain grass for the fattening of cattle and dairying. By the sixteenth and seventeenth centuries, this area was referred to as the 'woodland and pasture' part of Norfolk, 'sustayned cheefely by graseinge, by Dayries and rearinge of Cattell, yett it is able both to maintayne itself with Corne and to afforde an overplus to their neighboures of Suffolk'. In other words, local farming was deliberately mixed, and arable cultivation still remained an important component. But the new specialist emphasis was on enclosed grassland, punctuated by carefully managed patches of woodland.

It is important to stress that farmers usually enclosed land on a small scale, and piece by piece. Therefore, enclosure could be happening in any particular area for centuries. In east Norfolk, for example, although the process had undoubtedly begun by the fifteenth century, some men were still enclosing land 200 years later, and several open fields lasted until the eighteenth century. Furthermore, local obstacles could delay the process, for example the intermixture of small manors with different policies or, more important, rights of grazing that belonged to someone other than the owner or tenant. The most common form was 'half-year land', of which a fascinating example survived until recently on the cliff-edge at West Runton. On such land, the owner or tenant had to admit another person's animals after harvest, for up to six months. Where the grazing of sheep was not particularly important, as in east Norfolk, then these rights could be easily circumvented. At Burgh-by-Aylsham in 1589 the lord renounced his right of foldage over the open fields in return for the extinction of common rights over fifty acres of heath – which he then enclosed. At Horstead-cum-Stanninghall, an enclosure agreement of 1599 deliberately extinguished rights of pasturage or 'shackage'. A similar decision was taken at Kenninghall on the Breckland in 1610, when the lord's right of sheepfold was bought out and the land made 'whole-year'.

But other complications could occur: a farmer might choose to enclose a piece of land while another person still retained grazing rights over it. Thus, an Elizabethan map of Cawston marks some enclosures as subject to 'Autumn shack' and 'Lammas shack', which meant that they still had to be opened up to other people's animals in August and September.

The well known commission of enquiry held in 1517 certainly overlooked the extent of early, piecemeal enclosure in the south and east of Norfolk, but it did list a total of 10,454 acres enclosed, mainly in the western half of the county. Such land was not so much open field as commons and pastures which were increasingly brought under total personal control by landlords or their lessees. One result of this kind of 'improvement' was that landlords were able to increase the size of their sheep flocks. Improbable as it may seem, Sir Henry Fermor of East Barsham is said to have had, in 1521, as many as 15,500 sheep in twenty flocks. Inevitably, these developments led to a clash of interests between lords and tenants. Persistent complaints about the overstocking and enclosure of commons contributed in 1549 to Kett's Rebellion, which broke out in central Norfolk and, in certain parishes like Morley and Hethersett, resulted in the destruction of new hedges and ditches.

Norfolk had been famous since at least the twelfth century for its litigiousness. Even ploughmen were said to be interested in legal precedents, and in 1455 the county was criticised in parliament for having too many attorneys and legal suits 'more on account of evil will and malice, than of truth of the thing'. Divisions must have been even sharper in the sixteenth century: in 1537 a ringleader at Fincham thought that his landlord deserved 'a cartway betwixt his head and his shoulders', and at the end of the century certain poor inhabitants of Norfolk went to the extreme of declaring that 'wee were better to seke our lyvyng in Skotland'.

SELECT BIBLIOGRAPHY

Allison, K. J., 'The lost villages of Norfolk', *Norfolk Archaeology*, XXXI (1957), 116–62.
Allison, K. J., 'The Sheep-corn Husbandry of Norfolk in the sixteenth and seventeenth centuries', *Agricultural History Review*, 5 (1957), 12–30.
Davenport, F. G., *The Economic Development of a Norfolk Manor, 1086–1565* (1906).
'Deserted Medieval Villages', *East Anglian Archaeology*, Report No. 14 (1982), 40–101.
Leadam, I. S., 'The Inquisition of 1517, Inclosures and Evictions', *Transactions of the Royal Historical Society*, New Series VI (1892), 167–314 and VII (1893), 127–292.
Saltmarsh, J., 'Plague and Economic Decline in England in the Later Middle Ages', *Cambridge Historical Journal*, 7 (1941), 23–41.

12. Towns, markets and fairs

New towns.   Markets galore.   Losses and survivals.
Fairs.   The large towns.   New resorts.

GREAT AGRICULTURAL COUNTIES like Norfolk have many
attractive towns which seem to have grown naturally out of
their rural background. It would be hard to think of a more
dominating and distinctive regional capital than Norwich, or
more fascinating ports than Lynn, Yarmouth and Wells, or
more bustling and characterful market towns than Holt, Diss
and Swaffham. The secret is a deep and complicated interdependence, economically and socially, between town and
country – a relationship symbolised above all by the anima-
tion of market day – and an interdependence between a
region, other parts of England and the outside world.

Reference has already been made to the re-emergence of
major and minor towns in later Anglo-Saxon times. After the
initial shock of their conquest, the Normans provided a
stability and organisation which were ideal for the further
development of trade, industry and urban life. They stimulated the growth of existing towns like Norwich and Yarmouth, and created several important new towns, most of
which show signs of deliberate planning.

New towns

New Buckenham was planted in the 1140s and '50s by William
d'Albini, over a mile to the south-east of his existing castle
and village of Old Buckenham. On a virgin site which was
partially carved out of the adjoining parishes of Banham and
Carleton Rode, and beside a main road from Thetford and
Bury St Edmunds to Norwich, he built a new castle (the
earliest known round keep in England) and beside it laid out a
tight grid of streets about 200 yards square. The town con-

tained a large rectangular market place and was surrounded by a defensive bank and ditch. The main road was cleverly diverted by means of four right-angled bends to bring it through the market, but its original course is still visible as a curving hedge-line south of the town. Beside his castle, d'Albini built a small chapel which survives today as a stone and flint barn. Later, in the thirteenth century, a proper parish church was built for the townsmen, towards the northern edge of the original grid. Its parish is noticeably small, and excludes the nearby castle which still lies in the parent parish of Old Buckenham. Today New Buckenham ranks as no more than a village, but it is in reality one of England's best examples of a fossilised Norman town.

Castle Acre (Plate 22) is an even greater monument to Norman ambition, and in particular to the Warenne family, earls of Surrey. This tiny town has the aspect of a French 'bastide', especially from the south; it sits on a bluff above the river Nar and is wedged between a Cluniac priory and a huge castle, both of which were founded by the Warennes in the later eleventh century. The town itself was set within a ditched and walled enclosure about 200 yards square, sometimes interpreted as a second bailey to the castle. At the north end of the main street, which is a diversion of the Peddars Way, stands a thirteenth-century gate with circular towers. Pales Green, which used to exist inside the town, seems to have been the original market of *c.* 1100, though it may have been replaced at an early date by a broad street which now forms the main focus of the village, outside the gate. The parish church also lies outside the walled town, between it and the priory; it probably replaced an earlier chapel in the main street.

Castle Rising also shows traces of a planned layout of streets, was probably defended, had an open space for a market, and has the special distinction of a superb late-Norman church. However, its relationship to the adjacent castle is problematic. The grid of streets was parallel with the original east-west nucleus of the castle dating from the eleventh century; however a large extension of the mid-twelfth century (built, again, by William d'Albini) appears to encroach on the town and to divert some of its streets. The discovery of Anglo-Saxon pottery south of the castle suggests that an earlier settlement lay there and probably extends under the castle itself. Economically, Castle Rising developed also as a port. A street called Havengate Lane is said to have been a medieval wharf for ships which sailed up the sinuous Babingley river from the Wash.

The most important of Norfolk's 'new towns' in the Norman period was undoubtedly King's Lynn (Fig. 13) or, as it was first known, Bishop's Lynn. The site, beside the river Ouse (or Nar), consisted of marshes, muddy creeks and salt pans in a corner of the bishop's manor of Gaywood and just north of an existing village now called South Lynn. The nucleus of the town lay between two tributaries of the river called Purfleet and Millfleet. A little upstream was a large inland lagoon (hence Lynn, based on a Celtic word -*lindo* meaning a lake or pool).

The foundation of Lynn used to be attributed unreservedly to Herbert Losinga, first bishop of Norwich, at the end of the eleventh century, but recently Dorothy Owen has argued persuasively that its origins must precede the Norman Conquest. She points out that salt-making was a major industry around the Wash in late-Saxon times, for Domesday Book recorded 180 active salterns close to Lynn, and that it left behind large mounds of waste sand, up to twenty feet high, which would give dry sites to early settlers. Other writers have argued that the marshes were criss-crossed also by *natural* banks of estuarine silt which offered the same advantages. Certainly, enough people were living between the Purfleet and Millfleet by the 1090s for Losinga to be building a new church, St Margaret's, which combined the functions of parish church and small Benedictine priory. Rebuilt in the twelfth and thirteenth centuries, it sits on an irregular sandy hillock which is probably an abandoned saltern.

Again, the Saturday market and annual fair, which Losinga gave to the monks of Norwich soon after 1100, almost certainly existed before that date. For decades, the area had probably attracted traders in search of salt and wool (large flocks of sheep were recorded in Domesday Book on the coastal marshes). On a sheltered foreshore, Lynn's 'sand market' was held, as the term seems to imply, between the levels of high

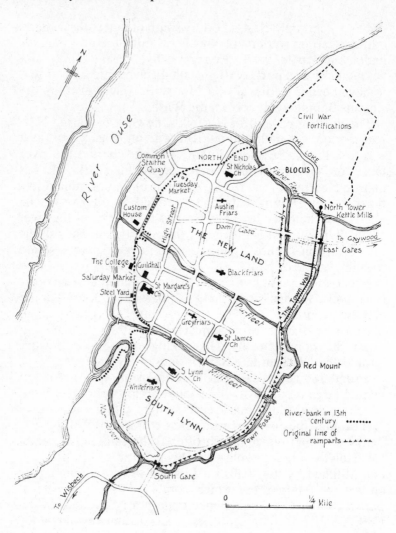

Fig. 13. Bishop's Lynn, later King's Lynn: a market-town and port which developed beside the estuary of the Great Ouse.

Plate 20 Barton Broad: a man-made industrial monument of the Middle Ages. Broads were originally dry pits from which peat was extracted, but later flooded. Islands and promontories still betray linear balks between individual workings.

Plate 21 Silfield: a medieval hunting-park of 750 acres, fossilised. Later hedges abut, but never cross, the park-pale. Lower Park Farm (centre) is the moated site of a hunting-lodge. Beyond is the industrial hamlet of Spooner Row.

Plate 22 Castle Acre: feudal power and foreign conquest. Soon after 1066, the Warennes, Earls of Surrey, created a walled town wedged between their vast new castle (right) and their Cluniac priory (off picture, left) – thus diverting the Roman Peddars Way.

Plate 23 Harleston: a triangular market-place of the Middle Ages; both of the long sides are visible (left and right). The central block of buildings represents later encroachment which gradually filled the open space.

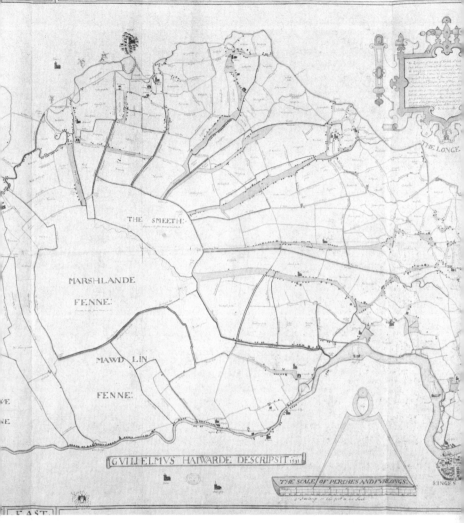

Plate 24 Marshland: William Hayward's map (1591) shows the radial pattern of parishes focussing on the Smeeth and Fen. Notice the great drove-roads and sea-bank against the Nene estuary and Wash.

Plate 25 Denver: flood and tide controlled. Great Ouse (top right to bottom left) with Denver Sluice; two man-made Bedford Rivers (right); Well Creek, a navigable stream (bottom-right); the modern Cut-off Channel (top) and Relief Channel (middle-left).

Plate 26 Cromer: the small fishing port which, from 1785, became a genteel resort. The pier and lighthouse were both great attractions. The tallest church-tower in Norfolk (160 ft) bears witness to earlier, medieval prosperity. Drawing of J.S. Cotman, engraved 1818.

and low water – perhaps, as Alan Carter has suggested, in order to escape royal dues. It may have begun as one of several trading points, but later emerged as the principal local market under the bishop's special protection. Lying beside St Margaret's church, it is today called the Saturday Market Place. Its triangular shape was probably dictated by another creek entering the river at this point, but it now lies one hundred yards inland because the river has since receded.

The town continued to grow organically. A new chapel dedicated to St James appeared on the eastern, inland, side by 1146, but the main developments were northwards along the bank of the river. In about 1150 the third bishop of Norwich, William de Turbe, granted a newly built chapel of St Nicholas to the monks of Norwich. This lay well north of St Margaret's, between the Purfleet and Fisherfleet, in an area known as 'Newland'. The grant has often been interpreted as the origin of Newland, but Mrs Owen points out that the area must have been already settled by 1150 to warrant a separate church, and that its origins probably go back to nearer 1100.

The Newland had its own market in the Tuesday Market Place, its own common staithe and its own place of worship. Because of its later foundation, however, St Nicholas' chapel remained subordinate to St Margaret's until modern times. The main axis of the Newland was a causeway which had probably existed for centuries, as an approach to a ford and ferry across the Ouse. Around this causeway and the Tuesday market, a new pattern of streets emerged, tied to the original nucleus by Damgate and again related to man-made salterns or natural banks of silt. Therefore the plan, as with Losinga's town, is a distorted grid – the land was divided rapidly and logically, but some lines were determined by pre-existing features. A written survey of *c.* 1279 describes the Newland, and shows it to be fully developed with a dense pattern of houses, shops, warehouses, mills and staithes. This area remained the property of the bishop of Norwich until 1536, when Henry VIII received the whole of Lynn in return for the revenues of St Benet's and Hickling. At this point, Bishop's Lynn became King's Lynn.

One interesting feature of the early town plan is that the bank of the river gradually shifted westwards, away from the town. This led to the reclamation of a long strip of ground, up to a hundred yards wide, upon which new streets, alleys and quays were built. The original eleventh-century river bank is marked by a series of curving streets: from the west end of St Nicholas' chapel in the north, past the edge of the Tuesday market, and down the line of King Street, Queen Street and Nelson Street. Late-twelfth-century houses recently discovered were built along a road, or series of quays, lining the river bank. Gradually, as the river receded, new buildings appeared on the far side of the road, at first warehouses belonging to houses opposite but by the fourteenth century merchant establishments, like Hampton Court, consisting of house, warehouses and private quay. For the shift of the river, several possible reasons can be suggested: the river itself was probably depositing silt on its edges, added to which the townsfolk were constantly tipping rubbish and building new wharves like the one found by excavation under Thoresby College.

Markets galore

Maurice Beresford has commented that 'medieval Norfolk was very lightly urbanised'. This was true in the sense that Norfolk has never had many large towns (four in the eleventh century, and three thereafter), and is still true today by national standards. But his judgment does not do justice to the numerous markets and small towns which appeared like a rash on the face of Norfolk, most of them from the mid-twelfth to the mid-fourteenth centuries, and constituted a major 'commercial revolution'. Evidence can be found for at least 138 medieval markets, which gives a higher density than any other English county. At some point in the Middle Ages, one in every five to six parishes had a market, or, to put it another way, a medieval market could be found for every 10,000 acres. The map on pages 154–5 shows their distribution. They were peppered fairly evenly throughout the county, but clustered most thickly in the centre, south and east where the population was densest. However, a few gaps need explanation. For example, no market was established in the Peat Fen which had few inhabitants, and only one in an area of approximately seven miles radius around Norwich, within which competition was actively discouraged.

The precise siting and spacing of markets were determined rather haphazardly by the speculation of manorial lords and by a degree of trial and error, rather than by deliberate planning or legal control. In 1348 the owner of Haveringland was even granted a market 'for good service in the French Wars'. Bracton, the thirteenth-century legal writer, judged that markets should be at least six and two thirds of a mile apart, but in practice they were frequently closer. The important market of East Dereham, for example, had smaller rivals at Shipdham, Gressenhall, Whinburgh and Elsing, all of which were within a radius of five miles. Not surprisingly, three of them do not appear to have been particularly successful but Shipdham, which also belonged to Ely, certainly was. In 1204 the de Vaux family failed to establish a market at Watton because it was deemed prejudicial to one already existing at Saham Toney, the next parish. Within a year, however, they did obtain a charter for a Wednesday market at Watton, and from that time the relative fortunes of the two parishes seem to have changed. Many years later, in 1299, Robert de Toney obtained a charter for a Monday market at Saham, so he was still, at the very least, trying to compete. Now Watton is the local market town and Saham Toney is a village on its sprawling outskirts. As an example of even closer rivalry, West Walton was said by Blomefield to have had two separate markets owned by two separate lords, the prior of Lewes and the bishop of Ely.

Nevertheless, a few landlords carefully weighed the geographical advantages and disadvantages of different places, and as a result sometimes chose virgin sites away from existing settlements (as had happened at New Buckenham). Thus, Harleston grew up in the early thirteenth century as a fair-stead and later market in a corner of Redenhall parish where roads converged on a good crossing of the Waveney. Meanwhile the market of Setchey was established in a corner of the Bardolph manor of North Runcton, where a major road crossed the navigable river Nar. It is significant that both Harleston and Setchey had chapels-of-ease subordinate for centuries to their parent parishes and churches. One of the

Fig. 14. The markets of medieval Norfolk: giving dates of charters where known, or of other documents which mention markets already functioning. A few markets which certainly existed are not marked (eg. which Kirby,

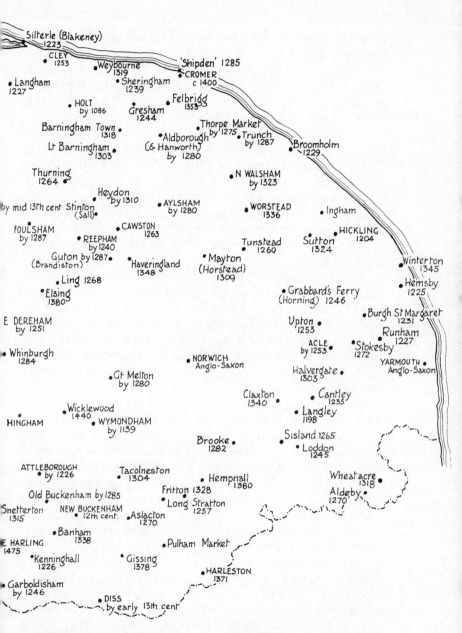

which Billingford?). Capital letters denote markets which survived into 16th century. (Sources include official *Calendars*; MS index in PRO; *PP*, 1888, LIII; Blomefield).

earliest examples of this parent-child relationship is at Wimbotsham, a large manor which belonged to Ramsey abbey. At
its southern end the market of Downham was certainly in
existence by 1050, and may be considerably older. It grew up,
probably with the active encouragement of its monastic landlords, on a sloping hillside which came unusually close to a
river, later called the Great Ouse, and where the latter could
be forded or bridged to connect the fenland and upland. Its
thirteenth-century name of Dunham*hith* shows that it was
also an inland port. Indeed, proximity to navigable rivers,
bridges and ferries was another vital factor which is clearly
related to the layout of local roads. Other good examples can
be seen at Stoke Ferry on the Wissey, and Wheatacre set
within a loop of the Waveney which had two weekly markets
from 1313.

The date when a charter was granted does not necessarily
represent the origin of that market. It may have existed
earlier, unofficially or experimentally, before an owner decided to pay for royal approval. At Heacham, for example,
the prior of Lewes had set up a market, on a piece of common
land in the King's highway, before he obtained a charter in
1272. At Reepham a market had existed for at least twenty-
five years before a charter was granted in 1276–7. On the
other hand, it appears that some markets were never chartered. These include the more important prescriptive ones
which were founded early, such as New Buckenham, East
Dereham, Acle, Downham and Lynn, and occasionally small
ones, such as Aldborough and Thorpe Market, which fortunately happen to be mentioned in other sources. Therefore
the true total of medieval markets is undoubtedly higher than
Fig. 14 records.

It must be emphasised that medieval markets were not all in
existence at the same time. Not only were they founded over
at least 200 years, but some were short-lived and failed to
develop because of competition from their neighbours. In
1258 a local lord tried to set up a market at 'Penesthorpe',
probably in the parish of Helhoughton, but gave up the
attempt because of the proximity of another market at East
Rudham, about two miles off. Other markets were simply in
the wrong places. An early market and fair near St Benet's

abbey were moved in 1246 because they disturbed 'the due tranquillity of religious life'; the new site was at Grabbard's Ferry near Horning. A Tuesday market was granted to Langley abbey in 1198 but the monks eventually gave it up in 1343 because their income was reduced by flooding and 'excessive hospitality'. On occasions, rivalry between markets and traders led to violence. For example, in 1342 several persons tore down stalls at the Thursday market of Walpole, and as a result were temporarily outlawed.

The actual day chosen for trading could lead to success or failure (all seven days of the week were available). Thus in 1339 Oliver le Gros changed his new market at Worstead from Tuesday to Friday because it was 'to the hurt' of the market at Sutton belonging to William de Clynton, Earl of Huntingdon. Similarly Weybourne market was switched from Mondays to Fridays. By contrast, out of a tight group of six markets around Acle, two traded on Mondays and three on Fridays—which seems rather suicidal. No evidence exists for changes of day, so perhaps it is not surprising that only Acle itself took root as a town, and lasted as such until modern times.

In spite of the difficulties, however, it was quite possible for two or more markets to co-exist, though only a few miles apart. In 1253 the sheriff of Norfolk had to enquire whether a new market at Cley was prejudicial to one at Holt, less than four miles away. Although Cley's market was suspended for a time, both continued for centuries, Cley on Fridays and Holt on Tuesdays.

The majority of markets and small towns developed out of existing settlements. The plans of villages are therefore worth careful study when it is known that they once contained markets. For example they may reveal an early nucleus associated with church and manor house, with later expansion around a market place or market street. Shipdham still has a Market Street marking its north-easterly development towards East Dereham. Rather differently, the small triangular market place of Foulsham lies half a mile south of its church and earlier nucleus. Frequently the medieval church, on its Saxon or Norman site, lies on one edge of the settlement and at some distance from the market place. Examples can be seen at Watton, East Harling and Holt. Though one first looks for an open space suitable for a market (or for its outline), it is worth considering other possible effects of economic growth; witness the size and complicated plan of Methwold, the tight clustering of houses at Worstead, or the web of roads converging on Docking.

Nevertheless, the legal existence of a medieval market did not always leave obvious or lasting topographical effects. Villages like Cantley, Garboldisham and Felbrigg show no clear traces of former commercial or industrial importance, though they all had chartered markets and contained greens or wide streets which could have been used for trading. On the A149 between North Walsham and Cromer lies a tiny village which the average motorist will hardly notice, yet it bears the significant name of Thorpe Market. Its market was certainly alive in the thirteenth century, and the outlines of a triangular space can still be traced. The parish of Tunstead near Wroxham would also not be recognisable as a former centre of commerce, were it not for the name Market Street applying to a straggle of housing about a mile from the church. At Mayton near Coltishall only a moated manor house marks the site of a market licensed in 1328 (but it does lie on an early route connecting Norwich and Cromer), while at Grenstein near Litcham cropmarks alone pinpoint the site of a village and thirteenth-century market.

At the other end of the scale, the establishment of a market in the Middle Ages could lead to the development of a distinctly 'urban' community. Places like Downham Market, Burnham Market, Fakenham, Loddon and Aylsham are all recognisable, physically, as towns. They are bigger than surrounding agricultural villages, have a greater tightness of plan, contain actual or vestigial market places, and are the obvious focus of local routes. Some, like North Walsham and Wymondham, also have larger than average parishes for their areas, suggesting that they had been of 'primary' importance for a long time.

Documents sometimes give us glimpses of these early towns in their formative years. For example the market at East Dereham was already mentioned in the Ely Coucher Book of 1251 as a separate part of the bishop of Ely's manor, though no charters are recorded for it. It was worth ten marks a year, and was tenanted by twenty-one individuals who held a total of twenty-two messuages, one building plot, a workshop and a stall. Among the occupations implied in their surnames are a potter and three finishers of cloth (one of whom had a tenter-frame). This small community, which had already attracted immigrants from parishes like Bradenham and Massingham, was clearly commercial in character and was probably living around Dereham's market as we know it today.

Unfortunately, very little archaeological work has been done on these smaller towns and, in any case, the vital layers may have been destroyed by later development. Therefore our ideas about their origins and early growth, and about their relationship to the small agricultural nucleus from which they often sprang, can be no more than intelligent guesswork. Some markets may simply have been held on convenient patches of common land, which slowly changed character as the market took root; certainly one has this feeling about Wymondham, whose market grew up where a main road crossed a common, half a mile from the abbey church; or about the long thin market at Burnham which follows the bottom of a small valley created by the Goose Beck. Occasionally one suspects that positive planning was involved. For example, Watton has a markedly rectilinear setting of open spaces and streets to the west of an original nucleus, and is associated with the clear diversion of a north-south road. Similarly the little town and port of Wells, for which the abbot of Ramsey obtained a charter in 1202, shows a village nucleus and church on higher ground, and beside it, sloping down to the marshes, a neat urban grid and rectangular market place.

One of the most intriguing medieval towns is Reepham (Fig. 15). It has a rare, perhaps unique, feature dating from the early thirteenth century: an oval churchyard of about one acre contains two medieval churches and originally had three. Today the two churches of Whitwell and Reepham lie roughly in line and actually touch, while the church of Hackford lay a few feet to the south but was burnt down in the early sixteenth century. This strange arrangement is accompanied by a complicated pattern of parish boundaries. The churchyard lay at a

Fig. 15. Reepham in 1906: a medieval market-town which grew up at the junction of three rural parishes. A churchyard of one acre still contains two churches, actually touching, and once had three.

point where the three parishes converged, although Whitwell church was actually built on a small detached portion embedded in Hackford. What was the importance of this small plot of land, which led three parishes to site their churches so closely, perhaps even moving two of them? In all probability it had something to do with Reepham's development as a market. In 1276–7 a charter for a Saturday market and annual fair was granted to Sir John de Vaux who owned the manors of both Reepham and Hackford, but an unofficial market had certainly been in existence some years before. In 1240 the bishop of Norwich prohibited the holding of a market in the 'cemetery' of Reepham, and ordered the sheriff of Norfolk to ensure that another site be provided. This was probably when the present market place was established a few yards further west, and entirely within the parish of Hackford. Hence, by accident, the town and market of 'Reepham' grew up largely in the parish of Hackford, because both manors belonged to the same lord. But why were the three churches built so closely together? Until new evidence is found, we can only surmise that each parish and manor, including the royal manor of Whitwell, was eager to profit from the embryonic market which had originally sprung up, unofficially, in a graveyard.

Once designated or purposely laid out, market places did not always retain their original shapes. They often tended to shrink as encroachments were made around their edges, or islands of development were planted inside them. One reason was that temporary market stalls tended to be replaced by permanent shops, houses and market halls. This process had certainly begun in Norfolk by the thirteenth century, as the Hundred Rolls show for Norwich and Yarmouth. The normal result is a dense, irregular network of alleys, buildings and small yards; excellent examples can still be seen at Holt, Litcham and Harleston where the present markets are only small fractions of their original sizes (Plate 23). Internally, market places were subdivided for the sale of different commodities. For example, the court books of Holt refer to a Butchery, Mercery Row, a Yarn Market and a special building for the sale of corn; Fish Hill still survives.

161

Losses and survivals

Only ten new markets were licensed in the Charter Rolls from 1350 to 1475, as compared with about seventy before 1350: some of them merely confirmed or modified existing rights, and the rest came to nothing. More important, the great majority of early markets decayed, and the communities to which they were attached reverted to the status of mere villages. The decline of England's population by a third, or even a half, had led to sharp reductions in the volume of agricultural production, industrial output and trading. Most of the speculative markets established in the boom years of the late twelfth, thirteenth and early fourteenth centuries were now unnecessary. After 1500, only about 35 markets remained in Norfolk out of an original total of about 140 – which represents a reduction of about seventy-five per cent. Places such as Halvergate, Wormegay and Shouldham (once known as Shouldham Market) never again showed signs of weekly commercial activity. At North Elmham, David Yaxley has shown that a market which yielded a fair income in the 1320s, brought in almost nothing by 1401. A survey of 1454 did mention five stalls near the churchyard, but by the early sixteenth century trading had altogether ceased. A document of 1572 gave the *coup de grâce* by referring to 'the market place of Elmham, now called le Bell grene'.

The thirty-five remaining markets were fairly evenly spaced throughout the county, though again the main emphasis was on the centre and east. In this process of thinning out, it was the largest and sometimes the earliest markets which tended to survive. Most of them are still recognisable as towns today, like Aylsham and Fakenham, but not all. For example, Snettisham was still described in the late seventeenth century as having a considerable market; its market place is represented by a triangular open space which still survives near the Old Hall. Although the average distance between markets was now much greater, a few were still remarkably close neighbours like Snettisham and Heacham, Castle Acre and Swaffham, Cley and Holt, and the trio of Aylsham, Cawston and Reepham.

The weeding out of markets continued into the seventeenth and eighteenth centuries, as a result of competition, increasing specialisation and improved communications. By about 1600, Pulham Market was described as 'altogether decayed' because of the competition of nearby Harleston, yet its market crosses still remained as a reminder of former trading. At the same time, the incorporated borough of Castle Rising 'hath almost expired the ghost', though it continued to send two members to parliament until 1832. Further casualties followed in the seventeenth century: the markets of Heacham and Litcham never recovered after fires in the reign of Charles I, while Cley's was discontinued by 1673. Methwold was described in 1672 as 'a poore Market Towne' and faded out in the eighteenth century, while a similar fate befell New Buckenham, Foulsham and Stoke Ferry. By the beginning of the nineteenth century, the number of Norfolk markets was down to about seventeen.

Markets not only became fewer and larger, but also increasingly specialised. The agricultural economy was more diverse than ever before, added to which rural and urban industries had developed strongly since the middle of the sixteenth century. Thus, by the seventeenth century, Diss was famous for the sale of linen, yarn and cloth. East Harling and Harleston shared in the same trade, which dominated the south of the county. Wymondham gained a reputation for the manufacture and sale of small wooden objects produced from locally grown coppice-wood, such as spoons, taps and spindles; the nearby hamlet of Spooner Row was in existence by the fifteenth century and is a lasting reminder of that trade (Plate 21). Downham was noted for the sale of butter, fish and fowl; in the mid-eighteenth century, during spring and summer, about 3,000 firkins of butter were regularly sold to factors, who sent them by water to Cambridge and thence overland to London. Swaffham, being in the centre of a major corn-growing area, specialised for centuries in grain, but in the seventeenth century its craftsmen also had a national reputation for the making of spurs.

Swaffham is, in fact, an excellent example of those few medieval markets which took permanent root. It was developed by the family of de Sabaudia who were lords of the manor, and by the middle of the thirteenth century had two weekly markets. No doubt they were held in the same large triangle of open ground as today, where an ancient track running north-west to south-east was crossed by two other major roads, on the western side of the original village whose outlines can still be discerned. Swaffham survived the economic changes of the later Middle Ages, and prospered enough to rebuild its church on magnificent lines in the late fifteenth and early sixteenth centuries. In the reign of Henry VIII, it was enthusiastically described by John Leland as 'One of the quikkest markettes in al Northfolk . . . It stondeth much by handy crafte [men] and byers of grayne'. To Richard Blome in 1673, Swaffham was 'one of the chiefest Market-towns in the county', well furnished with corn and other provisions; it was large and well built, 'full of Inns and Shopkeepers who drive a good trade'. In 1775, it lost twenty-four houses in one of those bad fires which regularly afflicted towns. A few years later it had fully recovered and a French nobleman, François de la Rochefoucauld, was impressed by the quality and cleanliness of the town; by then it contained an impressive array of amenities – a free school endowed in 1724, assembly room, theatre, billiards room, bowling green, racecourse and a classical market cross appropriately crowned by a figure of Ceres. In the same period many of the older houses were being Georgianised and given fashionable new façades.

Fairs

The grant of a *weekly* market usually contained similar per-mission for an *annual* fair. Such events were another impor-tant part of commercial life, and at least 115 are known to have been established in Norfolk between 1227 and 1475. Normally a fair lasted two or three days, and was centred on a particular feast day, which can often be tied to the dedication of a local parish church. For example, Holme Hale was granted a three-day fair in 1252 around the feast of St Andrew, to whom its church was dedicated. A few fairs were considerably longer in duration: for instance, Swaffham had one of fifteen days, and Lynn one of sixteen. While the great majority of medieval markets had decayed by the sixteenth century, most local fairs survived longer. As late as 1759, Norfolk still had sixty-seven.

Fairs were held on any convenient piece of open ground, and the site was not necessarily the same for centuries: it could be a piece of common land, certain arable fields after harvest, meadows after haysel, or even, as at Creake, a churchyard. Clues to the sites of former fairs can still be found on OS maps or in local field names. For example, at Shouldham the 'fairstead' is a large field on the north-western edge of the village, while at Hempnall it lay at the western end of the parish, near the vanished chapel of St Andrew. At Cley the fair around St Margaret's day once took place west of the hall, but the enclosure award of 1823 allotted a green in front of the church for the purpose. The best examples are probably at Hingham and Wymondham where open spaces called Fairstead still survive distinct from their market places; they may well have had that use continuously since medieval times.

In their early days, these annual events were much more than the entertainments and sales of toys and knick-knacks which many of them became in the eighteenth and nineteenth centuries. For example, Thetford priory bought food and building materials from various East Anglian fairs in the fifteenth century. Similarly materials for the rebuilding of Raynham Hall in the 1620s were obtained from fairs as widely spread as South Acre, Thetford, Gresham and Reedham. In addition, some fairs became noted for particular specialisations. Aylsham fair was known for bedding, Sloley for pottery; St Winwaloe's fair at Wereham (later moved to Downham) was famous for the sale of horses, while Setchey was 'much noted for the beast fair', especially its Scots cattle. Best known of all was St Faith's fair, north of Norwich, which lasted for three weeks in October. In 1727 Daniel Defoe described it as 'after the Falkirk Tryst the largest and best known fair attended by Scottish drovers'.

The large towns

The very different plans of Norwich, Yarmouth and King's Lynn had been largely decided by events in Anglo-Saxon or

Norman times, between the tenth and twelfth centuries. Therefore, most of the booming population of the thirteenth century was accommodated by intensifying the settlement which already existed, rather than by greatly extending built-up areas. For example, at Norwich the banks of the Wensum were colonised more intensively in the later thirteenth century, as the pressure of population was fuelled by a high birth-rate and considerable immigration from rural areas. From local surnames it has been calculated that Norwich, in the thirteenth century, drew in people from at least 400 villages in Norfolk and from a further sixty in Suffolk.

It was in the later thirteenth century that these towns decided to provide themselves with defensive stone walls. This was done partly to meet the threat of French invasion, but also as a means of expressing urban pride and wealth. In all three cases, it took considerable patience and money raising, for the walls with their gates and bastions were not finished until well into the fourteenth century. In fact Norwich had already made earthen ramparts and ditches in the early twelfth century, and a newer ditch with nine gates from *c.* 1250, but it is not clear how large an area was enclosed. However, the stone walls erected between 1297 and 1370 were two and a half miles long and enclosed one square mile (Fig. 16). To avoid awkward salients, they swept in a generous curve around the whole built-up area south of the Wensum, including large areas of open ground, and excluded only the hamlet of Pockthorpe on the north-east. At Yarmouth, the town walls were planned in the 1260s but were not begun until 1285; they fitted like a tight glove around the compact town of about 140 acres, were about 2,200 yards long, and were punctuated by ten gates and fifteen or sixteen towers (Fig. 17). Two re-entrant angles, at the northern and southern ends of the circuit, mark where the boundaries of religious houses were deliberately incorporated.

The medieval defences of Lynn have an even more compli-cated history (Fig. 13), enclosing a large area which, by the seventeenth century, was only half built-up and half in the form of commons, fields, orchards and gardens. This led some historians to assume that, in late medieval times, the town had shrunk dramatically. Research now shows that the defences

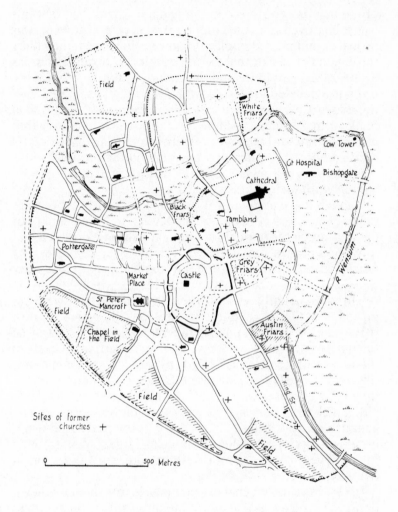

Fig. 16. Medieval Norwich: one of the largest medieval towns in Britain. A wall of 2¼ miles, with 40 towers and 10 gates, enclosed an area of nearly one square mile.

167

follow the line of a natural estuarine bank, once the boundary of the lagoon referred to in the name of Lynn, and that this was taken over as a convenient gift of nature. The bank was probably heightened in places and certainly strengthened by the digging of an external ditch. Four timber towers known as 'bretasks' helped to defend the circuit. Later on, from 1266, Lynn too decided to build a wall. However, it enclosed only the edge of Newland and ran 200 yards *outside* the original bank so that it could include a suburb which had grown up along the line of Damgate. Meanwhile, Losinga's town and South Lynn, the other two components of the thirteenth-century borough, were never walled and had to remain content with their defensive earthworks.

Though they varied in size, most medieval properties were rectangular blocks of land, which tended to be small in poor districts and large in rich. Modern excavation has shown that most boundaries remained very stable over centuries. At Surrey Street in King's Lynn, for example, thirteenth-century tenements were defined by wattle fences which had to be repaired frequently; in the fifteenth century they were re-placed, on the same lines, by stone walls which in turn survived until modern times. One interesting modification to the pattern of properties was caused by the arrival of friars in the thirteenth century. As relatively late religious communities who particularly ministered to the population of towns, they built premises wherever they conveniently could. They either picked up peripheral sites, as at King's Lynn which had so much space within its defences, or they purchased properties in a piecemeal fashion to build up larger blocks suitable for re-development, as four different orders of friars did in Norwich.

In recent years, much more has been learnt about medieval housing in towns, as a result of modern re-development and systematic recording. For example, although medieval survivals are relatively rare in Yarmouth, substantial parts of a medieval row, with contemporary doors and windows, were found in 1973 inside a supposedly 'Georgian' house. At Lynn numbers of medieval houses were identified and studied by Vanessa Parker in the 1960s. A common type consists of a timber-framed range along the street, of which the ground floor was probably used as a shop or workroom. At the back of the house and at right angles to the street, another range included an open hall with crown-post roof.

Although medieval houses were often heavily disguised in later centuries, their wooden roofs frequently survive, forgotten above later ceilings, and show interesting technical developments. At Lynn the earliest examples, dating from the thirteenth century onwards, support rafters by long braces which cross like a pair of scissors; later the value of a single central purlin stiffening the whole roof was realised, preferably supported by a decorative crown-post; finally, by about 1500, roofs were made more open with purlins against the rafters.

In Norwich too, major discoveries have been made since 1971 by the Norwich Survey and Norfolk Archaeological Unit. A new hall of the twelfth century has been identified, and over eighty undercrofts, vaulted in brick and stone, are known to have been constructed from the twelfth to the sixteenth centuries, 'easily the largest total in any English town'. However, the medieval buildings which still survive, like Strangers Hall and the Bridewell, were owned by the merchant class, so Alan Carter and his team have deliberately attempted to redress the balance by rediscovering lesser but more typical houses of the period. This could only be done by excavation, though valuable human detail has also come from parallel work on documents, particularly from the numerous deeds which survive for Norwich. Thus, for example, four clay-walled cottages of similar size were built in Alms Lane between 1350 and 1450. The best preserved had two rooms parallel with the street and separated by a cross-passage; one of the rooms was heated by a hearth sited against a wall. In Oak Street a two-roomed house with chalk floors was built in the fourteenth century, and again one of the rooms had a side-hearth. The owners of this property could be identified from 1300, beginning with one Cecily Thirken. Five others succeeded her in the next thirteen years, which suggests speculative dealing in a period of rising population. In the fifteenth century a landlord rebuilt the block as two, single-storeyed houses-cum-workshops under a single roof. By 1451 they were lived in by two owner occupiers. Within another

169

generation, a wealthy mercer called William Brewster had converted the pair into a single, two-roomed house which he let for rent. By 1570 the property had been bought by a wealthy man called Richard Bange who had re-converted it into two houses and had inserted an upper floor supported by an internal timber frame.

Medieval towns also invested in large public and institutional buildings. The tollhouse at Yarmouth is basically a first-floor hall of the thirteenth century and, though at first it may have been domestic, it is regarded as one of the oldest civic buildings in Britain. Norwich replaced its old tollhouse with a handsome new guildhall in 1407–12, while Lynn at the same time erected St George's Guildhall described as the 'largest surviving ancient guildhall in England'. Meanwhile, large sums of money were being spent on churches. By the end of the thirteenth century, St Nicholas at Yarmouth had grown to be one of the largest parish churches in Britain, with aisles thirty-nine feet wide. A further westward expansion was only abandoned when the Black Death struck in 1349. Towards the end of the Middle Ages, most urban churches were remodelled or replaced, producing masterpieces like St Nicholas at Lynn which was spectacularly rebuilt in early Perpendicular style between 1371 and 1491, or proud St Peter Mancroft in the centre of Norwich which was rebuilt in 1430–55.

In the sixteenth century, important structural changes overtook the major towns, particularly as a result of the Reformation. Norwich, having been over-provided with about sixty churches in the early Middle Ages, deliberately reduced the number. About six churches had already disappeared after the Black Death, but a further seventeen were secularised between 1520 and 1570 and their parishes absorbed by more viable neighbours. In all three towns, the dissolution of religious houses in the 1530s released large buildings and sites for new uses. For example, St Mary in the Fields at Norwich was taken over as a town house by the Hobart family, and in the eighteenth century provided the site for new assembly rooms and a theatre.

Hoskins' concept of a 'great rebuilding' applies as much to major towns as it does to the countryside. At Yarmouth, for example, the success of the new haven and the herring fishery after 1566 led to rapid re-development. Although some large buildings were erected, like the Duke's Head, the characteristic house of the Rows from the 1580s onwards was a relatively small three-storeyed house of brick or flint, with one room on each floor. It often had a passage through to a backyard, a winding staircase lit by small windows against the chimney stack, and cast-iron 'anchors' fixing joists to walls.

In Norwich the process of urban renewal had begun earlier. Cuningham's perspective view of 1558 already showed a city of two-storeyed houses with brick chimneys. Since about 1470, dwellings had been rebuilt or deliberately modernised, and such changes were accelerated by a steadily rising population as the sixteenth century wore on. Not only was the birth rate rising naturally, but many immigrants had arrived, including about 4,000 'strangers' from the Low Countries. In total, the population of the city probably rose from about 10,000 in 1580 to 20,000 in 1620, and to 30,000 in 1700. By the seventeenth century, Norwich was a major industrial and mercantile centre, famous for its New Draperies, and second only to London in economic standing. All these pressures led to the increasing subdivision of buildings to accommodate poorer families (already, 2,360 people were officially classed as poor in 1570), to the tendency to build higher, and to the development of new rows and yards behind older buildings. By the 1670s a standardised artisan's house had appeared: it was three-storeyed with a continuous line of dormer windows lighting the attics where work, particularly weaving, was done. A computerised study of probate inventories shows that several thousands of these houses must once have existed in Norwich, but today only five remain.

Lynn too was changing architecturally. New houses tended to be built parallel with the main streets, at first only one room deep (for example, the Greenland Fishery) and later rooms two deep (for example, St Nicholas House). Several wealthy merchants added prestigious towers to their houses behind the river front but only one, at Clifton House, actually survives. Most ordinary residents, however, could only modernise their existing houses. In the search for greater privacy and comfort, they subdivided medieval open halls by inserting new floors and ceilings, added brick chimneys to heat rooms on the ground and first floors, used large quantities of window glass which was now cheaper, replaced steep ladders by wider and more elegant staircases, and created more rooms with specialised functions (such as kitchens, dining rooms and studies). On the outside, houses were usually refronted in brick and given fashionable new gables (stepped, shaped or 'tumbled'). With the desire for greater symmetry and dignity, it was extremely common for older timber-framed houses to lose their overhanging jetties by the process of 'latching'. This meant moving forward, or re-building, the front wall of the ground floor by eighteen inches or so, to achieve an absolutely vertical façade. By such changes, the inner character and age of many buildings were utterly concealed.

Because of their economic and strategic importance, the two major ports of Norfolk were given improved defences in Tudor and Stuart times. In the sixteenth century, the walls of Yarmouth were strengthened by having large earthen banks raised behind them, by the construction of two large mounds as gun batteries, and by re-digging the outer ditch. In 1625 a boom was constructed across the river and some of the towers were filled with earth to make them withstand artillery fire. Then, with the outbreak of Civil War in 1642, a new outwork with ditches sixty feet wide and eight feet deep was thrown up to defend the more vulnerable northern end of town, and the whole circuit of walls given a series of projecting bastions. At Lynn, on the seaward side of the town, St Ann's Fort was built in 1570–1, followed by a nearby blockhouse in the 1620s. During the Civil Wars, an engineer called Christian added a new defensive system to the medieval banks and walls; it consisted of an outer ditch, about thirteen bastions and two outworks to north and south. Ironically, this work was interrupted by a siege in January 1643, when a Royalist garrison was invested by a parliamentary army under the Earl of Manchester. Parts of these seventeenth-century defences can still be seen as water-filled ditches, low banks and property boundaries.

A feature of urban life after the Restoration is the provision of new public buildings to cater for the rising expectations of local residents. From 1683 to 1707, thanks to its own homebred architectural genius, Henry Bell, King's Lynn was graced by the Exchange (later Custom House), the Duke's Head and an incomparable market cross which was regrettably demolished in the early nineteenth century. Norwich was provided with a whole string of new facilities: an asylum in 1714, assembly rooms in 1754, a theatre in 1756 and a hospital in 1771. At Yarmouth, such changes were connected with a fundamental shift in the economy of the town. Although it was a thriving port and market town, it began in the second half of the eighteenth century to develop as a resort attracting visitors. It had a theatre, assembly room, bath-house on the beach and an adjoining public room for refreshments and concerts, and numerous lodgings and inns. At this stage, the town was still largely huddled within its medieval defences and facing inland. Outside was a huge expanse of sand bank called the Denes, five miles long and up to three-quarters of a mile wide. Apart from a small huddle of buildings, a jetty, a few windmills and gun-emplacements, the Denes were open and constituted a considerable public amenity. They were used for grazing, drying linen and fishing nets, military training and horse-racing, and they gave visitors the pleasures of walking, riding and gazing out to sea.

The eighteenth and nineteenth centuries saw an increasing desire for urban 'improvement', often organised by specially appointed commissioners. Thus, obstructions were removed to ease the flow of increasing traffic, streets were paved and lit more effectively, and new public gardens were designed. Perhaps the most obvious and symbolic change was the destruction of medieval walls and gates: they had come to be regarded as undignified relics which prevented the proper circulation of air. All the city gates of Norwich were demolished between 1791 and 1801, and the walls were either used as quarries or began to disappear behind new suburban developments. Yarmouth similarly removed its gates after 1790, and began to lose sight of its crumbling walls. Lynn demolished its East Gate in 1790, but left its fifteenth-century South Gate untouched – today it is the only major town gate to survive in the whole of East Anglia.

In this atmosphere of improvement, entirely new roads

were created, slashing across older quarters in a recognisably modern way. Thus, Regent Street in Yarmouth was cut in 1813 to give for the first time a major east-west road linking the quay with King Street, the market and the Denes. Meanwhile the approach to Lynn from the south was made more direct and dignified by a broad new street called London Road (1811–13), and at Norwich the making of Davey Place (1812) provided a new direct link between the provision and cattle markets.

But the most important feature of urban life after 1800 was rapid expansion triggered off by an unprecedented growth of population, especially in the decades 1811–31. Although the trade of Lynn declined with the coming of the railways, its built-up area increased faster, from about 1830, than at any other time since the twelfth century, taking up open spaces both inside and outside its extravagantly-drawn medieval defences. The population of South Lynn grew fivefold in forty years, while in the vicinity of the new railway station the town also grew eastwards. Similarly, after 1830, the town of Yarmouth burst from its medieval constraints and began to colonise the Denes with new streets, terraces and hotels. Within a generation the town had more than doubled its medieval size, and was creeping along the Denes to both north and south. In other words, after 800 years of facing inland, Yarmouth turned itself around to face the sea (Fig. 17). Its two piers, Wellington and Britannia, and a marine drive were built in the 1850s; other popular amenities soon followed such as Winton's New Assembly Rooms and the Warwick Revolving Tower, 130 feet high. However, the really spectacular modern amusements, for which Yarmouth is now famous, did not appear until after the First World War.

Norwich saw the greatest growth, though its traditional industries were in serious decline by 1840 and it was becoming much less important by national standards. It too overstepped the walls which had comfortably contained it for 500 years, and began to encourage the undisciplined sprawl which is now one of its worst features. Most of the new growth occurred on the west and south-west, particularly along and between major approach roads. For example, between Unthank and Newmarket Roads, a tight pattern of streets and houses still

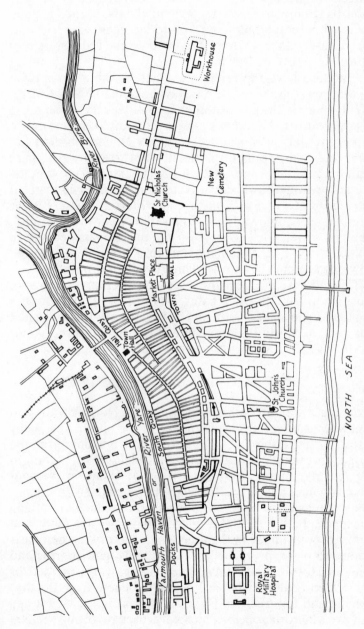

Fig. 17. Great Yarmouth in 1870: showing the medieval town beside the River Yare, tightly packed within its walls, and the more spacious Victorian developments spreading along the sea-shore.

reflects the hedges and fields which preceded them. Artisan suburbs sprang up as at Heigham or the 'New City' around Vauxhall Street; larger more well-to-do areas also appeared, for example along Thorpe Road and on the old common of Town Close (off the Newmarket Road). The nomenclature of the modern city graphically illustrates its suburban spread: New Sprowston, New Catton, New Lakenham, New Costessey, Upper Hellesdon. Another feature was the appearance of large industrial buildings such as the Yarn Company mill in 1836 (now Jarrold's printing works) or Bullards brewery of 1860, and of large public utilities like the three railway termini built between 1844 and 1882. In spite of external growth, the pressure within the old city was still considerable. In many of the old streets, such as King Street or Magdalen Street, large numbers of people still lived in insanitary alleys and courts. The first sewer was laid in 1869, and the first slum clearance followed in 1877. At the same time the Corporation acquired powers to compel landlords to improve their properties.

This sudden increase in the size of the three largest towns of Norfolk meant that a greater proportion of the county's population now lived in them. In 1801, twenty-two and a half per cent of Norfolk's population lived in the three major towns; by 1831 it was forty-one per cent.

New resorts

From the late eighteenth century onwards, Norfolk witnessed a new kind of urban development in the shape of holiday resorts or 'watering places'. Visitors, drawn mainly from the burgeoning middle classes, wanted the pleasures of bathing in the sea and sailing, and of walking or riding in pleasant scenery where the air was 'strongly impregnated with ozone'. They also came to expect various amenities such as bathing machines, bath-houses for indoor bathing, assembly and reading rooms; later in the nineteenth century the emphasis shifted to piers, promenades, bandstands, golf-courses and funfairs. Hospitals and convalescent homes were provided for the sick and elderly who also hoped to benefit from the dry, bracing and fog-free air. By 1900, for example, Mundesley had two sanatoria, one of which advertised revolving shelters for consumptive patients. A major stimulus was the arrival of railways in later Victorian and Edwardian times.

The town of New Hunstanton grew up on a virgin site overlooking the Wash, about a mile from the village of Old Hunstanton. It occupies a sloping hillside on the edge of the sea, at a point where the famous striped cliffs give way to salt marshes. Faden's map of 1797 depicted only two buildings on the clifftop, a lighthouse and ruined chapel (where St Edmund is supposed to have landed in the ninth century). Although the potential of this pleasant site had been recognised early in the nineteenth century, the town did not 'take off' until the 1860s, and was then encouraged by the local landowner, Hamon le Strange. The railway arrived from the south in 1862, and within forty years New Hunstanton was described as a 'well known and much frequented watering place'. A new parish church, appropriately dedicated to St Edmund, was built in 1865, and in 1879 given an enlargement called the 'visitors' aisle'. Other facilities included a pier 800 feet long, a 'union church' for all nonconformist denominations, hotels, a convalescent home, country club, town hall and theatre. In the parish of Old Hunstanton a golf-course was laid out in the '90s. The town itself was built on a grid-pattern of streets, with tall gabled houses of carrstone in a Tudor style. The centre was the Green, a large triangular space extending to the cliff edge.

Cromer (Plate 26) was first frequented as a watering place about 1785, when 'two or three families of retiring habit' were attracted by the long level beach, surrounding hills and woods, and 'the simple manners of the inhabitants'. In the Middle Ages Cromer had been a market town and centre of the Icelandic fishing trade, with an artificial breakwater to protect ships on a cruelly exposed stretch of coast. By the eighteenth century, however, it was no more than a small fishing village, four or five streets huddling around a large but decayed church. A tourist guide was written in 1800, and thereafter Cromer became a most fashionable resort; indeed one of Jane Austen's characters asserted that it was 'the best of all the sea-bathing places'. (One advantage, in the eyes of sensitive visitors, was that the sun both rose and set in the sea!) By 1845 the population had doubled, four hotels and a new inn had been built, and over seventy boarding and lodging houses were available. Among the facilities for visitors were a bath-house, reading and billiards rooms, and the inevitable bathing machines. All these were destroyed by a great storm in February 1837, but the town continued to develop. Investment was made in a new bath-house, jetty, breakwaters and esplanade, a cottage hospital and in the long-overdue restoration of the parish church. From 1876 Cromer entered the railway age; three companies were involved and two stations were built. By the 1890s the town was truly booming. The esplanade was rebuilt, yet again and very expensively, with a new pier and bandstand, while new buildings included a town hall with reading room, a lecture hall, a Catholic church and several large hotels designed by G. R. Skipper of Norwich. New streets full of private hotels and boarding houses spread outwards, particularly on the west and south-east. To the south, however, growth was checked by steep wooded slopes and the park around Cromer Hall. Much of the new building was in red brick with bay windows, gables, dormers and the occasional angle-turret. One mile to the south-east, in the former clifftop warren of Overstrand, appeared the inevitable golf-course.

Only four miles west of Cromer, similar developments occurred at Sheringham. The original village, now called Upper Sheringham, lies over a mile inland and was relatively untouched by modernity. By contrast, where a small valley met the coast, Lower Sheringham or Sheringham Hithe was a small fishing village which had grown up in the Middle Ages, and become a noted centre for the trade in Icelandic ling and cod. Its fisheries prospered again in the early nineteenth century, and this led to a sharply rising population and some new building, but the real expansion came in the 1890s with the arrival of the railway. Several bulky hotels and many boarding houses were then built, as the town spread inland and blossomed into a holiday resort. Exactly the same relationship emerged between the old village and upstart town as had happened in the Middle Ages at Downham Market and Harleston: a new church was built in 1895–7 but had only the status of a chapel-of-ease to All Saints at Upper Sheringham. It has now been upgraded to a full parish church, and has its own territory carved out of the old parish.

Not all towns, however, were successful in becoming resorts. For example, Thetford in the early nineteenth century
entertained hopes of becoming the eastern equivalent of
Bath, because it had an iron-bearing spring. A bath-house
was built, and a book was written extolling the medical effects
of its waters. But the expected boom never materialised, and
in 1838 the bath was abandoned. Thetford had to wait more
than another century for a 'boom' of a different sort.

SELECT BIBLIOGRAPHY

Bartell, Edmund, *Cromer, considered as a watering place* (2nd ed.
1806).
Blome, Richard, *Britannia* (1673).
Campbell, James, *Norwich*, Historic Towns Series (1975).
Clarke, Helen and Carter, A., *Excavations in King's Lynn, 1963–
70*, Society for Medieval Archaeology, Monograph 7 (1977).
Green, B. and Young, R. M. R., *Norwich, the Growth of a City*
(1981).
O'Donoghue, Rosemary, '. . . Some Aspects of Town Planning in
19th-century Norwich', *Norfolk Archaeology*, XXXVIII (1983),
321–28.
Owen, Dorothy M., 'Bishop's Lynn: the first century of a new
town?' in R. Allen Brown (ed.), *Proceedings of the Battle Confer-
ence, 1979* (1980), 141–53.
Parker, Vanessa, *The Making of King's Lynn* (1971).
Report of Royal Commission on Market Rights, *Parliamentary
Papers*, 1888, LIII, 108–31 for list of grants of markets and fairs
from 1 John to 22 Edward IV.

13. Mansions, parks and lesser houses

Norfolk méditerrané. Georgian country houses.
The latest country houses. The landscape of discipline.
Back to nature. The smaller domestic buildings.

THE MANY HUNDREDS of medieval manor houses in Norfolk, often more than one in each parish, gave rise to a vital institution of social, cultural and political life: the country house or, if large enough, the 'stately home'. From 1500 onwards, Norfolk witnessed a great rebuilding of its larger houses. Early examples still remain, often fragmentarily, such as a machicolated tower at Fincham, a stepped gable at Denver encrusted with pinnacles and mouldings, and terracotta panelling at Great Cressingham. The most important survival, however, is undoubtedly East Barsham Hall built for Sir Henry Fermor in the 1520s. This large brick building, rambling and asymmetrical, is capped by battlements, turrets and chimneys. It has bays of different lengths, divided by shafts, large windows with mullions and transoms, and decorative friezes at different levels. The main elements of the plan are a large open hall, two-storeyed porch, three-storeyed tower and a free-standing gatehouse. This building is particularly memorable because it sits comfortably in a hollow and, unusually for Norfolk, can be seen from above; it typifies the predominantly domestic requirements of the landowning class in Henry VIII's reign. Unfortunately, other fine buildings of the period have largely perished, such as Beaupré in the fens and the third Duke of Norfolk's palace at Kenninghall.

During the more settled reign of Elizabeth I, the local gentry set about rebuilding with even greater gusto. By this time, they wanted an exterior which was balanced and symmetrical, even though the interior was still irregular and

180

composed, broadly speaking, of the same rooms as late medieval houses. The typical plan was E-shaped, consisting of a main block with a central porch and two side wings which protruded forward. The façades were decorated with plain or stepped gables, large windows divided by mullions and transoms, tall chimneys (often in clusters), and initials or coats of arms above the main entrance. Fine examples of such halls survive at Flordon, Thelveton and Breckles, the last with a genuine priest's hole to remind us of the long-suffering Catholic gentry. Most of these buildings are of locally made brick, often with facings of imported stone, though in the south of Norfolk timber-framed versions can be found, as at Saxlingham Nethergate. Heydon Hall (1581–4) had extra sophistication with pediments above its windows, some balustrading and angle shafts topped by pinnacles; Stiffkey (*c.* 1575) occupied three sides of a square, had circular towers at its corners and a small detached gatehouse in front (Plate 10).

In the first thirty years of the seventeenth century, as examples like Kirstead and Gillingham show, the Elizabethan style of country house was still the normal choice of Jacobean landowners. In the hands of some designers, however, new refinements are visible. For example, Barningham Hall (1612) has strikingly vertical lines with slender shafts, tall chimneys stacks and dormers of two storeys. In the south front of Felbrigg Hall (1621–4), the traditional cross-wings are replaced by two-storeyed bay windows. They and the central porch are surmounted by a balustrade carrying the bold inscription 'Gloria Deo in Excelsis' and topped by a row of heraldic beasts.

All these charming halls are, however, dwarfed by the mighty Jacobean house at Blickling (Plate 29), built 1619–27 for Sir Henry Hobart, Lord Chief Justice. It was designed by Robert Lyminge, the architect of Hatfield, who died at Blickling and is buried in the church there. Behind the main southern façade is an internal courtyard, while at the back of the house two long wings, which have since been linked, protruded north. The design involved square turrets at the corners with ogee-shaped lead caps, stone quoins, canted bay windows (like Felbrigg which was almost certainly by Lyminge too), curved gables and a tall spire or lantern.

Internally the chief glory is a gallery 127 feet long, with a plaster ceiling covered with strap-work, pendants and allegorical emblems.

While Blickling was being built, another house of national importance, which provides an astonishing contrast, was rising less than twenty miles away. Raynham Hall, started in 1621 for Sir Roger Townshend, demonstrates the work of Inigo Jones and his associates (Plate 30). They insisted that classical proportions and harmony should once again govern architectural design, both externally and internally. Whereas Blickling uses certain classical features as applied decoration, for instance the columns which frame the main entrance, Raynham's east front is dominated by a large Ionic portico looking like the end of a Roman temple. On each side are wings surmounted by Dutch gables, with curving sides and pedimented tops. The main reception room on the first floor is indicated by a large Venetian window – a central arched opening flanked by two flat-headed ones. This and other Venetian windows, which originally existed on the main fronts, are among the earliest recorded in England. The whole building has a compactness and discipline which make it very different from its contemporary at Blickling.

The accounts of Sir Roger and his master mason William Edge reveal the organisation which lay behind the building of a great house: the site had to be prepared by stubbing up trees; brick kilns and lime kilns were built on the estate; new roads were constructed to carry materials; timber was cut at Raynham, Coxford, Horningtoft and other places; iron was shipped through the port of Wells and stone through Lynn. A special crane with an iron-tipped mallet was devised to drive in piles, and a model of the house constructed to guide the masons. At any one time, up to sixty workmen were employed, and the total cost was at least £3,500.

Later in the seventeenth century, Norfolk made other notable contributions to English architecture. A group of talented architects emerged, mainly gentlemen-amateurs, such as Sir Thomas Dereham (who built an unusual Italianate house at West Dereham; see Plate 16) and Sir Roger North of Rougham who wrote an important treatise 'On building'. The greatest, however, was Sir Roger Pratt (1620–84) who came

Plate 27 Hillington: a fine manorial map by William Hayward, 1592 (North to left). This section shows the old village with intricate patterns of roads, open fields and enclosures; the original also includes meadows, commons and heath. Later emparking has radically changed this village and parish.

Plate 28 Caister Castle: the heavily defensive lair (mainly 1432-5) of Sir John Fastolf, built of brick with gun-ports and machicolation. Mentioned in the Paston Letters, it became Paston property after 1459.

Plate 29 Blickling Hall: a great Jacobean palace designed by Robert Lyminge for Sir Henry Hobart, Lord Chief Justice, built 1619-27. Now the regional headquarters of the National Trust.

Plate 30 Raynham Hall: ancestral home of the Townshends. This house, contemporary with Blickling, was started in 1621 by Sir Roger Townshend, employing the new classical principles associated with Inigo Jones.

Plate 31 Holkham Park: aristocratic wealth and power, set in the farming landscape which was its main support. Notice the park defined by plantations, the three-mile avenue leading to the Hall itself, the parish church, a Roman road on the western (left) side of the park, and reclaimed marshland between park and sea.

Plate 32 Holkham Hall: the southern front, a vast symmetrical design with flanking pavilions, all built of yellow-grey brick and designed on strictly Palladian principles. On the extreme right, a conservatory of 1850.

of a Norfolk landowning family and, during the Civil Wars, travelled extensively abroad. His masterpiece was undoubtedly Coleshill House in Berkshire which, although now destroyed, is recognised as one of the most influential designs of the seventeenth century. Pratt designed five houses in all, of which the last was his own on the family manor of Ryston in west Norfolk. Although the house was greatly altered in the eighteenth century, it is still lived in by the family and contains Sir Roger's library and architectural notebooks. The latter reveal his meticulous approach to building and give detailed accounts. The cost of the house and its formal gardens was around £4,000. It was double-piled and symmetrical with principal rooms on the first floor, approached on each side by a flight of external stone stairs.

Two other buildings of the late seventeenth century deserve special mention. Sir Jacob Astley's house at Melton Constable was begun in 1664 and took over twenty years to complete (Plate 37). This classic English house has a compact double-piled plan, hipped roofs with a flat top which once carried balustrading and a cupola, tall rectangular chimneys and, internally, plaster ceilings depicting game-birds, fruit and flowers. Slightly later is Narford Hall, built for Sir Andrew Fountaine who was a noted collector and yet another gentleman-architect. On the walls of the hall are ten inset canvases painted by Giovanni Pellegrini, one of the continental craftsmen so frequently employed in England at this period. In the eighteenth century, this house of limestone and carrstone with its collections of porcelain, coins, bronzes and other curiosities was part of a cultural route around Norfolk recommended to discerning gentlemen.

As landed estates tended to grow in size, and some manors were absorbed by their neighbours, so an increasing number of early halls and country houses changed their status. Instead of being the residences of landowning squires, they became mere farmhouses occupied by tenant farmers. The sheer number of farms in Norfolk called 'Hall' reminds us that this process had been under way since the later Middle Ages and accelerated after the Restoration. Smaller houses frequently survived intact, but the larger ones were often cut down in size. Channonz Hall near Tibenham is a good example.

183

After 1731, the Buxton family moved to Shadwell on the Breckland which they made the centre of their expanding estate, and the old hall was let. In 1784 two-thirds of the Elizabethan house was demolished, and only the kitchen wing remained – as a tenant farmhouse.

Norfolk méditerrané

In the eighteenth century, the architecture of Norfolk was dominated by two palatial buildings which lie about ten miles apart in the north-west. Even today the houses of Houghton (Plate 33) and Holkham (Plate 32) shock us with a style and scale which seem alien to their bucolic surroundings. For example, they deliberately flout local traditions by using large quantities of imported materials such as Yorkshire or Bath stone, Italian marble and Jamaican mahogany. Furthermore, their design is consciously based on sixteenth-century Italian villas designed by Andrea Palladio, who in turn was inspired by the builders of ancient Rome. However, we can only understand the external dignity and internal opulence of Houghton and Holkham when we see them as the creations of a new race of Whig magnates, men of unprecedented power and wealth, soaked in the cultural traditions of renaissance Italy and classical Rome. Then it does not seem so strange to find Italianate palaces with pedimented windows and coffered ceilings, classical statues and renaissance paintings, set among the fields and farms of deepest Norfolk. Indeed, we must see a logical connection between them, because the rents from those farms were an indispensable part of the economic framework which helped to create and sustain their owners' magnificent and extravagant way of life.

Sir Robert Walpole, later Earl of Orford, is usually regarded as England's first prime minister. His family had lived locally since at least the thirteenth century, but as the most powerful and successful statesman of his age he no longer wished to live in the old rambling manor house of his ancestors. He therefore commissioned Colen Campbell, a leading exponent of the new Palladian taste, to design a classical mansion worthy of his rank. Built in the years 1722–35, it is symmetrical and consists of a main rectangular block of three storeys with two wings connected by curving corridors. With the help of James Gibbs, Walpole subsequently modified the design by substituting a dome at each corner of the main block, in place of Campbell's pavilions. The exterior was built of a beautiful variegated sandstone quarried at Aislaby in east Yorkshire, and brought most of the way by boat.

On entering the house, the visitor is struck by the contrast between a homely ground floor intended (in Lord Hervey's words) for 'hunters, hospitality, noise, dirt and business' and an unforgettable succession of state rooms on the first floor intended for 'taste, expense, state and parade'. The most magnificent of the latter are the 'Stone Hall', a cool white cube of forty feet, and the 'Saloon' which glows with deep red tapestries and gold leaf. The architecture itself was complemented by the plasterwork of Guiseppe Artari, carvings of John Rysbrack, furniture and painted ceilings of William Kent, and by one of the finest collections of oil paintings ever assembled by a private individual.

While Houghton was being finished, Thomas Coke, later Earl of Leicester, began a new house at Holkham where his family had held the manor since 1612. His old manor house, situated where the north-west wing now stands, was not demolished until 1757, and the project was not finally completed until 1764. Although construction was supervised by Matthew Brettingham, the design seems to have emerged from endless discussions between Coke, William Kent and Lord Burlington. The massive new hall, described by contemporaries as 'the finest house in England', consists of a main block with turrets at the angles and four linked wings, each of which would make a modest country house. The exterior is austere, even sombre, and was made of local yellow brick which Coke liked because it resembled Roman brick, as recommended by Vitruvius. External severity, however, belies an interior which is 'more consistently palatial than that of almost any other house in England'.

As at Houghton, the ground floor contains various domestic and service rooms, while the main apartments, including a dazzling suite of state rooms, are on the first floor. The latter include a large saloon with walls of crimson velvet, fireplaces of Sicilian marble and tables incorporating mosaics from

Hadrian's villa; a drawing room with an elaborate ceiling depicting fruits, foliage and masks; a cubic dining room with a famous antique bust of Lucius Verus; and, most memorable of all, a long sculpture gallery of white and gold which runs along the whole west front. A modern commentator has referred to the gallery as 'exquisitely chaste', while to Arthur Young it was simply 'the most beautiful room I ever beheld'. Unlike most Palladian houses, Holkham has no external staircase leading up to the first floor. The main door is on the ground floor and leads immediately into a marble hall. This, though based on the design of a classical basilica, is in reality a grand pillared staircase leading up to the state rooms.

Archives preserved at Holkham list 'every brick, nail, hod of lime, bushel of hair and leaf of gold': they show that no less than £90,000 was spent on building the hall, and a further £5,500 on furnishing it. It is no surprise to learn that, when he died in 1759, the Earl of Leicester left debts totalling £91,000 whereas his architectural rival Sir Robert Walpole, latterly Earl of Orford, owed only £40,000!

Georgian country houses

Holkham and Houghton are in a class of their own because of their scale, their architectural opulence and the wealth which was poured into them. Nevertheless, it must not be overlooked that scores of other country houses, large and small, were built in Norfolk during the Georgian period, and collectively they constitute a major feature of the landscape. They appeared in all parts of the county, mostly on the sites of earlier houses and frequently in landscaped surroundings. Their rhythmic and restrained façades of brick, coupled with their elegant reception rooms, epitomise the taste and leisure of landed proprietors whose power and wealth were as yet unchallenged. Socially, Georgian country houses range from major seats like Wolterton, Kimberley and Langley, also built in the Palladian style by families who were not far removed from the denizens of Houghton and Holkham, down to the relatively modest houses of numerous country squires and professional folk. Most of the houses were totally new, but some clearly represent the remodelling of earlier structures (for example Rokeles Hall or Ormesby Old Hall) to give them at least façades which accorded with the new taste.

Within the Georgian period, several different fashions are discernible. For example Rococo ideas were adopted during the middle years of the eighteenth century and are represented by some exuberant plasterwork at Langley and Gateley. Later, white or grey brick tended to replace red while, under the influence of architects like John Soane and James Wyatt, fashionable new features were introduced such as apsed extensions, windows with marginal lights, bay-windows and occasional Gothic battlements. But the basic style and vocabulary do not change much, and remained in use until the earlier part of Victoria's reign. Late examples such as Langham Hall (*c.* 1820) or Halvergate Hall (*c.* 1840) are clearly in the same tradition as Cavick House at Wymondham (1710–20) or Hanworth Hall (*c.* 1700). Exteriors are normally articulated by long sash windows, delicate glazing bars, string-courses and cornices; sometimes a more determined classical flourish is made by means of columned doorcases, pilasters and triangular pediments above the main façades.

Architects with national reputations occasionally appeared in Norfolk. For instance Sir John Soane worked on several houses in the 1780s, and his fine design for Shotesham Park, with its Ionic pilasters, niches and his own version of the Venetian window, shows his distinctive style in the making. In the main, however, Norfolk owners and local architects managed to create what was needed for themselves. Indeed, Norfolk produced several notable architects of its own such as Matthew Brettingham (1699–1796) who worked as Kent's understudy at Holkham and also at Gunton and Langley, or gentlemen amateurs such as John Buxton and the Reverend Thomas Gunn.

The latest country houses

Against the eighteenth-century achievement, the later history of country houses is sometimes overlooked. Yet building and re-building continued on a large scale; indeed new houses and landscaped parks were being created up to the eve of the

First World War, and it was in the Edwardian period that the number of country houses reached its peak. Not only did the nobility and gentry continue to build, but they were joined by an increasing number of *nouveaux riches* whose wealth had often come from outside East Anglia. Thus, in 1902–05 Pickenham Hall was greatly extended for a banker who had inherited a fortune from button-making at Moseley; Beechamwell Hall was rebuilt at the same time for the widow of a cotton manufacturer; and Kelling Hall was built in 1912–13 for a director of Shell and Royal Dutch Petroleum. Meanwhile, Norfolk also witnessed the creation of a new royal estate, from 1860 onwards, at Sandringham.

Most Victorian and later houses were rebuildings of, or extensions to, earlier seats, usually perpetuating the site of a medieval hall. But occasionally a completely new site was developed, as at Ken Hill at Snettisham where in 1879–80 Sir Edward Green commissioned a highly individual house on a hill overlooking the Wash, or at Bylaugh in 1849 where the Reverend Evans Lombe built an 'Elizabethan' palace on a new site, a half-mile from the old hall, on a slope commanding the Wensum valley (Plate 35).

The main characteristic of nineteenth-century architecture was its willingness to borrow from earlier styles. For instance the architect Edward Blore, who was widely employed, designed a large Italianate house at Haverland (now demolished) but used the Jacobean idiom elsewhere. At Costessey in 1826–36 J. C. Buckler produced a Gothic fantasy for Lord Stafford, which dwarfed the original Elizabethan hall; it was a 'superb folly' with gables, turrets, pinnacles and chimneys, all dominated by a massive 'keep'. In 1824–30 a local architect of note, W. J. Donthorne, produced another Gothic 'castle' at Hillington; this was built largely of local carrstone, again with a keep and battlemented turrets. Both of these extravaganzas have perished, but another still survives, happily, at Shadwell Park near Thetford. This prodigious house has been hailed by Mark Girouard as one of the masterpieces of Victorian Gothic. To a Georgian core and Blore's Jacobean block, S. S. Teulon in 1856–60 added asymmetrical Gothic ranges which doubled the size of the house. His new work included a free-standing tower with spire and a cruciform music hall which, with its Gothic pillars, windows and high wooden roof, has been likened to a Victorian cathedral.

In 1860 Sandringham House was bought by Edward, Prince of Wales, later King Edward VII. It was sufficiently remote from London to give privacy, yet was also reasonably accessible by road and rail. From 1863 that accessibility was improved when Wolferton station was opened, only two miles from the house. To cope with its flow of distinguished passengers, the station was later provided with 'royal waiting rooms'. The house, mainly a rebuilding of about 1770, was not an architectural gem: it was described by a contemporary as 'but a cottage compared with some residences in Norfolk'. After some hesitation, the prince decided, in 1870, to demolish it (with the exception of a conservatory recently added). Using an unknown architect called A. J. Humbert, he built a sprawling but homely house in Jacobean style which, with its abundant gables and bay-windows, has been likened to an outsize country hotel. Later additions included a bowling alley (eventually converted by the ageing prince into a library), a large ballroom and new ranges of bedrooms for staff. By the end of Edward's life the house had 365 rooms, 'more than any other English private house'. It was not simply a 'hunting box' which provided good sport, or a private home for a growing family. It was also used for large weekend parties, for annual balls, and as a place to entertain relatives who included most of Europe's royalty. For instance, the widowed Queen Victoria came twice and Kaiser Wilhelm II of Germany visited his uncle there in 1881, 1899 and 1902. Since Edward's death in 1910, Sandringham has remained one of the royal family's favourite homes. George V called it simply 'The place I love better than anywhere else in the world.'

From about 1900 the ideas of the Arts and Crafts movement began to be felt, for example in Edwin Lutyens' design for a new courtyard house at Overstrand. Most remarkable, however, are three houses built near the north-east coast on the 'butterfly' or 'suntrap' principle: Happisburgh Manor (1900), Home Place at Holt (1904–6) and Kelling Hall (1912–13). They have two or four wings jutting out at 135 degrees from the main block, in order to capture the maximum amount of sunlight throughout the day. Although these buildings are unusual in plan, they were deliberately made of traditional materials like flint pebbles, local brick and reed thatch.

In 1905–7 the Norwich architect George Skipper created a large baroque house at Sennowe Park near Fakenham. It was commissioned by a rich and flamboyant man called T. A. Cook, grandson of the founder of the travel agency. A modest Georgian house was extended into a main front of seventeen bays, large pilasters, rich window-surrounds and a covered porch for coaches; its skyline is similarly busy with dormers, balustrade, urns and statues. This extraordinary architectural confection, with its extended park and agricultural estate, represents not only 'the Edwardian country-house tradition at its most vigorous' but probably the last great investment of its kind in Norfolk. From 1914 onwards, it was increasingly difficult to maintain such houses, let alone build them.

The landscape of discipline

Before the middle of the eighteenth century, country houses were normally surrounded by geometrically planned gardens and parks. For example, an early seventeenth-century 'garden' survives to the east of Blickling Hall. It consists of a series of straight vistas radiating in star-patterns through two blocks of woodland; urns are set at focal points. The whole area amounting to eighty acres is roughly rectangular, and is enclosed by a mighty terraced walk and outer ditch which separate it from surrounding meadow and parkland. Another later example of the formal style is William Kent's avenue at Holkham, which is straight as an arrow for more than three miles (Plate 31). It begins half a mile south of the park boundary and incorporates a triumphal arch; in the park its northern end climbs a wooded hill surmounted by an obelisk eighty feet high. From this viewpoint Kent laid out eight straight vistas radiating through the trees, each focusing on some major feature such as a classical temple, the parish church, the town of Wells and distant plantations. Each of these views was subsequently blocked, except for the two main ones along the avenue itself, which commands the hall and indeed determined its precise site. The main axis continued beyond the house to the northern edge of the park, and was re-emphasised in 1845 when a tall pillar was erected to the memory of 'Coke of Norfolk'.

In several other places, geometrical layouts have survived only in smaller fragments. For example, Charles Bridgeman's 'mount' at Gunton still survives in a wood, but the vistas, terraces and serpentine paths which showed it off have all but vanished. Similarly only a ghost of his elaborate gardens at Wolterton can still be seen, in the shape of a large lake and some fine trees. Nevertheless, when more botanical and archaeological fieldwork is carried out in Norfolk's parks, we shall undoubtedly recognise more survivals, and be able to show that later landscape gardeners like Capability Brown did not always destroy formal designs, but often adapted or modified them.

To appreciate geometrical landscapes in their entirety, one can only use contemporary illustrations. Norfolk has two excellent examples in a bird's-eye view of Melton Constable engraved by John Kip in 1707 (Plate 37), and a map of Narford in the first volume of Colen Campbell's famous *Vitruvius Britannicus*, published in 1715. Each shows a large deer park wrapping itself around a highly formalised series of inner gardens. In each case the park is cut by long straight avenues of trees which cross at right angles at, or near the house. It seems that the north-south avenue at Melton, comprising four lines of trees, was up to two miles long. Both parks also contained rectangular lakes known as 'canals'. Melton had a long canal in front of the house, lining up with the great avenue. Narford also had a major canal but it was behind the house and, because of the lie of the land, off the main axis.

Around each house was a series of walled or terraced gardens. They contained geometrical flower beds, areas of grass and topiary, serried rows of trees, clipped hedges, gravelled walks, carriage drives and gardens for fruit and vegetables. Narford also had blocks of woodland, planned in various formal shapes but cut, according to developing taste, by serpentine paths leading to glades or arbours. It even had a small maze. Finally, various buildings and structures punctuated the vistas. The western avenue at Melton focused on a building with a polygonal tower, while Narford had gazebos, obelisks and a classical deer house. In both cases these extensive geometrical designs, expensive to create and to maintain, were dramatically transformed by the end of the eighteenth century – though again fragments may well survive.

The love and wealth lavished on seventeenth-century formal landscapes are also revealed in written documents left by two Norfolk gentlemen: they are the notebooks of Sir Roger Pratt and the so-called 'Green Book' of William Windham I. Around his new house at Ryston, built in 1668–73, Pratt laid out three brick-walled gardens and a series of straight avenues. For the latter he purchased 838 trees in 1672. He planted mainly oaks but also ash, white poplar, holly, 'best Dutch limes', spruces and cypresses. For his flower, vegetable and fruit gardens, he drew up equally impressive plans: for example he mentions five different kinds of nectarine, five kinds of grape and eleven kinds of pear.

Meanwhile, William Windham I was planting vigorously at Felbrigg. He acquired seedlings from other Norfolk gentry, and in his own nursery established in 1676 sowed acorns, ash-keys, haws, holly berries, beech-mast and the seeds of maple and sycamore. Subsequently he planted 4,000 oaks, 800 ashes and 600 birches, as well as beeches, crab-apples, walnuts, limes and Scots Pines. In 1683 he recorded the planting of forty-nine trees in a formal pattern described as 'the Quincunciall, Lozenge, or New-work Plantations'. This was an ancient mathematical form of planting brought back into fashion by Sir Thomas Browne of Norwich, in his book *The Garden of Cyrus*. A few of Windham's favourite sweet chestnuts have survived 300 years: witness the fine specimen east of the hall.

Back to nature

Because of the proliferation of large houses in the eighteenth and nineteenth centuries, landscaped parks increasingly asserted themselves in Norfolk's countryside. On his map of 1730, James Corbridge showed only sixteen parks, but he must have omitted many small examples. By 1797, Faden depicted over a hundred parks, large and small. They were thickest on the ground in the Breckland, on the Good Sands and within a twenty-mile radius of Norwich; conversely they were noticeably fewer in southern and central Norfolk, in Broadland and in Marshland. This variable distribution is a fascinating but largely unstudied reflection of important social differences: on lighter soils which were relatively thinly populated, it was easier for the aristocracy and gentry to build up their estates, whereas on heavier soils independently-minded farmers living in scattered but frequent farmsteads provided an important counterweight to such expansion. Another factor was the social and economic influence of Norwich, as one of the most important provincial cities in England. By the early twentieth century, the number of parks was at its maximum: about 170 are recorded on maps of the Ordnance Survey. The distribution was much as before, though Mid-Norfolk and the Western Escarpment had now relatively more examples. Even today, although much parkland has been converted to arable, we often see the characteristically thick belts of trees, the flint or brick walls and gate-lodges, and glimpses of grassland, lakes and fine houses. Indeed, because today's farming landscape is more open, parks often have an even greater visual impact than before.

Not only was the total number of parks rising in the eighteenth and nineteenth centuries, but individually they were often growing in size. For example Raynham's park stood at about 800 acres until, in about 1779, it was increased to 1,200 acres. By 1850 Holkham had by far the largest park in the county: it took in about 3,000 acres and its boundary wall was nine miles long. Quite frequently the ornamental landscape around a gentleman's or nobleman's house extended into several parishes. Thus, at Gunton, the park took up virtually all of its own parish and parts of Thorpe Market, Hanworth and Suffield. Because of this overstepping of boundaries, it seems likely that about a third of Norfolk's rural parishes contained parkland at the beginning of this century.

Between 1720 and 1750, the English landscape witnessed a

great cultural revolution. Instead of imposing rigid geometrical patterns on the irregular countryside, landscape gardeners increasingly emphasised curves, irregularity, diversity, secrecy, attractive glimpses and, above all, 'naturalness'. In Alexander Pope's words, they were prepared to 'consult the genius of the place'. Such landscapes were still man-made and contrived, but give an air of enhancing and beautifying nature rather than ruthlessly strait-jacketing it. The three main ingredients of the new style were trees, grass and water, though buildings of various kinds could still make a telling contribution.

The sheer number of trees planted at this time is staggering. For example, at Holkham over twenty years (1781–1801), no fewer than 2,123,090 trees were planted on about 720 acres, mainly to establish huge outer belts around the extended park. Over forty species were represented of which the most common were ash, oak, sycamore, English elm, Scots pine and beech. Thus, an 'open and barren estate', which was virtually devoid of timber in 1730, had been transformed by massive labour and investment. Belts often had carriage-ways and walks in them, and their inner edges were usually sinuous or scalloped, to make them look more natural. Another important form of tree-planting, normally associated with Capability Brown but used earlier by William Kent, was the tree-clump. These were dotted around grassland, and were usually oval in plan. Large woods could also be found inside parks; at both Blickling and Gunton are 'Great Woods' which are probably medieval and manorial in origin. Finally, trees were often grouped behind a great house, as a dark-toned backcloth, or partly to mask other buildings such as churches and stables.

Just as the landscapers of the seventeenth century patronised commercial nurseries, or established their own private ones, so later owners invested heavily in the sowing and rearing of trees. For example, in the 1760s William Windham III employed as his agent Nathaniel Kent (no relation to William) who planted large areas at Felbrigg, especially on the higher ground behind the house. Although this destroyed a greatly valued view to the north over heathland and the sea, it created a magnificent new asset now known as the Great

Wood. Some of Kent's plantations can still be identified within the Great Wood, such as the Oval which took up four acres and was ringed by silver firs, and later by beeches. These famous plantations were sown with acorns, Spanish chestnuts and beech-mast, on land which had been fallowed and dunged by sheep. In his well known *Hints to Gentlemen* (1775) which is one of the bases of modern forestry, Kent, drawing on his experience at Felbrigg, encouraged landowners to plant more trees and to establish a proper rotation of planting and felling.

An influential figure, especially in the key area of North-East Norfolk, was Robert Marsham, squire of Stratton Strawless. He was a naturalist and writer who took a scientific interest in trees and timber production. He was also a friend of Windham and Kent (whose home was at Rippon Hall in Hevingham), and taught Humphry Repton while he lived at Sustead. Some of the trees which Marsham grew from seed in his own nursery are still flourishing, and his planting on the edge of a large heath running towards Norwich can still be appreciated along the boundary between Stratton Strawless and Horsford.

In the early to mid-nineteenth century, the investment in tree-planting reached its apogee. In 1849 R. N. Bacon wrote that scarcely a landed proprietor in Norfolk had not added to his woods: 'the face of the country has consequently been not only very much changed but has become richly adorned'. Although new species of plants and trees had been introduced into Britain for many centuries (for example, laurel and sweet chestnut in Roman times; laburnum, almond and quince in the Middle Ages; larch, horse chestnut and cedar of Lebanon in the seventeenth century), the trickle of imports turned into a flood in the nineteenth century. Whereas Capability Brown had ten species of pine from which to choose, his successors in the middle decades of the nineteenth century, in designing their fashionable 'arboreta' and 'pineta', had fifty. For example, the Douglas fir was introduced in about 1827, the Sitka spruce in 1831, Lawson's cypress and western hemlock in the 1850s, all from the north-western side of North America. Another major component of parks and woodland was the rhododendron which was first imported from the south-eastern side of the USA in 1809. So much, therefore, of the characteristic coloration of bark, leaf and flower, and so much of the varied architecture of woodland (with its mixture of rounded and pointed shapes), are due to these comparatively late introductions which changed the face of the English countryside.

Water in the form of streams, ponds and lakes was another major feature, even where it was not easy to find or retain in the drier and sandier parts of the county. Some parks, as at Gunton, had more than one large lake. Again, landscape designers were keen to make the scene look as natural as possible, and to get away from the aggressively formal 'canals' of earlier generations. Normally, small natural streams were dammed with banks of earth, so that the resulting lakes would fill natural valleys. Even so, quantities of earth were often moved and natural contours modified to create, for example, shorelines, promontories and islands.

At Kimberley, Launcelot Brown created a lake of twenty-eight acres where two streams converged in front of the house. At Holkham, thanks to the combined efforts of William Games and Brown, a lake over a mile long, sinuous, wooded and with three islands, was created out of a small sandy valley running into a muddy creek. At Narford, one of the largest lakes in the county covers seventy acres. On its very edge is a medieval church which had previously stood among hedged fields and meadows. At Blickling is a lake which in 1787 was described as 'one of the finest in the kingdom'. Over half a mile long and up to 400 yards wide, it lies in an attractive curving valley and is screened by mature woodland.

Lakes were still being created in Victorian and Edwardian times. In the 1860s a landscape architect called W. B. Thomas was employed at Sandringham to fill in an earlier lake judged to be too near the house, and to replace it by formal gardens. He created two curving lakes further south, with islands and a rock garden. At Sennowe Park near Fakenham a lake was dug as late as 1905 with the aid of steam engines and a miniature railway.

Sometimes, because of the lie of the land, lakes had to be well away from the house itself, as at Felbrigg and Melton Constable: in such cases the purchase of a yacht ensured that white sails could be seen from the house, even if water could not! Occasionally owners embarked on even more elaborate water-engineering. For example, at Westwick, water was raised for some fine gardens and hot-houses by two archimedian screws. Each lifted water eleven feet and fed channels and tunnels about three miles long.

Many different buildings and structures were placed in parks as focal points and 'eye-catchers', or to provide special facilities. For instance, by 1729, William Kent had built his obelisk and classical temple on a wooded hill overlooking Holkham Hall; also in the 1720s the park at Houghton was given a quadrangular block of stables which is more imposing than many a Norfolk mansion, and a water-tower looking like a classical temple, probably designed by the Earl of Pembroke; Capability Brown built a Gothic menagerie at Melton Constable in the 1760s; Joseph Bonomi constructed a stone pyramid at Blickling in 1793 as a mausoleum for the 2nd Earl of Buckinghamshire; and an observatory tower was added at Gunton in *c.* 1840. In many parks, medieval churches were deliberately retained as 'Gothick' features islanded in grass and trees as the park grew outwards, or as the village shifted to a new site. There they remain, half private chapels and half parish churches to which villagers respectfully walk through the squire's gates. Good examples can be seen all over the county such as Raveningham, Merton and Stradsett. The most evocative, however, is surely Ketteringham where the struggle between squire and parson has been immortalised in Owen Chadwick's *Victorian Miniature*.

Most of the great landscape designers of the eighteenth century worked in Norfolk. For instance, the best known master of the new English style, Launcelot or 'Capability' Brown, worked on at least four estates and possibly six. His first commission was at Holkham in 1762 for which he was paid nearly £3,000, and within a few years he was also working at Kimberley, Langley and Melton Constable. It is also possible that he was employed at Honing and Ditchingham. More significant is the contribution of Humphry Repton who, in the earlier part of his life, lived in Norwich and then at Old Hall, Sustead. Although he took to landscaping at the relatively late age of thirty-nine, he soon built up a large following and worked on at least sixteen estates in Norfolk, mostly in the north and north-east. It was said that because of his love for Norfolk, he always charged local owners less than his normal fees. He worked on large parks at Blickling and Holkham, but also on relatively small ones at Northrepps, Honing, Hoveton St John and Bracondale. Being a competent water-colourist he developed the technique of writing and illustrating a 'Red Book' for each estate, which summarised his proposals; his illustrations had hinged flaps which enabled the owner to compare the view before and after improvement.

Sheringham Hall or 'Bower' is perhaps the best surviving example of Repton's work, and was his own personal favourite (Plate 36). Its Red Book of 1812 was printed by J. C. Loudon in the 1830s and has been recently reprinted in facsimile. By a few deft touches, Repton converted an area of woodland and farmland into a park of unparalleled beauty. The owners, Abbot Upcher and his newly married wife, thought this relatively small piece of undulating countryside 'a Paradise', but they did not want to continue living in the old farmhouse which was quite close to the village of Upper Sheringham. The new house which Repton designed with his son, John Adey Repton, was a modest but comfortable classical building; begun in 1813, it is H-shaped in plan and its main front has a portico and verandah. It faces slightly east of south, which was Repton's favourite aspect, and in so doing turns its back on the sea only three-quarters of a mile away. Repton argued that 'a view of the sea . . . ought not to be the first consideration' and would leave the house too exposed to the elements, especially in winter. In fact, the house was deliberately sited on the inland side of an isolated knoll called Oak Hill, and looks southwards across a park of grass and trees to the wooded escarpment of Howe's Hill.

Much of the woodland was already mature, but Repton thickened and extended it, for example by planting newly imported types of rhododendron, and made small changes to woodland drives and walks. Immediately in front of the new house, a few hedgelines were destroyed or thinned out, to convert meadows into grassy parkland studded with a few trees. Two main approaches to the house were laid out: one

Plate 33 Houghton Hall: fitting home for England's first Prime Minister. In the main block, west front, observe how the windows, steps (restored 1973) and rusticated ground-floor all draw attention to the state-rooms on the first-floor.

Plate 34 New Houghton: Norfolk's first estate-village, begun 1729. Twenty-four brick houses and eight almshouses were grouped symmetrically along the main approach to Houghton, just outside the park-gates. They replaced the medieval village, which was too close to the new Hall.

Plate 35 Bylaugh Hall: a Victorian masterpiece designed by Charles Barry, Junior, and built 1849-52 for the Rev. Evans-Lombe, whose wealth derived from northern industry. Now abandoned, like at least a score of Norfolk country-houses, and derelict.

Plate 36 Sheringham Bower: Humphry Repton's painting of 1812 showing the superb view which he proposed from the southern approach – over the new Hall, park and sea.

Plate 37 Melton Constable: Nature in subjection. John Kip's engraving of 1707 shows the earlier, geometrical layout of Melton Park, dominated by straight avenues focussing on the Hall itself.

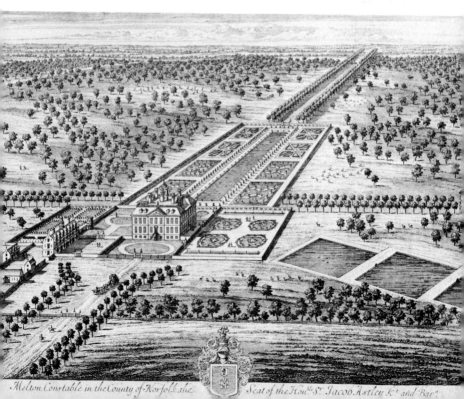

Melton Constable in the County of Norfolk, the   Seat of the Honble Sr. Jacob Astley Kt. and Bart.

Plate 38 King's Lynn: a stone house of *c.* 1200, with Gothic window, doorway and ashlar masonry, discovered when rendering was removed. Thanks to bureaucratic muddling this monument of national importance was tragically demolished in 1977.

Plate 39 Litcham: superficially a pair of Victorian cottages, this building reveals, in its gable-end, that it began as a single-storeyed house, probably before 1700, and has had at least two major remodellings since then.

from the old farm and village which was screened by a new plantation, and the other from a major road junction on the top of Howe's Hill. This descended the escarpment among woods, and then swung round a dramatic corner which Repton deliberately deepened into a cutting to reveal a superb view of the house, its rolling park, the wooded backcloth of Oak Hill and, beyond, the North Sea.

Parks in the landscape today are symbols of former wealth, power and taste. Never again, since the eighteenth and nineteenth centuries, have landowners managed so successfully to combine economic self-interest with ideas of enhancing and improving nature. The contrast with today's attitudes is startling. Yet this exercise of economic and political power had another side to it. Towards the end of his life, Thomas Coke wrote thus: 'It is a melancholy thing to stand alone in one's own Country. I look around, not a house to be seen but my own. I am Giant, of Giant Castle, and have ate up all my neighbours.'

The smaller domestic buildings

Though buildings threatened with destruction are now being recorded, and major surveys have already taken place in King's Lynn and Norwich, the study of Norfolk's smaller domestic, or 'vernacular', architecture is still in its infancy. The sheer number of historical houses, farms and cottages is staggering: many of them are not officially 'listed' and comparatively few have been properly investigated. They range in date from at least the fourteenth century through to the nineteenth, involve several different styles and plans, and are made of a fascinating variety of local materials.

Archaeological evidence, out of which the study of standing buildings must grow, suggests that most village houses in the Middle Ages were single-storeyed structures of timber, clay and thatch. At Thuxton, for instance, a complete croft of a deserted village was excavated in 1963–4. It contained the remains of two apparently contemporary houses (*c.* 1250–1350) which measured forty by seventeen feet and thirty-three by eighteen feet. Both were timber framed on a foundation of flint and clay. On the other three sides of a ditched

199

courtyard lay barns or animal sheds. Such farmsteads were probably commonplace in Norfolk, and were clearly not in the long-house tradition whereby animals were housed under the same roof as human beings. Early maps suggest that smaller and less substantial houses also existed, which would probably have had a short life and were frequently replaced.

Nevertheless, the lesser gentry and their wealthier tenants had timber-framed houses of a more solid kind, particularly in the fourteenth and fifteenth centuries. Numbers of these have survived and are now being recognised, for example Hall Farm at Garveston, the Grange at Bressingham, Williams Manor at Forncett St Peter and houses of Wealden type at Long Stratton and New Buckenham. Though these buildings vary in scale and plan, the dominant feature is a barn-like living room called the 'hall', which was open to the underside of the roof and heated by an open hearth. Later, halls were normally subdivided by inserting floors and partitions, so it is especially instructive to see them occasionally restored to their original dimensions, as in the miniature but perfect Bretts Manor at Wacton Common (Plates 40 and 42). At each end of a medieval hall one usually finds a two-storeyed section: one contained service rooms on the ground floor and chambers above, while the other contained a parlour to which the family could retire, again with chambers above. Many of these medieval houses must still await recognition behind later façades, particularly in the south of the county where early timber work has not been so frequently replaced.

From about 1500, a desire for more rooms, greater privacy and better forms of heating stimulated new ideas of design. At Thetford, for example, the Ancient House shows how a prosperous merchant chose to live in the early sixteenth century. Its ground plan looks medieval with a large hall, an entrance passage divided from the hall by a heavy oak screen, and two rooms at the lower end, one of which was probably a shop against the street. There the resemblance ends, for the hall was heated by a large brick fireplace and has a carved and moulded ceiling with a chamber above. Externally, the house has a continuous overhang ('jetty') at first-floor level, which indicates that the hall was never of the open medieval kind.

Perhaps the most common kind of new house was the

so-called 'Type J' and its derivatives, which have three major rooms on the ground floor and three above, and include an internal chimney stack (Plate 41). This plan was popular over several centuries from the reign of Elizabeth I until the end of the seventeenth century, and can be found in many parishes south of Norwich. For instance, Manor Farm at Pulham Market is a timber-framed house of about 1600, with close studding, arched fireplaces, panelled partitions and attics; the only hang-over from medieval planning is the inclusion of a screens passage between two external doors. Dairy Farm, Tacolneston, represents a variant with brick gables and timber sidewalls.

The techniques and organisation needed to 'raise' timber frames are sometimes revealed by financial accounts kept for institutional or parochial buildings. Thus, when the parish of Deopham decided to build a 'town house' in 1584, the total cost came to just over eighteen pounds, of which five pounds was for timber, and the job which took seventy days involved carpenters, 'claymen', labourers and carters. Furthermore, once houses were erected, they were frequently altered and modernised (Plate 39). For example, a new rector at North Barsham in 1614 wanted to improve his parsonage, so he erected new partitions, glazed windows which previously many only have had internal shutters, and inserted a ceiling over his parlour chamber so that he did not have to lie in bed and see the rafters.

The vernacular architecture of Norfolk is divided into two major zones. Approximately south of a line formed by the A11 and the river Yare, one sees large numbers of timber-framed houses ranging in date from medieval to seventeenth century. Many of them are substantial structures that have been adapted, increased in size and often re-faced according to changing fashion, but have never been totally rebuilt. They reflect the fact that, for centuries adequate supplies of timber were locally available from well managed woods. In the rest of the county, however, one is conscious that most houses are rather later in date, from the late seventeenth century onwards, and that the dominant building materials are locally made bricks and rolled pebbles.

It does not follow, of course, that timbered buildings never

201

existed away from the south, or that none actually survives today. At East Rudham, for instance, David Yaxley recently recorded a timber frame embedded in two brick cottages which superficially looked early nineteenth century. A survey of the Houghton estate in 1800 shows that more timber framing was then visible in that same corner of Norfolk. Indeed, timber houses, particularly when they are of higher than average quality, can survive anywhere: witness the Ancient House in Thetford, or Bishop Bonner's Cottage at East Dereham with its fine external plasterwork depicting fruit and flowers, or the town of Little Walsingham which has a surprisingly high proportion of timbered jettied houses.

This interesting dichotomy in the vernacular architecture of Norfolk brings us to W. G. Hoskins' concept of the great rebuilding of rural England. He argued that in most parts of England, local people felt wealthy and secure enough to rebuild their houses in the years 1570 to 1640. Since Hoskins wrote in 1953, however, other historians have pointed out that the 'great rebuilding' often happened *after* 1640, and furthermore that a region can display more than one wave of major rebuilding. In the greater part of Norfolk, north of the A11 and Yare, the main period of rebuilding certainly seems to be as late as 1660–1750. The red brick and tiled farmhouse of the early eighteenth century is a quintessential component of Norfolk's character (Plates 46, 47). Of two or two and a half storeys, its brick façade displays decoration ranging from simple string-courses, dentilation and segmental window heads to more elaborate cornices, pedimented door frames and quoins. Gables are usually straight-sided though a size-able minority are curved and stepped, and remind one of Holland. It should also be said that buildings superficially of this kind can turn out, on deeper investigation, to be remod-ellings of earlier structures, rather than totally new.

Such large scale rebuilding of villages and farms in durable brick depended on the widespread exploitation of local clays and brickearths. Though bricks had been made in Norfolk since the Middle Ages, the eighteenth century must have seen a rapid increase in the number of brickmakers or 'brickburn-ers', kilns and brickpits. Typically when in 1710 the Hobart family built a new barn at Great Park Farm, Wymondham, they fired 78,000 bricks on the site and paid three men to prepare over 7,000 faggots as fuel for the kiln. Hand-made bricks of this period range in colour from orange to deep red, and are usually from 2″–2½″ thick. Also in the eighteenth century the traditional steeply pitched covering of reed or straw gave way to various kinds of baked tile, which could be on as shallow a slope as thirty degrees. Large curved pantiles became fashionable, mostly red though sometimes of the more expensive dark-blue, glazed to prevent frost-cracking.

In the period of the 'great rebuilding', another favourite material was flint and other stone in the form of rounded pebbles or cobbles, which were gathered on Norfolk's beaches and sometimes carted many miles inland. In places like Weybourne on the coast or Hunworth inland, these sea-worn and patinated stones are the favourite building material, and their chalky or silvery colour combines beautifully with the reds and oranges of local bricks and tiles. In each wall a particular size of stone was used, but between different buildings the variation of size can be considerable. Invariably a cobbled wall is faced by brick at the corners and around doors and windows. This attractive combination of materials and colours continued in use after 1750, and large numbers of early-nineteenth-century cottages and post-enclosure farmhouses were built in the same way.

Another important building material, used from the Middle Ages to the twentieth century, was clay-lump. This consisted of large blocks of puddled clay and chopped straw, which were made in wooden moulds and allowed to dry naturally for one or two months. A standard size was eighteen by six by six inches. Particularly used in cottages and outbuildings, clay-lump was protected by a plinth of brick or flint, overhanging eaves and an outer skin of clay or tar.

How can this rebuilding in the period 1660 to 1750 be explained economically and socially? Presumably it must be connected with the emergence of great estates, and with the reorganisation and increasing profitability of larger scale farming in the late seventeenth and early eighteenth centuries. Earlier buildings of timber, clay and plaster must have existed, but a new prosperity and rising standard of living gave the confidence to rebuild on a large scale. An early shortage of timber in parts of the county (for example in Marshland, the Good Sands and the North-east) may also have resulted in the erection of less substantial buildings, which were less desirable to keep and easier to demolish. Meanwhile, in the south, the timber-framed legacy survived without wholesale replacement. Most of those buildings had been erected from the fifteenth to the seventeenth centuries: they may also be the result of a major campaign of rebuilding, or perhaps of more than one, in Elizabethan and Jacobean times for example, or even in the fifteenth century.

Finally, we must acknowledge that other waves of rebuilding, or building anew, have happened since 1750. For example, in the early nineteenth century large numbers of cottages and rows were built to accommodate an expanding rural population (see p. 243). Most of them can be seen as part of the vernacular tradition for they were made of local bricks, flint, clay-lump and reed – at a time when alien materials such as slate and mass-produced bricks were making their first appearance. Again, since the Second World War, many of Norfolk's villages and market towns have undergone massive rebuilding and expansion, the scale of which has been unprecedented. Nevertheless, in the same period, considerable numbers of people have taken up the challenge of restoring older buildings. Although many have failed disastrously, the more sensitive have soon learnt that success depends on understanding the methods and values of earlier generations – that is, the 'vernacular tradition'.

SELECT BIBLIOGRAPHY

Aslet, Clive, *The Last Country Houses* (1982).

Bradfer-Lawrence, H. L., 'The building of Raynham Hall', *Norfolk Archaeology*, XXIII (1928) 93–145.

Burke's & Savills Guide to Country Houses, Vol. III, East Anglia (1981).

Carter, George, Goode, Patrick, Laurie, Kedrun, *Humphry Repton, Landscape Gardener, 1752–1818* (1983).

Franklin, Jill, *The Gentleman's Country House, 1835–1914* (1981).

Glendinning, S. E., 'Manor Farm, Pulham Market', *Norfolk Archaeology*, 30 (1951), 223–25.

Pevsner, N., *Buildings of England, Norfolk*, 2 vols (1962).

14. Farms and drains

Drainage and reclamation.

In the seventeenth century the social and economic changes apparent in earlier times gathered pace. Of particular importance was the emergence of great estates in the hands of powerful families such as the Townshends and Cokes, and those changes of agricultural practice which are described as the Agricultural Revolution and were once confined to the eighteenth century alone. Various factors lay behind these developments, such as runs of bad harvests and a marked fall in agricultural prices, especially for grain and wool, which lasted until *c.* 1750. The cumulative effect was to drive out smaller farmers so that, in terms of farming families and holdings, the depopulation which began in the mid-fourteenth century continued in bursts whenever conditions deteriorated. A report for the Horsford estate, made in 1696, showed how landlords positively preferred fewer, more substantial tenant farmers; otherwise 'you must deal with pedling and triffling fellows who will take your land for a tyme and starve it'. This was especially true of open-field or 'champion' areas like the Breckland or Good Sands, where the landlord with his aggressive use of commons and foldcourses usually had an advantage over small producers. Indeed, in the seventeenth century we must look for that fascinating economic watershed between the older manorial agriculture based on copyhold tenure and a new system of rationalised tenant farms.

The enclosure of land within hedges and ditches continued steadily on all save the lightest soils. While most of South Norfolk was probably enclosed by 1600, large parts of the centre and east followed in the next century. For example, successive maps show that Longham was almost completely enclosed by the early eighteenth century. The process had probably been going on spasmodically for three centuries or more, and was no doubt encouraged by the Coke family after they bought the manor in 1610. On similar lines, seventeenth-century maps of Cawston and Haveringland show large blocks of enclosed land eating into extensive open fields. The accounts of various travellers and commentators attest the same trends. For instance, Thomas Skippon in 1668 described South Norfolk, between Attleborough and Diss, as for the most part in meadows or pasture; further north, up to the Wensum valley, he still found 'good enclosed country'.

The actual mechanics of enclosure varied from place to place. In parishes where the population was low, as in many parts of the Good Sands and Breckland, it was no great problem for a landlord to buy or take in land from his struggling tenants and smaller competitors, and then to enclose as a personal decision. Sometimes, however, agreement was necessary between the lord and his surviving tenants. For example, a Chancery decree of 1627 for an unknown Norfolk parish records that the whole community had agreed to enclose as 'It would raise and turne to a far greater benefitt to every of them then the enjoyinge of it in common'. At Kenninghall in 1610 the townspeople purchased the sheep-walk and so made their land 'whole-year'. Similarly parsons were sometimes able to consolidate their glebes and enclose them, as at Hargham in 1697–8.

Against this topographical background, it is no surprise to learn that farming was becoming more innovatory and specialised. By the end of the seventeenth century, Norfolk not only had many distinctive landscape regions, but several different styles and blends of farming. For example, the area around Walsingham was noted for its saffron, sold at about twenty-seven shillings per pound, and Stiffkey Hall in 1636 had special 'saffron chambers' and kilns for drying this valuable crop. Clover, sanfoin and turnips were being grown as fodder crops on the Good Sands by the mid-seventeenth century, and the 'champion country' generally was renowned for barley and malt. Large amounts of surplus grain were regularly exported from Lynn and a chain of small ports along the north coast. North-east Norfolk and Flegg also yielded abundant corn and were described as 'the most fruitfull, fatt and mouldie of any part in England'; the land was so easy to work that one horse 'though but a jade' was quite sufficient to pull an improved Norfolk plough. Meanwhile the Marshland and fens grew vast quantities of hemp, flax, rape, oats and woad. The heavier lands in the woodland half of the county were noted for their butter and cheese, most of which was sent to London. (Norfolk cheese was described by contemporaries as having a white colour.) Similarly, coastal districts were said to produce the best honey.

Agricultural methods and practices were also changing. Seed-drills and horse-hoes were being used on certain estates before the end of the seventeenth century; improved rotations were agreed between landlords and farmers and carefully enshrined in leases; drains filled with brushwood and straw were making heavy land more tractable; the ancient practice of marling, used in Norfolk from at least the thirteenth century, was greatly intensified in order to make light land more productive. Meanwhile, coastal marshes and fenland were being increasingly used for the fattening of cattle, which were often driven on foot from northern England and Scotland. For example, Setchey on the edge of the peat fenland was noted for its 'rich pasturage' for large herds of cattle.

Nor was the natural harvest of wildfowl neglected. The first duck decoy in England is said to have been made at Waxham in the reign of James I, and others were created in various low-lying parts of Norfolk down to the nineteenth century. One of the most famous, Micklemere in Wretham Park, remained in use until this century. Such ponds had a complicated system of curving side-channels, tunnels of netting, and screens, so that birds could be lured into the tunnels and trapped in the nets.

The fattening of large numbers of cattle led to a progressive improvement of low-lying pasture. Along the North Alluvial Plain, individual owners were reclaiming marshland from the sea by building costly walls and cutting ditches. For example, John Coke reclaimed 360 acres at Holkham in 1660 and another 670 acres were taken in sixty years later. At Salthouse a Dutch expert, John Van Hasedunck, was employed. In 1637 Sir Henry Calthorpe threw up a bank between Wiveton Hall and the quay at Cley, to reclaim marshes in the lower Glaven valley, but objectors argued that it would encourage the silting of Cley harbour and it was therefore removed (to be built again in the nineteenth century).

In the east of Norfolk, vast tracts of pasture and marshland had been in use since at least Saxon times, and slowly improved over the centuries by the piecemeal digging of drains and embanking of rivers (Plate 15). Defoe unequivocally described the area as 'the richest meadows and largest . . . that are anywhere in England', but such riches were constantly under threat. In the seventeenth century, for example, the sea regularly breached coastal dunes and manmade defences. One of the worst disasters was in 1609 when seventy-six parishes were affected, mainly in the valleys of the Waveney, Yare, Bure, Thurne and Ant. An act was subsequently passed 'for the Speedye Recoverye of manye thousand Acres of Marsh Groundes . . . latelye surrounded by the Rage of the Sea'. The main weakness was between Winterton and Happisburgh where the shore was flat and the sand dunes were easily washed away. Commissioners had to survey the damage, decide liabilities and costs, and to repair the breaches by 'Peres, Wals, Jettes, Pyles, Strengthes, Fortificaccions, Defences and other thinges whatsoever'. This did not prevent recurrent crises and, even though the defences generally held in the later seventeenth century, a new round of trouble began soon after 1700.

The main defences were sand dunes fortified by piles and rails. The latter held down faggots and were consolidated by stones and clay. 'Hedges' of faggots helped to catch windblown sand, while marram grass and brambles were encouraged to stabilise the surface. Windpumps, that is windmills driving scoop-wheels, were suggested for the marshes as early as 1625 but the earliest surviving example, at Oby, is dated 1753. Although numbers of these pumps were built in the eighteenth century, the situation gradually got worse. In 1784 the curate of Horsey, who had to ride over regularly from Winterton, complained that several times he had narrowly escaped drowning. Faden's map of 1797 shows about nine breaches along that vulnerable coast. It was not until the early nineteenth century that a new Commission of Sewers was able to control the menace of flooding. Under the direction of an eminent geologist, William Smith, the line of irregular sand banks was converted into a broad bank of uniform height, which is still one of the sights of the county. At the same time greater investment was put into internal drains, under-draining, the top-dressing of grass and, from the 1840s, into steampumps which supplemented the earlier technology of wind power. The marshes were divided into 'fields' of ten to fifty acres by man-made ditches five to ten feet wide and, although the soft soil compacted and fell in level, the system of embankments and drainage ensured luxuriant grazing for large numbers of cattle, horses and, to a lesser extent, sheep. William Marshall in 1795 described the life of the 'marsh-men', tending their animals, selling their noted 'hay butter' at Yarmouth and living in lonely cottages surrounded by flat expanses of grass and water.

Drainage and reclamation

Although many people thought, with Camden, that man should not 'intermeddle at all with that which God has ordained', vast works of drainage and reclamation were undertaken in the Peat Fens during the seventeenth century. A contemporary map of Hilgay Fen shows the situation faced by those who wanted improvement. A large common fen of about 1,300 acres was surrounded by private or 'several' fens which were embanked, drained by 'lodes' and entered by 'droves'. As lord of the manor, Sir Henry Willoughby had driven a 'cutt' right across the common fen (now followed by Main Engine Drain) to drain that and his main 'several'. Most of the early lodes are still embedded in the later system of dykes and have a 'primary' or even natural look. They are mostly sinuous rather than straight, and sometimes coincide with parish boundaries (for example, May Lode which forms the boundary between Hilgay and Welney).

The desire to avoid regular flooding and to make land more productive led to endless discussion and to the production of conflicting reports, surveys, and pamphlets. For example, Mr Richard Atkyns of Outwell published a report on 'fenny grounds' in 1604. Occasionally, talk led to positive action. Dugdale records that, in the early 1600s, a group of London businessmen reclaimed 3,000 acres of Upwell Fen, creating 'Londoners Fen' from the Upwell-Welney causeway in the west to Denver Common in the east. In so doing they probably created Cock Fen Drove which still survives today, but the drains broke down and local people opposed the scheme. In 1605, Sir John Popham, Lord Chief Justice, and other investors were more successful. With the consent of the commissioners of sewers they constructed a major drain called Popham's Eau which still substantially survives. This ran straight for over five miles from the river Nene in the west to a great convergence of watercourses at Nordelph in the east. The purpose was presumably to divert floodwater from the Nene towards the New Podike and Great Ouse, and also to drain a notorious morass known, significantly, as 'crosse water'. However, all these schemes were localised and piecemeal, 'pretending the benefit of the whole countrey thereby, but intending a private end'.

The first really comprehensive scheme for improving the drainage of the peat fens came in 1630 under an agreement known as the 'Lynn Law'. A group of investors headed by the fourth Earl of Bedford employed a Dutch engineer, Cornelius Vermuyden, to plan a system which would drain 190,000 acres. He imaginatively suggested a long straight cut of twenty-one miles from near Earith to Denver – two-thirds in Cambridgeshire and one-third in Norfolk. It was designed to take floodwater more directly towards the Ouse estuary or 'outfall', and at the same time to steepen the gradient. The old winding course of the Great Ouse around the Isle of Ely was to be effectively bypassed. In 1631 the 'Old Bedford River', as it was later known, was completed. It was seventy feet wide, streaking as straight as an arrow across the flat expanses of the fens, and still one of the most astonishing human achievements in the East Anglian landscape. A contemporary described 'lusty sweating Pioneers hard at worke, digging, delving, casting up and quartering out new streams and Rivers'.

At the same time, another important drain was cut in Norfolk, across Methwold and Feltwell fens. Known as Sams' Cut, it drained north-westwards into the Great Ouse below Ten Mile Bank, and ran almost straight for about seven miles,

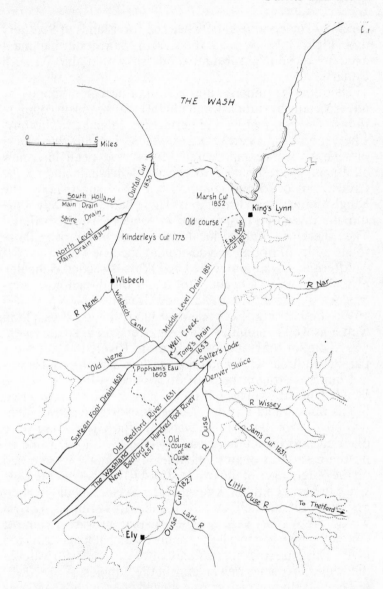

Fig. 18. The Norfolk Fenland and its environs: showing principal water-courses, natural and artificial (after H. C. Darby).

211

carefully angled to pass between the two islands of Southery and Hilgay. Also by 1636, the Earl of Manchester had managed to reclaim a substantial marsh within the Wisbech estuary.

These major undertakings were not accepted happily by all, especially by ordinary fenland folk who relied on common rights. The contractors had permission to make drains anywhere, and to take earth from anywhere, but only the owners of 'severals' were compensated. Most serious of all, large new allotments were granted to private individuals and to the Crown, out of former common fens. Not surprisingly, the King's Council soon learnt that 'There hath been lately some tumults raysed and force used in some parts of Norffolk.' They therefore ordered local magistrates to imprison those found guilty of rioting and destroying the new works.

After the disruption of the Civil Wars, a second campaign of reclamation was begun, still under the direction of Vermuyden. A new act for draining the Great Level was passed in 1649, emphasising that reclaimed land should be usable in winter as well as summer. The engineers' main achievement was to dig, in 1651, the 'New' Bedford River, 100 feet wide, parallel with the 'Old' and on its eastern side. Its course was not quite as straight because of obstacles which had to be avoided, like the village of Mepal, but generally the two great drains ran parallel about 1,000 yards apart. The New River was open at both ends: the waters of the Great Ouse were diverted into its southern end by Hunters Sluice, while its northern end was open to the tides. High banks were raised on the outer edges of the two Bedford Rivers so that the wide space in between them, known as the Washes, could be used as a reservoir and deliberately flooded. In Vermuyden's own words, the Washes were designed 'so that the water in time of Extremity may goe in a large roome to keep it from rising too high'. This long strip of grassland, often covered with water in the winter, becomes rich grazing in the summer.

The Old Bedford River was sluiced at both ends, and was brought into use in time of flood. Similarly, the great loop of the Ouse cut off by the Bedford River was converted into the main drain of the south-eastern fenland (called the South Level). It was cut off near the western end of the Isle of Ely by

Hermitage Sluice, so that its waters were diverted down the New Bedford, while its northern end was controlled by the famous Denver Sluice (Plate 25) built in 1650–1. This lower sluice was not welcomed by towns like Cambridge and Thetford which saw their navigational interests threatened, and it was blamed for both the deterioration of the natural river and the silting of the estuary. It was 'blown up' in 1713, when freshwater floods coincided with high tides but, after another round of arguments, was rebuilt in 1748–50.

The New Bedford was not the only achievement of this period in Norfolk. Below Denver Sluice and on the east side of the Ouse, St John Eau was dug to Stowbridge to cope with freshwater flooding when the main river was full. Also, to take the pressure of waters from the Middle Level converging on the New Podike and Salter's Lode, Tong's Drain was cut in 1653. This was a double channel with sluices at both ends, and it too was provided with a 'wash' inside strong banks, so that it could act as a reservoir when the risk of flooding was at its greatest.

As a result of this work, large blocks of fenland were allotted to the investors or 'adventurers', and can still be traced in parishes like Feltwell, Methwold, Hilgay and Welney. Some impression is left on local place names (for instance, King's Land in Methwold) but more important is the pattern of fields and drains within the allotments. For example, in the middle of Methwold Fen, to the south of Sams' Cut, the adventurers created a ladder pattern of main drains and cross-drains, and 'fields' which were smaller and squarer than nineteenth-century reclamations further east.

SELECT BIBLIOGRAPHY

Darby, H. C., *The Changing Fenland* (1983).
Darby, H. C., *The Draining of the Fens* (1956).
Plumb, J. H., 'Sir Robert Walpole and Norfolk Husbandry', *Economic History Review*, 2nd series, 5–6 (1952–54), 86–166.
Saunders, H. W., 'Estate management at Raynham . . . 1661–86 and 1706', *Norfolk Archaeology*, XIX (1917), 39–66.
Thirsk, Joan, *The Agrarian History of England and Wales, Vol IV, 1500–1640*, 40–49.
Wells, Samuel, *History of the . . . Bedford Level*, 2 vols (1830).

15. The setting of Norfolk husbandry

The Good Sands.   The new Breckland.
Agricultural improvement elsewhere.   Fenland under
threat.   Improved communications.

IN THE EIGHTEENTH and nineteenth centuries even more profound changes overtook Norfolk's farming landscape as landowners and farmers seized new economic opportunities to improve their estates and farms. As before, many of the changes involved enclosure. At first this was done by private and local arrangement, mostly on a piecemeal basis and without the help of a parliamentary act. Thus Tittleshall in Mid-Norfolk, the ancient home and burial place of the Coke family, was finally enclosed by 1779, and at Felbrigg William Windham III completed the enclosure of his parish by buying the scattered lands of a young yeoman and establishing him in a newly consolidated farm. Local acts of parliament which legalised enclosure did not become commonplace until after 1770 (although Stokesby had one as early as 1720). By 1800 about seventy such acts had been passed for Norfolk; most of them related to a single parish, though a substantial minority covered two or more. The climax came in the period 1800–20 when about 200 acts were passed as the farming community responded energetically to higher prices and increased demand during the Napoleonic Wars. The pace slowed after 1820 and seventy more enclosures were achieved in the next fifty years, mostly as a result of general acts which were passed from 1836 onwards in order to simplify and cheapen the process. The last enclosure in the county related to Saxlingham Common in 1873. By that time about 400 parishes had been parliamentarily 'enclosed' in some way or other.

Enclosure acts and the resultant awards had five main

effects. First, they converted open fields into better shaped fields totally under private control. The largest acreages which remained were on the lighter soils: for example Northwold on the Breckland had 3,000 acres of open field to enclose in 1798, while Horsham north of Norwich divided 1,022 acres in 1802. Second, half-year lands, in which people other than the main tenants had rights of pasture for part of the year, were extinguished. Third, parcels of land which were dispersed and intermixed – whether arable, meadow or 'old enclosures' – were re-alloted. Fourth, a huge acreage of common land was ploughed, sometimes undoubtedly for the first time ever, and converted to conveniently sized fields. Finally, the opportunity was taken to improve the drainage of marshes and fens, whether on the coast or along major and minor valleys. This was normally done by digging ditches, underdraining and raising embankments. In Broadland, acts also provided for the digging of navigable dykes and the construction of staithes, so that barges could take out agricultural produce such as grain and malt and bring in heavy goods like coal, marl and timber.

The most dramatic effect was undoubtedly the rapid disappearance of common land in the shape of greens, road verges, heaths, warrens or sheepwalks. Although of course local lords and their tenants had enclosed and encroached upon commons for centuries, Nathaniel Kent in 1794 calculated that Norfolk still had 143,000 acres of 'waste', and Faden on his map of 1797 also shows how numerous, and sometimes extensive, the commons were, even in the anciently enclosed south. However, by the end of the eighteenth century common land had acquired a bad reputation among agricultural pundits, and was often associated with pauperism and crime. As Kent said, 'the larger the common, the greater number and more miserable are the poor'. So these areas of permanent grazing, bequeathed from medieval or earlier times, were quickly converted into farmland and ploughed. An American traveller in 1810 described how heaths near Oxborough were being broken up by breast-ploughs, and the turf then burnt in smoking heaps. By 1844 it was calculated that only 27,000 acres remained, which meant that over eighty per cent of the commons had disappeared in fifty years.

Furthermore the attrition continued and a large acreage was requisitioned during the Second World War. Today Norfolk has roughly 8,000 acres left of its ancient common land.

Occasionally the loss of commons led to open protest and even violence. For example the village of Ashill near Watton developed a remarkable radical tradition in the nineteenth century. An anonymous letter sent to a local newspaper in 1816 accused local farmers of greedy exploitation and threatened them with violence and death: "You do as you like, you rob the poor of their commons right, plough the grass up that God sent to grow . . . [and] lay muck and stones on the road to prevent grass growing.' At Swaffham in 1869 grievances were orchestrated by a local coachbuilder and led to the appointment of a parliamentary select committee. As a result fifty acres of the common were earmarked for allotments and a further five acres for recreation. At Fakenham in the following year, stakes and railings dividing the common were actually pulled up and burnt, and a local association was formed for the 'Defence of the Rights of the Poor'. Enclosure, however, was not averted in spite of the words of a local protest song, 'Don't be fidgety, we shall get our common back again.'

When open fields or commons were enclosed, the result was generally a geometric landscape which bore all the marks of having been designed first on a drawing board. Large rectangular fields were defined by ditches and banks whose dimensions were normally specified in the relevant act. Ditches were usually three to five feet wide and two to three and a half feet deep. New hedges were normally planted on the banks, or rather at the top of the scarp above the ditch: they consisted mainly of whitethorn planted at six-inch intervals and more widely spaced trees such as oak or holly. Laying or plashing of hedges was not a Norfolk tradition, and they were usually cut back to the stub every twenty or thirty years, or were 'buckstalled' by cutting off the top about two feet above the bank. In some coastal parts of the county, hedges were not necessarily planted and bare banks were the main divisions between fields – 'mere mud walls' as Marshall called them. At the same time new roads and tracks, public and private, were laid out with constant and specified widths, and old roads were frequently straightened and narrowed. It is therefore a frequent experience in Norfolk to be driving along a twisting country road which suddenly changes character: to run in either straight lengths connected by sharp angles, or to run dead straight for half-a-mile or more, as between Hindolveston and Fulmodeston or between Hingham and Great Ellingham. One can usually see that the fields on each side of the straight are distinctly regular and geometric in plan, and realises that one is crossing a former open field or a common.

Other landscape features characteristic of this period, though not necessarily of parliamentary enclosure, are the numerous plantations and coverts established to encourage game. They were often planted on former commons, and their names frequently show the connection: witness Witton Heath, Eccles Common and Shouldham Warren which are all heavily planted with trees today. By the mid-nineteenth century Norfolk had a great reputation as a game county, in which landowners and tenants (with their new-fangled breach-loaders and percussion caps) could get good sport and where poaching became a way of life among the lower orders.

Norfolk also has thousands of pits from which 'marl' was extracted in the eighteenth and nineteenth centuries: in some areas one sees one or more pits to each field. Of course the digging of marl had been carried on since at least the Middle Ages, but it was especially needed to improve the texture of farmland when open fields and commons were enclosed. In talking of the successful farmers of West Norfolk, Arthur Young had no doubt that 'marling is the great foundation of their wealth'. Cartloads varied from 7 to 120 per acre, and the effect was expected to last twenty years or more. If the marl-pit was close to the field, then twenty-five to thirty loads could be carted in a day. The actual material varied from one district to another: for instance a hard chalk was dug around Swaffham, a chalky clay at Thorpe Market, soft chalk at Thorpe-next-Norwich, and clay at Hemsby in Flegg. In addition farmers also used the rubble of old buildings known as 'mergin' and great quantities of 'town muck' from Norwich which were carried by barge to agricultural parishes in east Norfolk. Today marl-pits are being deliberately filled and ploughed out, but large numbers are still visible as tree-filled depressions or as ponds. They represent, as John Sell Cotman's painting of 1808 reminds us, an enormous investment of human time and labour. However, they should not be confused with other kinds of excavation such as ponds for watering animals, pits for the extraction of clay and daub, and the remains of medieval moats – all of which are common, particularly on the heavier lands.

Before the late eighteenth century, farms tended to be rather haphazard and unplanned collections of buildings of different dates. This is beautifully illustrated in a survey of the Houghton estate, written *c*. 1800. From the 1790s, however, farmsteads were frequently replanned and rebuilt, especially on major estates. Compact, geometrical layouts were recommended in order to make the running of the farm as efficient as possible. Durable materials were used such as locally made brick, cobbles and tile, and concrete made its first appearance in the 1870s. Cattle sheds were increasingly built around yards, in order to conserve manure, while implement sheds faced outwards towards the fields. On the largest farms, the number of buildings could be surprisingly high: for example in the later nineteenth century Henry Overman's farm at Weasenham had sixty-seven different features including a knife house, apple house, a building for sick cattle and three 'lying-in hospitals' for cows. But the most obtrusive building on most farms was undoubtedly the barn.

Norfolk still has many fine barns of timber, brick, flint and other stone, built at various times from the fifteenth to the eighteenth centuries. Good examples can be seen at Hales (Plate 43), Paston and Dersingham. Yet it was from the 1790s that the county acquired a national reputation for its barns, 'superior to those of every other county'. Farmers preferred them to stacks in the open air, and they had to be large enough to accommodate the unthreshed corn from expanding acreages. The largest, as at Syderstone or South Creake, were over 100 feet long and had two or three pairs of doors and threshing floors. Arthur Young declared himself against the new trend: 'I cannot approve of the rage all Norfolk farmers have for barns . . . I believe half the land would be covered with barns to receive the corn from the other half.' During the nineteenth century, barns were increasingly used for storing grain which had already been threshed by machine. Because some of the grain was for feeding livestock, the barn and cattle sheds had to be in close proximity.

All these changes, and others unmentioned, were related to the chosen system of husbandry. This deliberately alternated grain and fodder crops, supported greatly increased numbers of sheep, cattle and horses, and produced much larger quantities of corn, particularly barley and wheat. The system was acclaimed by observant visitors like François de la Rochefoucauld and William Gilpin, and was disseminated by specialist agricultural writers such as Nathaniel Kent, William Marshall and Arthur Young. By the end of the eighteenth century Norfolk had become the best known and most productive region in Britain, exporting grain and animals worth well over a million pounds each year. It was no accident that George III or 'Farmer George' named one of his new enterprises at Windsor, 'Norfolk Farm'.

The Good Sands

Most commentators were convinced that the heartland of advanced, modern agriculture lay in the Good Sands. 'At Swaffham the Norfolk husbandry begins,' said Arthur Young, assuming that visitors could only approach from the south. An area which in the seventeenth century had contained huge acreages of open fields, commons and sheepwalks was radically re-designed. The classic description, though with characteristic over-statement, came from Young's *Tour* of 1767:

All the country from Holkham to Houghton was a wild sheep-walk before the spirit of improvement seized the inhabitants . . . Instead of boundless wilds and uncultivated wastes, inhabited by scarce anything but sheep, the country is all cut into enclosures, cultivated in a most husband-like manner, richly manured, well peopled, and yielding an hundred times the produce that it did in its former state.

Here the old sheep-corn husbandry, based since at least Anglo-Saxon times on open fields and commons, had given landlords and their tenants the space, control and resources which they needed to introduce sweeping changes. So, by the 1760s, the richest farmers of Norfolk were, paradoxically, on the poorer soils, but they were growing 'some of the finest corn in the world'. Although most changes had been foreshadowed in the seventeenth century, the transformation had largely occurred since about 1720.

Some of the new, large farms on the Good Sands were described by contemporaries in the most glowing terms. Mr Barton's spread of 3,000 acres at Rougham contained nineteen different groups of buildings, carried over 2,000 sheep, and was esteemed 'the largest farm in the county'. From his 2,500 acres at Dunton, Mr Mallett, who began his career as a farm worker, was said to have made a fortune of £70,000 in thirty-four years (no doubt an exaggeration). When de la Rochefoucauld visited this farm in 1784, he described the farming system of Mallett's successor, Mr Case: he grew wheat, turnips, barley and clover, fattened bullocks, fed 180 pigs mainly on peas, ran 1,000 sheep and employed 26 labourers and 80 working horses. Mr Curtis' farm at Summerfield near Docking, consisting of 2,500 acres, was dubbed the 'best in Europe'. The landlady, Mrs Henley, had cleared and enclosed the land from former sheepwalk, establishing clipped hedges and shelter belts which were 120 feet thick. An attractive farmhouse had been built for the tenant, as well as large barns, stables, granaries, a pond and a large stackyard. Mr Curtis, the tenant, grew 'immense crops of corn' and was one of the leading foxhunters of Norfolk. He was succeeded by Mr Dursgate who was noted as the 'richest farmer in the county'.

Even more famous, at a later stage, was Lodge or Abbey Farm at Castle Acre, a property of the Earl of Leicester. At the beginning of the eighteenth century, the sandy rolling country north of that town was covered by three huge open fields, divided into hundreds of small strips. From 1714 onwards, the strips were progressively exchanged and consolidated, and four modern farms began to emerge. For over sixty years new hedges were planted annually, and enormous

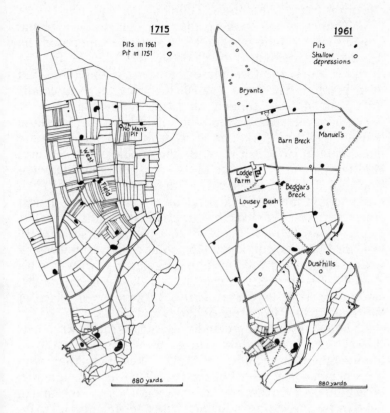

Fig. 19. Lodge Farm, Castle Acre: a complicated open-field landscape converted by consolidation, enclosure and marling into a famous tenant-farm (after Hugh Prince).

221

effort was put into marling and dunging the land (Fig. 19). In 1735 Thomas Abell took up the area that was to become Lodge Farm. In one period of five years he supervised the digging and spreading of over 5,000 loads of clay. By the end of the century, the farmhouse, barn and outbuildings had been erected. The farm flourished during the Napoleonic Wars, and its rent trebled. In 1822, during the post-war depression, a teenager called John Hudson was granted the tenancy by T. W. Coke, an event which is depicted on the monument in Holkham Park. By the middle of the century, Hudson had made this 'one of the most celebrated farms in England'. He invested massively during the period of High Farming and ran his 1,500 acres on a truly modern, almost American, scale. For example, he clayed the whole farm after 1822 and again in 1838; used 36 working horses and 16 working bullocks; employed 110 people to harvest one year's wheat; and bought 200 tons of oil-cake each year to feed his animals. His success was spectacular: the farm carried 200 cattle instead of its earlier thirty, 3,000 sheep in place of 800, and doubled its output of barley and wheat.

Although several major landlords, such as the Townshends of Raynham and Sir John Turner of Warham, worked to improve the Good Sands, it was the Cokes of Holkham who were deemed 'the fairest of the fair'. Their large estate had been built up since the late sixteenth century by taking land in hand or by purchasing individual fields, tenements and manors. For example, in ten years at the beginning of the eighteenth century, the estate spent £12,500 on acquiring more land. By the nineteenth century it amounted to 42,000 acres: 70 to 80 farms in 26 different parishes in the north-west *and* centre of Norfolk.

The pace of improvement on the estate varied according to the district or even the individual parish. For example, Fulmodeston was virtually enclosed by 1614 whereas Castle Acre was not reorganised until the eighteenth century. Furthermore, the term 'enclosure' itself covers several different kinds of change. At Flitcham, for instance, Abbey Farm in 1700 consisted of 276 acres of arable in open fields, 211 acres of meadow and pasture, and 1,535 acres of 'brecks' and sheep-walk. In 1733, immediately after the open fields were enclosed, Abbey Farm was redesigned: the land was marled, large rectangular fields were laid out and new hedges planted, the brecks and sheep-walks were also divided, and a new house and barn were built for the new tenant.

Between 1776 and 1816, and especially during the Napoleonic Wars, the rents of the Coke estate doubled and triggered off another round of improvement. Over a period of some sixty years, twenty-three farms were completely rebuilt. One of the first was Leicester Square Farm at South Creake which was rebuilt after 1790 with a 'style of expence rarely met with'. The farm of 865 acres was provided with a fine new house, a symmetrical set of farm buildings and an impressive barn designed by Samuel Wyatt. In about 1810 Grenstein Farm at Mileham, consisting of 496 acres, was created out of several earlier units and enclosed commons. It was provided with two barns (one for hay and the other for chaff), a horse yard, bullock yard, turnip house, hospital for animals and several other buildings. The last and most expensive rebuilding, costing £5,458, was at Egmere in the years 1850–56.

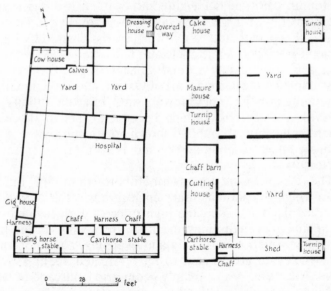

Fig. 20. Waterden: a 'model' farmstead on the Holkham estate, greatly praised by Arthur Young in 1784 (after Susanna Wade-Martins).

223

Designed by G. A. Dean, it has the usual barn, stackyard and stables but shows an increased emphasis on stock with six cattle yards and looseboxes with feeding passages.

At the heart of this enterprising estate was the home farm at Holkham itself. This was basically the amalgamation of two earlier farms which made up the park. In the 1790s it was described enthusiastically by two southern farmers as 'a perfect paradise', 3,000 acres within a ring-fence. The most notable building was the huge barn, 130 feet long, designed by Wyatt in 1790 as the centre for Mr Coke's 'sheep-shearings' which were held annually until 1821 and at times catered for as many as 7,000 guests. Instead of being in the usual position at the edge of a farm complex, this barn lies in the centre of a large yard and is surrounded by cattle sheds, stables and storehouses.

The new Breckland

Improvement came later to the Breckland but was no less profound. Until the late eighteenth century, this region consisted mainly of large open fields and extensive uplands of heath, sheep-walk and rabbit warren criss-crossed by lonely wandering tracks. Some enclosure had taken place but most of it was immediately around villages. Eighteenth-century travellers like the second Earl of Oxford and William Gilpin commented on the area's blowing sand, bracken, rabbits and bustards (a large bird which became extinct in the early nineteenth century), but had shown no affection for it. They dismissed it as 'absolute desert' and as a 'miserable entrance' to Norfolk.

The first enclosure act was for Hilborough in 1768, but the main weight of parliamentary enclosure was felt during the Napoleonic Wars when the high price of corn justified the ploughing of even this marginal land. Between 1800 and 1820 the transformation was rapid and sweeping: a total of forty-nine enclosure acts is said to have affected about 115,000 acres. The result was a mainly geometric landscape of large rectangular fields bounded by hedges and tree belts, punctuated by coverts and plantations. The Scots pine, originally a native species, was reintroduced in large numbers, and still remains dominant today with its irregular profile and warmly tinted bark. Established roads were often straightened, as between Bridgeham and Brettenham, while large numbers of new straight tracks were laid out to serve outlying fields. The pattern of buildings was to some extent altered as well. For instance, new farms were sometimes created on former heaths or warrens. Waterloo Farm at Sturston, which was reclaimed and marled in about 1845, is a good example: its name commemorates the fact that, as a warren, the land yielded 'at a single netting, the same number of rabbits . . . as men were killed at Waterloo'. Similarly, a few new hamlets sprang up to accommodate the labouring population at places like High Brettenham and Little London at Northwold. The occasional field barn was also built in outlying parts of larger farms. The regular geometry of each parish's landscape was only broken when it hit a medieval road or ancient parish boundary.

The owners of large estates were key figures in the movement to enclose and improve the Breckland, and their large houses and parks were already conspicuous on Faden's map of 1797. For example, in about 1785 Sylvanus Bevan had purchased 2,000 acres around the decayed villages of Riddlesworth and Gasthorpe, and spent about £7,000 on building a classical mansion, farm, barns and cottages. He created large new enclosures out of common fields, clayed them and surrounded them with hedges containing his favourite crabapples and sweetbriar. He also watered meadows, reclaimed a fen in the valley of the Little Ouse, and planted nearly a million trees in and around his park. Some of Breckland's tenant farmers also gained considerable reputations. For example Mr Wright of Kilverstone was, in the eyes of Arthur Young, 'one of the best farmers in England'. He farmed about 2,000 acres which had been entirely reclaimed from waste in the middle of the eighteenth century. By means of marling he had turned his sandy soil into a profitable enterprise, producing fine crops and carrying 900 sheep.

Investment was renewed in the middle decades of the nineteenth century when, for example, covered yards for cattle were built at Thetford, Wretham and Hilborough, but from the 1870s onwards the Breckland was devastated by

225

agricultural depression. Much of the arable land tumbled back to rough pasture, and for many people its only obvious use seemed to be for the shooting of game. In the early years of the twentieth century, the area provided some of the largest 'bags' ever recorded in England. Nevertheless, some landowners still managed to use the poor soil more productively. At Kilverstone, Lord Fisher planted half a million new trees and grew worthwhile cash crops like asparagus and blackcurrants. Nearby at Shadwell Court, John Musker, a man whose wealth came from the grocery business, developed a viable system of mixed farming dependent on lucerne, cocksfoot, carrots and barley, and also built up a thoroughbred stud.

By planting large numbers of trees in their parks and on their farms, landowners of the eighteenth and nineteenth centuries transformed the Breckland landscape, which, since prehistoric times, had been open and windswept. For example, St Payne Galway absorbed a large heath and most of the parish into his park at West Tofts. Around his estate, he made a plantation over nine miles long which was greatly applauded by Nathaniel Kent.

Agricultural improvement elsewhere

Although the Good Sands and Breckland changed most radically, and in the process acquired a national reputation, we must not overlook developments in other parts of the county. On or below the Western Escarpment, for example, open fields and commons were enclosed, new plantations and parks established, and marshes embanked. One of the outstanding achievements, from 1870 onwards, was the creation of a new royal estate at Sandringham.

When it was bought by Edward Prince of Wales for £220,000, the estate consisted of about 7,000 acres and was described by a contemporary as the 'wildest and most out-of-the-way place imaginable'. Queen Victoria on her first visit in 1871 also complained about the 'rather wild-looking, flat, bleak country'. Indeed, apart from two manorial woods belonging to Dersingham and Wolferton, the house and park were largely an oasis surrounded by sandy heathland to the west and newly enclosed farmland on the escarpment to the east. Nor was the rent roll of £7,000 particularly impressive. However, earlier owners had shown that agricultural improvement was possible, and that the heathland between Sandringham and Wolferton, traditionally a rabbit warren, could be made to grow trees.

The prince immediately undertook major improvements. He laid out new roads, improved tenant farms and built a new home farm, a stud and a soaring water tower at Appleton. The greatest impact came from the planting of thousands of trees: some within the park, or as belts dividing large fields, but most as large blocks of woodland on the former warren. Today the area is noticeable for its exotic conifers mixed with broad-leaved trees and thickets of rhododendron. Not surprisingly, shooting became the principal activity of the royal household. In the 'Big House' clocks were always advanced by half-an-hour, thus encouraging residents to make maximum use of daylight. Between 1870 and 1910, the annual count of game shot, particularly pheasant and partridge, rose from about 7,000 to 30,000. Meanwhile the estate was steadily growing: today it comprises about 20,000 acres and includes, wholly or partly, thirteen parishes.

So general was the drive for improvement that one eminent commentator, William Marshall, thought the reputation of the Good Sands much exaggerated. He argued passionately that it was *eastern* Norfolk which was the true home of the 'Norfolk system' because for generations it had accepted advanced methods and principles – placing emphasis on enclosed fields, ditches and hedges, marling, barns and other substantial buildings, alternation of arable and pasture, the rationalisation of holdings, management of woods, and four-to six-year rotations using crops which alternately fouled and cleansed the land. The result was a landscape of much greater intricacy and irregularity. In this 'very old-inclosed country' of small farms, frequent enclosures, high hedges and fine trees 'the eye seems ever on the verge of a forest'. Nathaniel Kent, Marshall's contemporary, described what local people had been doing for centuries: 'Whenever a person can get four or five acres together, he plants a whitethorn hedge around it, and sets an oak at every rod distance, which is consented to by a kind of general courtesy from one neighbour to another.' Of course the eastern side of Norfolk witnessed many of the engrossing trends which occurred in the west: farms were often amalgamated and certain 'men of fortune' built up estates and swallowed their neighbours. But a more numerous peasantry and yeomanry, exploiting richer soils, ensured that 'there was not *room* to make a Mallet, a Dursgate or a Martin' (all large farmers in the west).

Marshall's opinions were based on his experience as agent, from 1780–82, to Sir Harbord Harbord at Gunton. By 'east Norfolk' he primarily meant the north-eastern corner of the county from the southern slopes of the Holt-Cromer Ridge across to the Broads and the island of Flegg. Nevertheless, his argument can also be applied to South and Mid-Norfolk which had a similar demographic and agricultural history. Moreover Marshall's interpretation of the agricultural history of Norfolk has major implications for economic and topographical historians today. It emphasises, surely correctly, that the 'wood pasture' area of medium to heavy soils is an older, more evolutionary, landscape. It probably incorporates elements of great antiquity from Anglo-Saxon, Roman and even prehistoric times, and yet it has slowly evolved, particularly since the Middle Ages, as its scattered but numerous peasantry intelligently and industriously exploited a naturally rich environment.

Fenland under threat

The great drains, sluices and reclamations of the seventeenth century led to consequences which were not foreseen by Vermuyden. When the peat was converted into more productive grassland or arable, its level began to drop because it dried, wasted by bacterial action, shrank and blew. While the bands of silt nearer the Wash remained stable at some twelve feet above sea-level, the peat fens, which had been at roughly the same height, shrank steadily, sometimes dramatically, and are now ten to fifteen feet lower than they were. Large areas of the Norfolk peats are not more than three feet above sea-level and are still shrinking.

This 'deepening concavity of the peat fens', as Sir Harry

Godwin called it, brought grave new problems: serious flooding was commonplace throughout the eighteenth century, and has remained a threat until the present day. The peat under major rivers and drains did not shrink at anything like the same rate, and therefore watercourses were increasingly 'perched' above the ground on each side. As a consequence, the fenland is a place where you often go uphill to cross water. To maintain watercourses, stronger and higher banks were necessary as the land on each side shrank; even so, they sometimes leaked or broke. Furthermore, if disaster was to be averted, water in the small drains around fields had to be *raised* into the main drains and rivers. For a century and a half it was the windmill driving a scoop-wheel which provided the necessary lift. Faden's map of 1797 shows large numbers of those mills dotted around the peat fens of Norfolk: for example, he marks thirteen windpumps along the bank of the Great Ouse, in the six miles between Brandon Creek and Denver Sluice, all sited at points where local drainage converged on the banks of the river.

Unfortunately, as the peat continued to shrink, every improvement contained the seeds of its own destruction. By the end of the eighteenth century, windmills were no longer coping with the pressure of water, and most of the peat fens of Norfolk were once again classified as 'drowned' or 'waste'. Arthur Young described the desolation of about 20,000 acres in Stow Bardolph Fen; by that time, Tong's Drain was virtually useless. Even when water could be raised into the Great Ouse and its feeders, it did not necessarily get away because of silting in the estuary and the sheer volume of water coming from both the South and Middle Levels. Conditions were at their most difficult when heavy freshwater flooding from inland coincided with high spring tides and an adverse wind.

Two factors which combined to save the fens in the nineteenth century were the making of new cuts to improve the outfall and the introduction of steam engines. Whereas windmills were often becalmed when they were most needed, steam engines gave consistent and predictable power. From 1820 onwards, they were constructed all over the fenland, and windmills fell into disuse. For example, a forty horse power engine was installed at Magdalen Fen in 1834, and four years later a twenty horse power engine in Feltwell Fen. Once again, the very success of new machines started another dramatic round of shrinkage. It was reckoned that, between the 1840s and '70s, Hilgay Fen shrank over four feet at a rate of 1.7 inches per year. Methwold Fen sank five to six feet in fifty years; to lift water, increasingly powerful pumps had to be introduced at regular intervals, in 1883, 1913, 1928 and 1938. Much of Methwold Fen now lies at about sea-level, and is still shrinking steadily as new and even deeper drains are cut by modern machinery.

Four great works of engineering have been undertaken since 1800 to improve the flow of water through the lower Ouse into the sea (Fig. 18). First, a six-mile loop of the river, just south of Lynn, was by-passed by the Eau Brink Cut, itself three and a half miles long. This scheme had been talked about since the early eighteenth century, but was consistently opposed by the people of Lynn who thought it threatened their port. An act was eventually passed in 1795, work started in 1817, and the cut was opened in 1821 at a total cost of £300,000. It certainly improved the drainage of the interior, but not as much as some people had hoped. After similar vacillations, the Middle Level Drain was completed in 1848. This was a major new cut, straight for ten miles, taking water from the Middle Level to a lower junction with the Ouse at St Germans, and therefore relieving the traditional outlets at Salter's Lode and Tong's Drain. It involved the construction of Norfolk's only aqueduct at Mullicourt, where it passes under the medieval Well Creek.

The two other schemes are quite modern, and came after disastrous flooding in 1947, when 37,000 acres of the South Level alone were under water. In the 1950s a relief channel was cut from Denver to just south of Lynn to take pressure off the lower reaches of the river. Then in 1964 a cut-off channel was opened which runs down the eastern side of the fens from Mildenhall to Denver. It collects floodwater from all the tributary rivers as they enter the fens, and therefore bypasses the drains of the South Level. Ironically, this cut had originally been proposed by Vermuyden in 1642.

Another form of reclamation was carried out in the

Plate 40 Wacton: a small medieval house, timber-framed and recently restored. It consists of an open hall in the centre and a two-storeyed section at each end. The lean-to is later, and the original house would have had internal shutters.

Plate 41 Diss: a timber-framed house of six principal rooms, typical of southern Norfolk in the late-16th and 17th centuries. The integral chimney-stack heated two ground-floor rooms; the front door, in line with the chimney, gave access by a small lobby.

Plate 42 Wacton: interior of house shown in Pl. 40. The open hall with its queen-post roof, restored by the removal of later floors, ceilings and walls. The two arched doors led to service-rooms with chambers above.

Plate 43 Hales Hall: interior of the great barn, looking west, built in the late 15th century by Sir James Hobart, and 184 ft long. Brick walls support a magnificent roof of tie-beams (27 ft long, 15 inches square), queen-posts and collars.

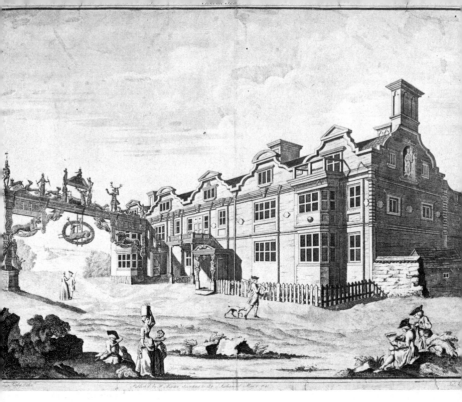

Plate 44 Scole: The White Hart, built *c.* 1655, with its sumptuous brick facade and 'the noblest signepost in England', drawn by Joshua Kirby in 1740. The sign was demolished *c.* 1800.

Plate 45 Stalham: at the staithe, Jan. 1933, one of the last trading wherries, frozen in. The artificial 'cut' leading from the River Ant to this staithe is 1½ miles long.

estuaries of the Ouse and Nene. Both were subject to silting, and their channels were constantly shifting as new sand banks and shoals developed. A Norfolk Estuary Company was set up and, in 1852–53, made a new cut of two miles continued by 'training walls' to straighten the Ouse estuary and cut off a former natural loop just north of Lynn. This new cut explains why North Lynn Farm and a slice of that parish now lie on the wrong side of the river. Over a longer period, the Nene or Wisbech estuary was progressively improved. Kinderley's Cut was begun in the 1720s but not completed until 1773; it was extended seawards in 1830 by the Outfall Cut and finally by the Marsh Cut of 1832 which straightened the river from Kinderley's Cut into Wisbech itself. The effects were dramatic: the bed of the Nene was lowered ten feet, the port of Wisbech greatly improved, 3,000 acres of marshland were drained, and a new bridge and road spanned an estuary which had been notoriously difficult since at least the thirteenth century when King John lost his treasure. Instead of licensed guides conducting travellers over treacherous sands, a straight road four miles long, served by a new bridge (Sutton Bridge) and a massive embankment, connected Long Sutton in Lincolnshire to Cross Keys in Norfolk.

The reclamation of salt marshes on the Norfolk side of the Nene estuary has been particularly marked, though most of it lay legally in Lincolnshire. By constructing straight roads, drainage ditches and defensive banks, investors have created rich new farmland, and the work has continued into the twentieth century. Similar 'polders' were won from the Wash itself. Large-scale work outside the old Sea Bank began in the eighteenth century as East Marsh was embanked as far out as Hungry (or Ongar) Hill. This was extended by Captain Bentinck in 1775, and then a very long strip reclaimed along the eastern edge of the Nene estuary in 1791. The line of that embankment of 1791 has largely remained the county boundary to this day. East Marsh is distinguishable on the modern map by a group of eighteenth-century habitations like Roon and Clipston Farms, and by its natural drainage channels which were retained. Later intakes are marked by names like Balaclava Farm and Kamarad Farm. Similarly, on the east side of the Ouse estuary, a large new embankment was built before 1797 to improve two long strips of salt marsh north and south of the Babingley river. Again, the natural drainage of winding streams was retained. In the nineteenth century more intakes were made, creating Estuary Farm and a new road from North Wootton. In this century, several other major compartments have been won from the sea. They are defended by strong machine-made banks, which mostly run in straight lengths connected by sharp angles, and internally have numerous close-set parallel drains.

Improved communications

The roads of Norfolk were traditionally maintained by a combination of private charity and public investment. While individuals, manorial courts and parish vestries tried to cope with local problems, the county accepted responsibility for major works and bridges. For example, a county rate was levied in 1576 for the total rebuilding of Wroxham bridge, which entailed the purchase of 30,000 bricks, four tons of squared flint, seven tons of freestone, twelve 'greate steppes' of freestone and sixty large timber piles. Because of these overlapping responsibilities, the road system was inevitably patchy; it was also affected by the vagaries of soil and season. Contemporaries certainly gave conflicting opinions. To Celia Fiennes, Norfolk miles were long and the roads were 'pretty deep . . . especially after raines', and William Marshall thought the roads of east Norfolk 'unpardonably bad'. Yet Nathaniel Kent found Norfolk roads 'free from sloughs in all parts' (except the marshes); because the soils were absorbent, ruts were shallow and roads 'better in their natural state than in almost any other county'. One road, at least, was exceptionally 'natural' and needed no maintenance. It ran, in John Ogilby's words, 'along the beach' from Cromer to Yarmouth. Providing the traveller avoided high tides and storms, he could proceed for thirty miles without interruption by headland or estuary.

The droving of large numbers of animals, particularly cattle, is an important aspect of communications from at least the seventeenth century onwards. The main entry for Scots and northern cattle was through Wisbech and across the

Great Ouse at Magdalen and Stow bridges. In 1750 alone, it was calculated that 20,000 Scots cattle entered Norfolk through Wisbech. Well established droving routes also linked the grazing areas of east Norfolk to their main market at Smithfield in London. In the 1790s, a noted Norfolk drover normally took seven days to take a 'drift' of fattened beasts from St Faiths to London (112 miles).

After the Restoration of Charles II, the increasing volume of private and commercial traffic undoubtedly quickened the pace of change. For example, Norfolk was one of the first counties in England to experiment with the idea of turnpike trusts. 'The great Post Road from London to Norwich,' as Blomefield called the A11, had caused recurrent problems – especially where it crossed Attleborough Fen. In the 1580s –90s, an attempt to collect a special rate had largely failed, while a century later the road had to be saved by private charity. A pillar at Besthorpe, dated 1675, commemorates the magistrates' gratitude to Sir Edwin Rich who had given £200. In 1696, however, an act of parliament was passed to improve the road between Wymondham and Attleborough. Soon after, Celia Fiennes was stopped by 'a barr at which passengers pay a penny a horse in order to the mending the way'. By 1746–7, the whole of the A11 from Norwich to Thetford was turnpiked, and a flurry of acts between 1766 and 1832 ensured that all ten main roads leading into Norwich were brought under the control of trusts. Another important focus was King's Lynn. Nevertheless, only 271 miles or 7.3% of Norfolk's total mileage was ever turnpiked, and most roads survived 'in their natural state' until modern times.

Another significant development was the improvement of accommodation, stabling and postal services. By 1673, Norfolk had four 'stages' in the principal towns (Norwich, Lynn, Yarmouth and Thetford) and fifteen 'post-towns' scattered throughout the county. Although inns had been a feature of Norfolk's roads for centuries, a major effort was now being made to improve their quality. The Duke's Head beside the Tuesday market in Lynn is a superb example of a late seventeenth-century urban inn, with its handsome façade and galleried courtyard. The best rural example is surely the White Hart or Scole Inn (Plate 44), standing at one of the major entrances to the county, beside the Ipswich-Norwich road. This elegantly classical building with its bold brick detailing of Dutch gables, large rectangular chimneys, cornices, quoins and panels, was erected by John Peck in 1655. It was long famous for a great carved sign which straddled the road; it carried twenty-five different features including the arms of local families and towns, depictions of the 'virtues' and various mythological scenes. Although, in the words of Sir Thomas Browne, this was 'the noblest signnepost in England', it was taken down about 1800. The inn also provided a large garden, bowling green, grazing for horses, occasional cockfights and, internally, a large round bed 'big enough to hold fifteen or twenty couples'.

The steady improvement of main roads and the better design of vehicles meant that travelling times were progressively shortened. For example, the distance from Norwich to London is about 100 miles: in the fifteenth century the journey took four days; by the early eighteenth century three days; by 1741 two days (at least in summer); by 1761 less than one day; by 1823 it could be done in ten and a half hours. Stage wagons began plying between the two cities in 1729, the first regular coaching service started in 1762, and mail coaches appeared in 1785. Meanwhile carriers had built up weekly services to 150 places within thirty miles' radius of Norwich. Not only did turnpike trusts improve the surfaces of main roads, but enclosure acts greatly reduced the number of gates ('falgates') which had to be opened on the edges of commons and open fields. It has been estimated that at least twelve gates had to be negotiated on the twenty-two miles between Norwich and Holt. These features of the unenclosed landscape are still commemorated in minor place names, for example the two hamlets in Cawston parish called Southgate and Eastgate.

Improvements given to the road system did not detract from the importance of waterways. On the contrary, they showed a parallel development, particularly for the transport of heavy goods. Thus, when two weighty tombstones were brought in 1612 from London to Felbrigg, they came by sea to Yarmouth and then by the river Bure to Coltishall. Similarly, in the late eighteenth century, marl was transported from

Thorpe-next-Norwich to Woodbastwick, not by a short overland journey of seven miles, but by barge through fifty miles of winding rivers. Passenger services were also available from an early date. For instance, in 1668, a daily service plied between Norwich and Yarmouth, costing sixpence a head.

A certain number of diversions, cuts and staithes were made in Norfolk during the Middle Ages, but in subsequent centuries we see an increased desire to improve on nature. For example, between 1549 and 1613, Yarmouth spent £39,000 on its harbour and haven. For centuries the burgesses had struggled to keep a clear outlet from the river Yare into the North Sea, through shifting sand banks. Six times they cut channels at various points through the lower end of the great spit, which in the Middle Ages was much longer than it is today – even at one stage extending as far south as Corton and Gunton. Each time the new works were destroyed by tides and storms. Finally the existing haven was established in 1613 by a Dutch engineer, Joas Johnson, and secured by the construction of major piers of timber and stone. An inland example of similar works can be seen at the lower end of the river Ant, which has clearly been diverted into the Bure west of St Benet's, and away from its original eastward course along the Hundred Dike to the Thurne. The new channel cuts through a wide causeway which was the principal road to the medieval monastery; it is therefore very likely to be post-Dissolution in date.

One result of building Denver Sluice in 1651 was to reduce the navigability of the river Little Ouse, much to the chagrin of Thetford corporation. Accordingly, they and other interests, in 1670, acquired an act of parliament to improve the Little Ouse and also to join it to the Waveney by cutting through the watershed at Lopham Ford. (After all, the two rivers had, in later Pleistocene times, been part of the same through-valley). In the event, the link was never made. The Little Ouse was, however, made navigable as far as Thetford and later provided with its unusual single gates or 'staunches', while the Waveney was ultimately made navigable to Bungay by means of three orthodox locks.

After this precedent, several other rivers were made the subject of improving acts. The river Nar, after an act of 1751,

235

was made navigable again at least as far as Narborough, while the old silted course of the Nene, from Upwell to Wisbech, was reopened as the Wisbech Canal following an act of 1794. On the other side of the county, nine miles of the middle Bure from Coltishall up to Aylsham were improved after 1779. The river was scoured for most of its course, though some new cuts were made, and five locks were installed. In 1826 the North Walsham and Dilham Canal was opened, which was an improvement of the river Ant from Wangford bridge upstream for eight miles to Swafield and Walsham; from it a special cut of one mile was dug to serve Dilham. Other ambitious schemes were never put into practice: for example to make the Wensum navigable from Norwich up to Dereham and Fakenham, or to connect London with both King's Lynn and Norwich.

Major new channels were sometimes cut where no rivers had existed previously. For example, the New Cut which runs dead straight for two and a half miles from Reedham to St Olaves connects the Yare with the Waveney, and is a monument to municipal warfare. It was built in 1832 by William Cubitt, so that Norwich could get direct access to the sea *via* Lowestoft and Oulton Broad, thus bypassing its troublesome rival Yarmouth. Unfortunately it was never a financial success and the main beneficiary, ironically, was the port of Lowestoft. Similar works were carried out in Marshland (see p. 230).

In the eighteenth and nineteenth centuries, usually as a result of enclosure and drainage acts, large numbers of minor cuts were made from navigable rivers to staithes. Sometimes they were well over a mile long. Good examples can be seen at Stalham (Plate 45) and Sutton from the river Ant, at West Somerton from the Thurne and at Geldeston from the Waveney. On the western network of rivers, they were comparatively infrequent but examples can still be traced at Oxborough from the Wissey and at Wormegay from the Nar. In spite of modern demolitions, staithes may still retain a few commercial buildings, of which the most common survival is probably an inn. Geldeston, for example, has an inn called The Wherry and the remains of malthouses and a brewery, while warehouses still survive at Stokesby and Acle. Sometimes a sizeable industrial hamlet grew up around a staithe as at Loddon and Aylsham. At the northern edge of the latter, a hamlet called Dunkirk sprouted in the late eighteenth century around an artificial basin: it contained a mill, malting, granary, boatyards and warehouses for coal and timber.

Sometimes cuts were deliberately designed for the dual purpose of navigation *and* drainage. For example, a chain of broads and marshes between Hickling and the sea was improved by digging straight drains, and by constructing dikes at a higher level which connected with the river Thurne. Floodwater therefore had to be raised by windpumps like the restored example at Horsey Mere. At the same time the major dikes were made navigable and provided with staithes so that marsh produce such as reeds, sedge and hay could be taken out and coal brought in.

Thus, by the early nineteenth century, before railways began to reduce the volume of water transport, the waterways of Norfolk were alive with constant traffic. In the west, rivers draining into the Wash carried many barges or 'lighters' made of elm and drawn by horses walking on a 'haling' path. In the east, special kinds of sailing barge had been developed, suitable for navigating shallow winding rivers through a relatively flat, marshy and open countryside. Although the 'keel' with its square sail had an early importance, it was the oaken 'wherry' which became the enduring symbol of Broadland, partly because it was painted so many times by artists of the Norwich School and later frequently photographed. With its enormous brown sail gliding majestically through rivers, broads and cuts, the wherry provides a superb example of how human industry and ingenuity can use nature without violating it. Estimates suggest that the Yare alone carried some 200 wherries in the early nineteenth century, each bearing a load of twenty to forty tons.

The first railway in Norfolk was constructed by the Stephensons between Norwich and Yarmouth, and was opened with pomp on 30th April 1844. On a single track a train of fourteen carriages covered the twenty miles in fifty minutes. The Norwich–Cambridge double-track, through Wymondham and Thetford, followed in 1845, and the Norwich–Ipswich line, through Diss, in 1848. The journey to

London could now be done in about four and a half hours. Other lines soon appeared in the western and central parts of the county, and provided useful employment. Morton Peto, a major contractor in the 1840s, provided good conditions for his navvies, even to the extent of erecting temporary rooms to serve as a club on wet days and a church on Sundays. The main developments in the north and east, amalgamated in 1893 under the Midland and Great Northern Joint Company, did not happen until after 1870. By the end of the century, lines had spread into most corners of Norfolk and formed a loose network connecting the major towns. One of the last constructions was the Wissington Light Railway, built privately in 1905 to help fenland farmers. Inevitably, too, certain schemes failed, such as the proposed line linking Kelling, Cley and Blakeney.

The relatively soft and undulating landscape of Norfolk normally posed few problems for railway surveyors and engineers, though a fair number of cuttings and embankments were made and major parks, as at Holkham and Melton Constable, had to be avoided. The principal challenge came from the crossing of wide rivers. This occasionally necessitated the building of major bridges, as at Runham across Breydon Water or at Hilgay across the river Ouse. The piecemeal work of several early companies meant that lines sometimes cross without interconnecting (as at Fakenham and Lakenham) and that certain towns were provided with more than one station. Norwich in fact acquired three stations while Fakenham, Aylsham and Cromer each had two. In 1862, five of the primary companies serving Norfolk were amalgamated into the Great Eastern.

The social and economic consequences were profound. Railways enabled people who were dissatisfied with their lot to migrate more easily; transported agricultural produce more speedily to markets within the region and outside; led to a rapid decline in coaching, droving, innkeeping and the profitability of turnpikes; accelerated the decline of northern ports such as Wells and Cley, but at the same time encouraged the growth of resorts like Hunstanton and Cromer.

SELECT BIBLIOGRAPHY

Barringer, C. (ed.) 'Faden's Map of Norfolk', *Norfolk Record Society*, XLII (1975).

Gordon, D. I., *A Regional History of the Railways of Great Britain, Vol. 5, The Eastern Counties*, (2nd ed. 1977).

Kent, Nathaniel, *General View of the Agriculture of Norfolk* (1794).

Marshall, William, *The Rural Economy of Norfolk*, 2 vols (1795).

Parker, R. A. C., *Coke of Norfolk* (1975).

Riches, N., *The Agricultural Revolution in Norfolk* (1967).

Tate, W. E. and Turner, M. E., *Domesday of Enclosures* (1978).

Wade-Martins, Susanna, *A Great Estate at Work* [Holkham] (1980).

Young, Arthur, *General View of the Agriculture of Norfolk* (1804).

Young, Arthur, *Six Weeks' Tour* (1767).

16. Villages of contrast

DURING THE EARLY eighteenth century, village life remained fairly static or declining. Blomefield, the county historian, frequently commented on the low ebb of rural communities, their continued shrinkage as holdings were consolidated by landlords, and the neglected state of churches. For example, Appleton contained only four or five houses and its church was filthy and ruinous; Thorpe Parva had four houses, and its church only survived as a ruinous tower. But in the second half of the eighteenth century, villages again entered a period of change and growth, for two basic reasons. First, after 1750, the population began to rise again, faster than at any time since the thirteenth century. Norfolk's growth was at its steepest (eighteen per cent) during the decade 1811–21, and most rural parishes reached their peak around the middle of the nineteenth century. The increase has been variously explained by, for example, earlier marriage, and by parochial relief and improvements in basic medicine which at least kept people alive. The second major reason is that new land was frequently available for building, as a result of enclosing common land.

Some villages grew outwards from earlier nuclei. For example the former market town of East Harling developed a new 'suburb' on its western side after its green was enclosed in 1805: new houses were soon built along the edges of its characteristically straight enclosure roads. Similarly Mattishall expanded westwards over a former common, and Horsford grew a northern extension with the significant name of St Helena. Hamlets also grew, both in population and built-up area. For instance, a street leading from Horsham St Faith to its watermill expanded into a hamlet called Waterloo, while Crossdale street in Northrepps showed similar thickening along a single road. In other places, substantially new hamlets were created to accommodate a bourgeoning population. At least seven of them, amusingly, were called Little

London. On a large common south of East Dereham, a mile-long hamlet called Toftwood appeared along the road to Shipdham: it still preserves its predominantly nineteenth-century character today, in spite of modern infill and expansion (Plate 49). Sometimes developments were more in the nature of loose straggles of houses and cottages, such as the rectilinear growth of Hainford over its former heath, also incorporating the name Waterloo. However, the most remarkable example of new rural settlement was surely in Marshland. Here, after an act of 1796, over 7,000 acres of common fen were drained and divided among the owners of 525 common rights; as a result new farmsteads and cottages straggled along an enclosure-road for more than three miles.

Nineteenth-century villages and hamlets also grew *inwards*. As the pressure of population made itself felt, so gaps in existing streets were filled, and yards or back gardens were built on. At the same time, older houses were frequently subdivided into tenements and could be occupied by several families and dozens of people. For instance, Brooke in 1811 had 77 houses for 109 families, while at Docking in 1831 no fewer than 279 families were fitted into 133 houses. The densely packed nature of nineteenth-century housing can be seen particularly well in southern Norfolk where older timber-framed houses were frequently subdivided, and extended backwards or sideways. Each unit or 'tenement' had essential facilities like external doors, an internal staircase or ladder, and a separate chimney or at least flue (Plate 50).

Villages and hamlets also grew inwards by enclosing central greens, usually with a local act of parliament. At Sloley and East Ruston, for example, the 1851 census attributed an increase of population to the enclosure of commons and the building of cottages on the allotments. This produced another familiar characteristic of rural Norfolk: 'double-banking' where old houses lie well back from a village street (in fact, just outside the edge of a former green) while newer ones are closer to the road (actually on the green). Often one can still see traces of a substantial hedge and ditch which originally bounded the common (Fig. 21 and Plate 46).

However, where villages expanded they did so at different rates, and some did not grow at all. These variations can best

241

Fig. 21. Deopham: the main focus of settlement in the parish since medieval times. In 1814 the Green was enclosed and divided: on it, straight roads were constructed and new houses built in front of older ones. The outline of the former Green can still be traced today as ditches, hedges and scarps.

be explained by distinguishing between parishes which were 'open' and those which were 'closed'. In an open community the ownership of land was fragmented among a relatively large group of people, and land could therefore be bought and developed in response to the natural growth of population. By contrast, closed villages were under the control of one or two major landowners who deliberately kept them small, or only allowed modest growth. A major reason for this policy is that each parish was still responsible for financing its own poor until 1865; therefore in controlling the growth of his village's population, a landlord avoided burdening himself and his tenant-farmers with high poor rates.

In practice, one finds that a considerable number of villages represent intermediate stages where, for example, landlords were non-resident or the ownership of land was not too much fragmented. Even so, it has been calculated that in parts of Norfolk thirty to forty per cent of all villages were 'closed'. This certainly seems true of the north-western side of the county, north of the A11, and is nowhere clearer than on the Good Sands (Plate 34). In any area, though, one finds a mixture of open, intermediate and closed villages, because all their economies were interdependent. Frequently, small villages did not have enough labourers to run their farms, and they therefore had to draw on their larger, more open neighbours. From Gooderstone, for example, some labourers walked five miles each day to work in parishes like Cockley Cley, Shingham or Beechamwell (Fig. 11); similarly Castle Acre became notorious for its use of the 'gang system' whereby men, women and children were taken in carts to parishes which were sometimes more than ten miles away.

New cottages in the more open villages were mainly financed by tradesmen, craftsmen and small capitalists, and were frequently described as 'inferior' or 'miserable'. Rooms were often small, walls thin, bedrooms were in short supply and sanitation was primitive. In addition, gardens could be small or non-existent. One particular form of building, done for the sake of cheapness, was especially criticised – the terrace or 'row' which frequently bore the name of the owner. To make matters worse, these small landlords were often lax in doing essential repairs. Nevertheless, even though many of

243

the worst and flimsiest have since been demolished, hundreds of nineteenth-century cottages have survived, and been modernised to form a major feature of Norfolk. They are normally plain boxes of two to four rooms, often with leans-to, and with one or two end chimneys. They can be built of almost any materials, and range from studwork and clay-lump in the south through various kinds of brick in the centre of the county, to mixtures of cobbles, brick, carrstone and clunch in the north. Bricks were the commonest material but, to keep down costs, they were quite frequently laid on their sides in a pattern known as 'rat-trap'. Many of these cottages have roofs of imported slate, at a lower pitch than those of older vernacular buildings. They frequently cluster around important institutional buildings like National schools, Primitive Methodist chapels and public houses.

Because they at least provided some hope of accommodation, open villages attracted large numbers of immigrants. For example, Castle Acre in 1843 contained 249 families, of whom 103 came from other parishes. Lakenham expanded sevenfold in the first forty years of the century and had the 'worst class of cottages'; in 1841 it contained 1,159 inhabitants who had been born there and 1,718 who had not. So great was the pressure that, in spite of new building and conversions, these villages became grossly overcrowded. In one cottage at Docking, the single bedroom accommodated a father, mother, three grown daughters (one of whom had a baby), a younger daughter and two teenage sons. As a result of this 'cottage herding', open villages were frequently associated with extreme poverty, social unrest, bastardy and crime. The worst strictures were usually reserved for Castle Acre which was seen as the most immoral place in Norfolk, 'the coop of all the scrapings in the country'. However, for us today the most potent symbol of rural poverty and discontent is the Union workhouse. From the late eighteenth century onwards, seventeen of these large grim buildings were erected in Norfolk, and several were attacked and burnt by local mobs. Some have been converted to modern uses, but the most atmospheric is the lonely and sinister ruin lying between Great Snoring and Thursford.

Closed villages were a world apart. If new building took

place, it was either a modest expansion of the village or simply a rebuilding of existing houses to improve them – sometimes with the stated purpose of attracting and keeping a good class of tenant and worker. Occasionally, as at Brandon Parva and the Wrethams, cottages were actually demolished or allowed to fall down 'to reduce the liability of maintaining the poor'. Such tight policies meant that landlords of closed parishes often had less accommodation than they needed to farm their acreages. For example, Markshall had five cottages on an estate of 830 acres when it really required twenty-five workers; on their estate at Sedgeford the Church Commissioners farmed 2,000 acres and had no cottages at all.

Little wonder, therefore, that extra labour had to be recruited from larger and more open villages in the vicinity. This exploitative relationship can still be seen on the modern map; for instance, Lakenham having an arc of closed villages to its south, such as Intwood, Keswick, Caistor St Edmund, Arminghall, and Trowse; or Docking which is virtually surrounded by depopulated parishes like Fring, Shernborne, Choseley, Stanhoe, Barwick and Barmer.

Landowners created closed villages in order to avoid the social and financial problems which afflicted other places, but it would be wrong to suggest that they acted purely selfishly. Some of them, like Lord Ashburton at Bodney or Lord Spencer at North Creake, invested heavily in rebuilding their employees' houses to a high standard. A few went further to create 'estate villages' with 'model cottages'. Good examples, ranging from Victorian to Edwardian times, can be seen at Stow Bardolph, Shadwell, Woodbastwick and Glandford, but two deserve special mention.

At Holkham Thomas William Coke began building cottages in the 1790s. By 1840 he had erected fifty substantial and comfortable dwellings which were regarded as among the best in England. They lay in rows and semi-detached pairs, with wash-houses, privies, pig styes and dirt-bins. Even so, half the estate's cottages were still in poor repair. By 1900 another hundred had been built or remodelled. The two main clusters of estate housing were in the main village, north-west of the hall, and in a semi-circular layout south of the park, at New Holkham.

A large number of model cottages was also built on the Sandringham estate. By 1885, the Prince of Wales' agent could claim that about seventy had either been rebuilt or enlarged. Each family now had three bedrooms, two living rooms, outhouses, earth closets and a garden of at least twenty perches. Built of carrstone or brick, the cottages were mostly semi-detached and stood back from the road. The main focus of these developments was the village of West Newton, which became virtually embedded in the extended park: it has been described as 'King Edward's own village' (Plate 48). Today it has an impressive array of cottages, ranging in date from 1864 to 1949. But housing was not the only concern. By 1885 three schools had been built, two churches restored, the careful tending of cottage gardens encouraged by an annual show, and well regulated social clubs were being introduced to replace public houses. After only twenty years of benevolent landlordism, the agent could say of the labourers, 'their whole tone is improved.'

Between 1831 and 1861, the populations of most villages reached their peak, and thereafter began a long slow decline which lasted well into the twentieth century. Some have continued to shrink until the present day. This reversed trend was mainly caused by the number of people migrating to large cities and industrial areas, or emigrating overseas to the colonies, because they wished to escape from poverty, over-crowding and unemployment. For example, in 1836 Ship-dham sent forty-four people to a new life in Leeds, while Edgefield bade farewell to 123 who emigrated to North America (one-sixth of its entire population). The population of rural Norfolk as a whole began to decline in 1861, but already 149,000 natives of the county were living in other parts of England, above all in London and the Home Counties. Even when the outflow began to exceed the high level of births, housing conditions remained bad. Accommodation was still in short supply because few new houses were being built (except in estate villages), and because the worst and most isolated cottages were being abandoned. In the 1890s Erpingham RDC tried to build its own houses, but was opposed by the county council. It was not until the 1920s that 'council housing' became a normal feature of rural Norfolk

Plate 46 Hardingham: a typical 18th-century farmstead, built of local brick on the edge of a former green. A scarp (right) shows the original boundary of the green, enclosed 1816.

Plate 47 Itteringham: a Norfolk farmhouse with shaped gables, pantiles and end-chimneys, dated 1707. The door, sash-windows and dormers are clearly later modifications.

Plate 48 West Newton: a formal estate-village, created by the Prince of Wales. These semi-detached 'cottages', dedicated to Princess Alexandra, were built in 1864. Note the use of carrstone, generous gardens and regimented design.

Plate 49 Toftwood: a mixed row of 19th-century cottages built on former common land. Raw materials include brick, flint and clay-lump. Modern restoration is noticeable with new doors, windows and even painted flint.

Plate 50 Brundish: a timber-framed house of *c.* 1600 converted into three Victorian cottages, each with front door, fireplaces and stairs. An extension behind gave extra accommodation.

Plate 51 Wicklewood: a tower-mill built in the early-19th century, derelict when photographed in 1949 but since restored. Windmills, with their strong vertical lines, have been major features on the Norfolk skyline since about 1200.

Plate 52 East Harling: two welcome characteristics of modern Norfolk, the 'new vernacular' style of housing and the conversion of old agricultural buildings to new uses, usually residential.

Plate 53 Tivetshall: a modern farmscape, open and increasingly desolate. Trees on the skyline are over a mile away. The green lane, at least medieval in date, is already mutilated and will disappear when the left-hand ditch is completely filled.

with its familiar rows of 'semis', often set apart from the old village.

Rural populations quickly responded to the introduction of new forms of employment, when available. For example, Salthouse and Cley grew in the 1840s while embankments were under construction; Edgefield was boosted around 1850 when its Great Wood, once the property of Binham Priory, was being felled. Occasionally, genuine attempts were made to generate new industries in rural areas. Thus from the 1840s Taverham grew because of the success of its paper mill, which provided newsprint for *The Times*, while a silk mill at Ditchingham attracted settlement to that area. But the most remarkable example of industrial development happened later, against a background of agricultural depression, in the north of the county.

In 1850 the consolidated parishes of Melton Constable and Burgh Parva had a small population of just over 100, living either in Lord Hastings' elegant establishment or in scattered farms and cottages. Then in the 1880s, railway companies (which in 1893 became the Midland and Great Northern) chose Melton as a major junction and depot, while his lordship agreed to sell the necessary land. Four lines converged on it from Cromer, North Walsham, King's Lynn and Norwich – the last two respectfully skirting the park. A station was built, with platforms 800 feet long and a specially appointed waiting room for Lord Hastings, followed by works for the construction of carriages, wagons and locomotives. To the north-east of the station, between 1885 and 1910, a new industrial village (Fig. 22) was created on a grid pattern of streets (not unlike twelfth-century Lynn or New Buckenham). About 170 new houses were erected for railway employees: they were mainly in solid terraces, built of dark-red brick with mock timber gables, and looking as if transplanted from the industrial Midlands. The residents were provided with various facilities such as corner shops, a hotel, a school, a cooperative store and an institute for meetings and entertainments. In thirty years the population of this 'Crewe of Norfolk' increased tenfold, and by 1911 stood at 1,157. Thereafter it slowly declined. Finally, about eighty years after its start, Melton's career as a rail-centre was officially termin-

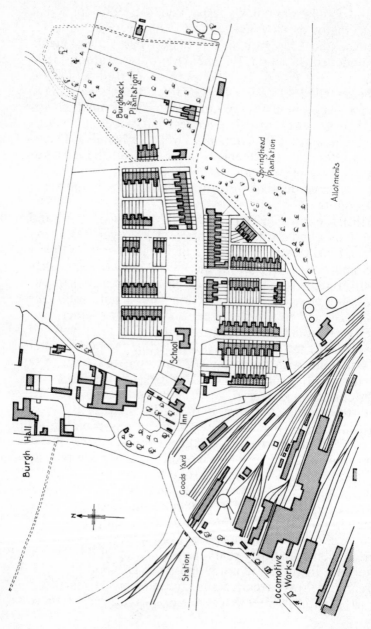

Fig. 22. Melton Constable: the 'Crewe of Norfolk', in 1906. A late-Victorian railway development comprising station, workshops, housing, public amenities and allotments. House-building continued after this date.

ated. Between 1959 and 1964, British Railways progressively closed the lines and withdrew both passenger and goods services. In 1971 the station was demolished while the works were converted into an industrial estate. Now Melton Constable lies like a stranded whale in a vast agricultural area which has turned to other forms of transport, but it remains a worthy monument to the age of steam.

SELECT BIBLIOGRAPHY

Digby, Anne, *Pauper Palaces* (1978).
Holderness, B. A., 'Open and close parishes in England . . .', *Agricultural History Review*, 20 (1972), 126–39.
Report by Edward Twistleton on the Dwellings of the Labouring Classes in Norfolk and Suffolk, from Edwin Chadwick's *Report on the Sanitary Condition of the Labouring Population of Great Britain* (1842).
Reports to the Poor Law Board on the Laws of Settlement and Removal, *Parliamentary Papers*, 1850, XXVII, 21–72 (Report by G. A. à Beckett on Norfolk).
Springall, Marion, *Labouring Life in Norfolk Villages, 1834–1914* (1936).

17. Contemporary prospects

IN THE FIRST forty years of the twentieth century, the rural population of Norfolk continued to decline because, apart from a short break during the First World War, farming was still in the grip of serious depression. Inevitably, though, the landscape was still changing. For example, the acreage of arable land in 1936 was about twenty per cent less than it had been 100 years earlier. Many fields had been put down to grass, while the least economic land was simply abandoned. Related to this was the spread of large-scale forestry, particularly after the Forestry Commission was established in 1919. The main impact of its large coniferous plantations is to be seen on the Breckland, where the commission bought or leased huge tracts of land, mostly former heath. In 1880 the Breckland of Norfolk and Suffolk still contained 54,000 acres of heathland; by 1968 this had declined by seventy per cent to 6,600 acres, largely as a result of afforestation. Thetford Forest now covers over 50,000 acres or 80 square miles, and other plantations of the Commission, north of Norwich and around King's Lynn, amount to a further 8,000 acres.

While the depression lasted, some farmers, who had the necessary capital or optimism, tried new crops – such as tobacco on the Breckland, lavender and flax in the north-west and potatoes in the fens. A significant trend, from the 1920s, was the gradual adoption of sugar beet, which led to the building of one of Britain's first beet factories at Cantley on the river Yare. But the most successful experiment was the growing of fruit and vegetables in both the west and east of Norfolk. For example, Richard Allen of Wiggenhall St Germans had grown corn but from about 1895 started to plant thousands of fruit trees and a large acreage of strawberries. Such pioneers proved that they could grow high quality produce with profit, and this encouraged the growth of orchards, market gardens and new factories, at Lynn and Yarmouth particularly, for jamming and canning.

Another visual effect of the agricultural depression was the gradual decay and disappearance of windmills and, to a lesser extent, watermills. Because of the importation of foreign grain and the adoption of rollers in place of stones, the ancient craft of local milling went into an irreversible decline. The related windpump of the marshes and fens was also in jeopardy because it was being replaced by steam and, later, by diesel power, and also because some drained land was abandoned during the depression. Windmills had been a feature of the Norfolk landscape since the twelfth century, and had existed in their hundreds in the eighteenth and nineteenth centuries. The postmill, revolving on a single great post of oak, was the traditional type which had been constructed for many centuries, and frequently rebuilt because of fires and structural failures. It can be seen depicted in two medieval churches, on a brass at Lynn and on a carved bench end at Thornham. More common by the nineteenth century, however, was the towermill with its tarred brick tower, swivelling cap and painted sails (Plate 51). We have the paintings of the Norwich School and the work of early photographers like P. H. Emmerson to remind us of how dominant these magnificent, moving structures were against the wide Norfolk sky.

Major and portentous changes also began to overtake the fragile environment of the broads which were, until the mid-nineteenth century, remote, inaccessible and sparsely inhabited. This area was, to those who knew it, an unspoilt rural, or aquatic, paradise with pure crystal waters, carpets of yellow and white water lilies, great expanses of reed-bed, fen and alder carr, and an abundance of wildfowl and fish. But, from the 1870s onwards, the broads were 'discovered'. Early pioneers like George Davies published attractive books and photographs (his *Handbook* quickly ran to over fifty editions), and a triangle of railway lines was built around northern Broadland and brought in day visitors, holiday-makers, yachtsmen and fishermen. Davies, who is regarded as 'the man who found the Broads', wrote prophetically in 1883, 'There is no better "playground" in England, and certainly none easier of access or more cheaply to be enjoyed.' Before his death in 1927, he had seen the growth of a hire fleet of 160 yachts, a score of pleasure wherries and, most significant of all, a dozen or so motor cruisers. Today, it is estimated that

251

the broads carry some 2,000 hirecraft (the majority are powered cruisers), 500 day-launches, 3,000 privately registered launches and 2,450 sailing dinghies. As more people came to enjoy the area, from the 1870s onwards, they inevitably demanded, and were provided with, new facilities. Some parishes, like Neatishead and Irstead, saw no more than the building of a few detached houses or 'villas' on the edges of watercourses and broads, but other places on major routes, such as Brundall, Horning and Potter Heigham, were more intensively developed with chalets, bungalows, public houses, houseboats and boatyards. Since the Second World War, tourism has become a major industry which put local waterways and villages under ever-increasing pressure. The twin villages of Wroxham and Hoveton, which face each other across the river Bure, neatly summarise Broadland's development over the last century (Fig. 23). The first is dominated by an exclusive area, called the 'Avenues', with large detached houses, boathouses and private staithes; the second is a seething, commercialised resort crammed with boatyards, shops, eating places and amusements.

But more profound than the obvious signs of human development were slower-moving ecological changes. As the resident and visiting population grew, the rivers and broads became polluted by human sewage, and their chemistry began to alter. At first this led to an enrichment of plant life and to an increase in the numbers of fish but, after the Second World War, conditions deteriorated markedly. A new factor was the massive use of chemicals on surrounding farmland. The waters became brown, murky and full of algae; water plants could no longer grow; the reed-beds thinned out; and all these changes inevitably had their effect on the wildlife of fish, insects, animals and birds. Ironically, the freshwater dykes of the marshes are now ecologically richer than the rivers and broads themselves.

While the farming community was in deep depression, the major towns of Norfolk were still growing. For example, Norwich expanded greatly between 1914 and 1939 as large new estates, public and private, were built along and between the major approach roads. In fact, the large-scale provision of council houses is a striking characteristic of which the city has

Fig. 23. Broadland discovered and exploited:
two advertisements from G. C. Davies' *Handbook*, 41st edition, 1901.

been very proud. Mile Cross, an estate of about 2,000 houses built from the early 1920s to 1934, is now proposed as a conservation area. The suburban growth of Norwich was particularly marked on its west, north and east, but to the south was severely restricted by agricultural estates which were unwilling to sell land. This gave Norwich the curiously lopsided shape which it still has today.

Environmentally, the Second World War was an important watershed. On the one hand, Norfolk suffered considerable physical damage. For example, the southern end of medieval Yarmouth was devastated by enemy bombing, while Norwich is said to have lost 2,000 houses, 100 factories, many shops and several medieval churches. In the county as a whole, about thirty airfields were laid out, mainly to sustain the great bombing offensive against Germany. For the first time, modern earth-moving machines tore holes in the traditional countryside – a sinister omen of things to come. On the other hand, the war dramatically revived local farming which has remained prosperous ever since.

Most country roads were surfaced between the wars, but after 1945 villages were provided with important new amenities such as mains water, electricity and, in places, mains sewerage. Visually this led to the progressive disappearance of pumps, wells, ponds and outside lavatories, and to the proliferation of wires, aerials, poles and pylons. Changes in the social fabric of the countryside were even more significant. Because of over-population and agricultural depression, farm workers had been leaving the land for a century or more, but they left even faster after the Second World War because, ironically, farming was becoming more prosperous and mechanised. From about 41,000 in 1951, they have declined momentously to about 11,000 today.

Meanwhile, villages began to attract new and largely middle-class residents such as commuters, weekenders and the retired. New houses were built, particularly around the larger villages, and older properties restored. As the number of private cars rose, public transport slowly deteriorated: hence the dismantling of many of Norfolk's railway lines in the 1950s and '60s. Similarly, because of changing lifestyles, some of the older rural institutions weakened still further. Today, one in every eight churches is redundant or falling into ruin; hundreds of nonconformist chapels have been converted or demolished; a quarter of Norfolk's villages have no shop, and a half no longer have a primary school. The widespread fashion of erecting village signs, whatever one thinks of their tastefulness or historical accuracy, illustrates well how predominantly middle-class and suburban values have now penetrated rural life.

Modern villages can be divided into two main categories: those which are large and growing, and those which are small and static. Growing villages tend to be open villages of the nineteenth century, usually within comfortable commuting distance of major towns; their size means that certain levels of public service can be provided at an economic cost. Thus, the Structure Plan of 1976 has earmarked eighteen villages for residential development, twenty-five villages as 'service centres' with such facilities as a middle school, surgery and library, and fourteen others as 'minor service centres'. The rest of Norfolk's villages, which include most of the 'closed' communities of the nineteenth century, are to have 'little change in their character or services'. In built-up areas, they will change little, and their appearance will only be affected by the standards of local restoration and small-scale infill. Of course, these communities will still have to cope with genuine problems such as poor public transport and the effects of an ageing population. People of pensionable age account for nearly half of the migration into rural areas; thirty per cent of the population of Blakeney is now over sixty-five. Nevertheless, the negative achievement of modern planners in preventing undisciplined and sporadic development, such as took place in the 1930s, is undeniable and quite unprecedented in earlier generations. Without such controls, the county would have experienced ribbon development on a massive scale along its major roads, rivers and broads, while the coastline would have been as developed as present-day Runton or Caister.

The standard of post-war design in rural areas was not high. Regrettably the bungalow was accepted as the normal kind of house, though its squat shape with low-pitched roof and large windows fits badly with earlier vernacular buildings. Particularly damaging are large and ostentatious bungalows, which were often built of unsympathetic materials and have sham 'period' features like bay-windows, latticed glass and external shutters. Their effect is made worse by equally aggressive gardening with the accent on dinkyness, excessive formality and openness – all qualities which are the very antithesis of the rural tradition. However, we can point to some early exceptions to the generally low standard. Loddon RDC was justly praised for its patronage of the architects Tayler and Green, who from the later 1940s designed small rows and estates in several local parishes. Their houses are simple and strong in outline, yet varied and unregimented. Furthermore, they consist of materials which harmonise with their surroundings. But it was not until the 1970s that a general improvement was discernible. Gradually a new style, based at last on the shape, textures and detailing of traditional buildings, took root and was deliberately encouraged by the new district councils and their 'design guides'. Houses in this style, often called the 'new vernacular', can now be seen all over the county (Plate 52). They may not be convincing from all angles, and their details can still be carelessly ungrammatical (especially those over-large porches and barbarous 'Georgian' doors which incorporate fanlights), but the general advance in the quality of design is undeniable, and they fit their surroundings far better than their predecessors.

The population of the county has grown considerably in the last thirty years. From 566,000 in 1961, it rose by over ten per cent each decade to 695,000 in 1981 and is growing at four times the national average. The expansion was mostly absorbed by towns, including smaller market centres which had stagnated in the later nineteenth century; it was caused partly by a natural rise in the birth rate and by improvements in living standards, but also by deliberate planning decisions. Thus, the Structure Plan of 1976 designated six towns, including Fakenham, Diss and North Walsham, as 'growth centres', and twelve other towns, of the size of Watton, Aylsham and Wells, were zoned for lesser growth. Meanwhile King's Lynn and Thetford signed 'overspill' agreements with Greater London, and have built large residential and industrial estates on their fringes as well as redeveloping parts of their historic centres. In 1951, Thetford was a small market town which some said had been asleep for nearly a thousand years. Its population then stood at 4,447. In the 1960s it grew by nearly ten per cent each *year*, and now has nearly 20,000 inhabitants and a built-up area which has more than quadrupled.

In Norwich, the 'flight to the fringe' continued after 1945. By 1961 the population passed 160,000 and had doubled since 1871. The boundaries of the city were extended in 1965, and one of the newly acquired areas was Bowthorpe, 600 acres of farmland around a deserted medieval village. This is now being built as a major new suburb which, when completed, will house 13,500 people. One of its three 'villages' is substantially complete: around its centre which contains shops, a pub, village hall and school, is a mixture of private and local authority houses, at a density of twenty per acre. They are designed in the 'new vernacular' and certainly have more character than Norwich's earlier post-war suburbs. The intention has been 'to create a genuine Norfolk development rather than an anonymous one'. Whatever one's reservations about trying to create 'instant' communities and environments, Bowthorpe is a bold architectural and social experiment which deserves to succeed.

Norfolk's villages and towns altered rapidly enough after the Second World War, but the changes in the countryside were even more radical. The vastly improved productivity and profitability of modern farming has been achieved by the reduction of labour costs, by ever-developing mechanisation, by the use of chemical fertilisers, herbicides and pesticides, and by the injection of enormous sums of money, both private and public. Such an 'agricultural revolution', for it is nothing less, meant that the landscape too had to alter: we now see much more arable and less grassland, fewer and larger farms, larger prefabricated buildings, and much larger fields. In fact, since about 1950, the pace and scale of change have been totally without precedent. By the late 1970s, forty-five per cent of Norfolk's hedgerows had already been uprooted and nearly one per cent of its hedgerow trees were disappearing annually. The process continues year by year, so that in some East Anglian parishes seventy per cent or more of the landscape features depicted on maps of the nineteenth century

257

have disappeared: whether hedges, ditches, banks, individual trees, road verges, green lanes, ponds, moats or parish boundaries. So artificially high is the price of cereals that all other forms of land use such as meadows, marshes, fens, parks or woodland, are in danger of destruction, no matter how irreplaceable they are as ecological resources. We were recently told that one-quarter of the Halvergate marshes have already been ploughed, yet if ever land were naturally designed for grazing, this is it. In parishes like West Dereham, Winfarthing, Crownthorpe and Southrepps, one frequently sees long arable vistas which are featureless for a mile or more (Plate 53). Small subtle valleys, which were traditionally defined by hedges and terraces, are ignored by the arable plains which sweep down and across; the streams, if they survive, are straightened and canalised; the flat plateaux, which desperately need trees and hedges to punctuate them, are left desolate. Most of these changes have taken place without any rounded assessment of the landscape or planning consultation, yet with the massive support of the taxpayer. To make matters worse, thousands of trees and saplings in woods and hedges have been killed by Dutch Elm disease. In the next twenty-five years, the number of trees in the county is expected to decline by about 8,000 annually so, merely to halt the decline, the county council suggests that it is now necessary to plant 40,000 trees a year.

Yet the Norfolk countryside is still full of variations. By crossing a ditch, you can pass from a barren landscape, ecologically impoverished and depressing to the soul, to the land of a farmer who has found a compromise. He farms efficiently and apparently profitably, makes many changes, destroys many features, yet still manages to leave the landscape rich and stimulating, with a sense of enclosure and continuity. As a result, the farming landscape is now a patchwork of good, bad and indifferent. The principles of compromise have been obvious all the time, but have never been properly codified or officially recommended. Farmers could have been helped, quite easily, to identify those features of greatest value, historically, biologically or visually, so that they could be retained. It could still be done, so far as future changes are concerned. Meanwhile, in just thirty years, large areas of a fragile and beautiful landscape have been savaged by modern technology, insufficiently controlled by forethought, sensitivity and a sense of responsibility.

It would be wrong, however, to end this survey on a note of gloom. 'Rare and beautiful Norfolk,' as John Sell Cotman called it in 1841, is undoubtedly less rare and beautiful than it was, but we have some grounds of hope. In the first place, an increasing number of people care about the county, its buildings and its landscape. Organisations like the Norwich Society and the Norfolk Naturalists Trust were among the first of their kind nationally, the Norfolk Society was formed in 1972, and new groups are appearing all the time. The new University of East Anglia has stimulated valuable research into many aspects of the region's life and environment. Various bodies now protect nearly 29,000 acres of Norfolk as nature reserves. This represents only 2.2% of the total area, but it does safeguard some of the most precious parts of the coastal marshes, heaths and broads. In addition, the National Trust and various private owners are doing sterling work in conserving and beautifying great houses, their gardens and parks.

Meanwhile, the growing demand for environmental information has called into existence new interpretative schemes such as 'Norfolk Heritage'. The general public is now more interested in, and concerned about, issues such as access to the countryside, drainage and pollution. The standards of restoration and new design do genuinely appear to be rising. We see this best in the infilling of rural and urban sites, in the conversion of agricultural buildings (Plate 52), and in the regeneration of older suburbs (like the Arlington scheme in Norwich). Councils at various levels, led by pioneering Norwich, have undoubtedly become more conscious of the importance of the environment, and are willing to spend more resources on its protection. Large statutory organisations which have the power to change the countryside fundamentally, like the Anglia Water Authority and the Forestry Commission, are wakening to their responsibilities and trying to find new compromises between development and conservation. Commercial interests are gradually realising that it makes no sense to destroy the very qualities which people have come to enjoy. Landowners and farmers are showing regret for what has happened in the last generation, and a willingness to repair some of the damage. For example, the large-scale replanting of trees along the A140 is a joint scheme involving local farmers and the county council. This and similar planting elsewhere will certainly be an appreciable asset in twenty years' time.

Perhaps our best encouragement comes from the 'battle of the broads'. Here we see an awesome clash of powerful interests, agricultural, commercial and environmental, yet the pronouncements of local authorities and conservationists have a new strength and determination. The Broads Authority, formed in 1978 and fortified by three years of scientific research, 'is not prepared to accept broads and rivers which are polluted and dead, rivers which look like monotonous canals, commercialised villages with no character or great expanses of crops with no wildlife'. Already Cockshut Broad has been purified of nitrates and phosphates, and is growing the water-lilies and other aquatic plants which only eighty years ago flourished all over Broadland.

But we should have no illusions. The balance of modern change still tends to erode and destroy, rather than enhance, the county's character – a strange achievement for a generation which has acquired a higher standard of living than any of its predecessors. The task of reversing many current trends, in the broads and elsewhere, is truly enormous, and the cost will be high in time, effort and money. Unfortunately, most of the successful conservationist schemes create no more than 'oases' in a desert of mediocrity. We desperately need strategies and philosophies which will arrest the decline of ordinary, average places – expanding villages as well as conservation areas; the average farmer's land as well as Horsey Mere or Holkham Park. It remains to be seen whether we can muster the restraint, vision and political will which are needed, first to save our unique and priceless inheritance, and then sensitively to develop it.

SELECT BIBLIOGRAPHY

Broads Authority, *What Future for Broadland?* (1982)
Davies, G. Christopher, *The Handbook to the Rivers and Broads of Norfolk and Suffolk* (1882).
Mosby, J. E. G., *The Land of Britain, Norfolk*, Report of the Land Utilisation Survey of Britain, Part 70 (1938).
Nature in Norfolk: A Heritage in Trust (1976).
Norfolk County Council, *Farmland Tree Survey of Norfolk* (nd).
Norfolk Heritage, *Water Transport in Norfolk* (nd).
Tarrant, J. R. and Baird, W. W., *Hedgerow Destruction in Norfolk, 1946–70* (3rd ed. 1975).
Yaxley, David, *Portrait of Norfolk* (1977).

Index

FLINTS - HISTORY OF P26.
SHORELINE + RIVERS   P27
Holme to Weybourne marsh
area, known as North Alluvial Plain P31
woodland dates at- Breckland P41
Iceni People P29

Wolterton - garden designed by Charles Bridgeman
Barningham Hall P181   P191